ESTHER
Reflections From an Unexpected Life

Esther

reflections from an unexpected life

Jennifer Westbrook Spivey

Ambassador International

GREENVILLE, SOUTH CAROLINA & BELFAST, NORTHERN IRELAND

Esther
Reflections From An Unexpected Life

Unless otherwise indicated, all scriptures are from the New King James Version.

Cover design and page layout by David Siglin of A&E Media

ISBN 978-1-932307-90-0

Published by the Ambassador Group

Ambassador International
427 Wade Hampton Blvd.
Greenville, SC 29609
USA
www.emeraldhouse.com

and

Ambassador Publications Ltd.
Providence House
Ardenlee Street
Belfast BT6 8QJ
Northern Ireland
www.ambassador-productions.com

The colophon is a trademark of Ambassador

DEDICATION

In honor and memory of my paternal grandmother,
Anne Stearns Westbrook
whose godly example continues to inspire and encourage me

To my little princess,
Lindsay Grace Spivey
in whom I see all the qualities of a queen being developed

And mostly to my mother,
Penelope Harris Westbrook
who always knew I could

ACKNOWLEDGEMENTS

As with every journey, God sends people along the way whose gifts prove indispensable. I wish to thank...

Margaret Hofstad Harris, my maternal grandmother and source of much encouragement (she even likes how I write the church newsletters!)

Betty Myers Smith, whom God uses every single day to bless and strengthen me

Andrea Michele Gaines, whose friendship has been one of my greatest blessings and most valuable treasures for close to half my life

Ethylene Brannon Spivey, my husband's precious grandmother; though my time with her was short, her influence in my life has proved lasting

The congregation of Northland Church, all of whom make serving the Lord and His people an absolute joy

Thanks to the most important men in my life, too

Michael Lee Spivey, my husband and my dearest friend

George Grey Westbrook, my dad and still my hero

Tyler Grey Spivey and Jacob Adkins Spivey, who are not "double trouble" at all, but are two of my most favorite people ever

TABLE OF CONTENTS

Foreword 11
Introduction 17

Week One 25
Week Two 59
Week Three 89
Week Four 113
Week Five 135
Week Six 155
Week Seven 177
Week Eight 199
Week Nine 223
Week Ten 245

Afterword 269

FOREWORD
BY THE AUTHOR

At our church on Sunday morning, the service opens with songs of praise. Our music minister has started the call to worship, and the people respond in excitement. As the second song closes, I catch the music minister's eye. Even though the service began several minutes ago, I notice that our pastor is not yet in the sanctuary. Before there is an awkward moment of silence in the service, I leave my seat in the front row to greet the congregation. Reaching for the nearest microphone, I think to myself that this random little ritual must make the sound man insane — the same microphone is rarely chosen twice, and each time I come to the stage unannounced, it leaves him in a mad scramble to find out which one I will choose. From his booth in the back, he smiles at me in spite of the frustration that I cause him, so I welcome the people with a smile and a few announcements. Meanwhile, my husband walks in through the back of the sanctuary. I realize that he has been in the parking lot doing some greeting of his own: he pastors this congregation, and he wants to shake everyone's hand himself. At the time that our service was beginning, he must have seen a family running a few minutes late!

We understand running a few minutes behind. With three children of our own, Sunday mornings can get crazy! Jacob and Tyler, our twin sons, identical to each other and to their dad, are ten. Lindsay, the little princess, is eight. With three so close in age, you come to expect the unexpected. Of course, "unexpected" seems to be a common theme for us. When Michael and I married, he was a police officer and I was a music teacher. However, six weeks after the wedding, Michael announced his call to the ministry and accepted a youth pastor position 1300 miles from our hometown. This announcement turned out to be the beginning of a great adventure — with each other and with the Lord. Ten years later, here we are: Michael now pastors his own church, and I am "filling in the blanks" where I can!

On several Sundays, I "fill in those blanks" by greeting the congregation while Michael is waiting for that last car to pull in. Because he feels confident that our music minister will start the service on time, he can spend these few moments with some of his flock. While timeliness is very important to my husband, people are infinitely more important. Smiling because my husband is sweet and God is good, I raise the microphone and pray that my words will be encouraging and uplifting as the service begins.

Since the microphone is already in my hand, sharing a verse seems appropriate. As Paul admonishes in 2 Timothy 4:2, I remember that we are to be ready "in season and out of season". Though my choice of microphone may have been a surprise to the sound man, my being on the platform is not a surprise to the people. They smile at me, and I share a little from my heart — a little of what God had spoken to me through the week, or a favorite passage. Because these times are random — I am never sure week to week whether or not I will speak — I do not really prepare specifically for this moment, though I am prepared. My words are an outcome of my time spent with the Lord during the previous seven days, and He never disappoints.

On one special Sunday morning, however, I did attempt to specifically prepare for this time. Because it was our church's anniversary service, Michael asked me to be prepared. After the music, I would open the service; but this time as part of the plan. All week I prayed, practiced, studied, and praised. I searched the scriptures for just the right verse. Part of the inspiration was that our district superintendent and his wife would be there, and I wanted to impress! I had hoped that the music would be extra-phenomenal, that the people would be extra-friendly (and I have to admit it: that the crowd would be extra-large!), and that my three little angels would be extra-angelic. My expectations for this service were pretty high!

I had pretty high expectations for myself as well. I was looking for something powerful, something inspirational, something to "knock their socks off" as I opened this special service. I wanted to make my husband and my church proud, and really "blow away" the district superintendent and his wife. Isaiah 50:4 states, "The Lord GOD has given Me the tongue of the learned, that I should know how to speak a word in season to him who is weary. He awakens Me morning by morning, He awakens My ear to hear as the learned". I had high hopes that the word that the Lord would lead me to speak would be just that!

The Sunday of our three year anniversary came. Michael looked sharp driving to church that morning in his new suit. "The brothers", as Jacob and Tyler are always referred to by their sister, were especially handsome — all cowlicks were behaving. Lindsay happened to find the right shoes in the jungle some may refer to as her closet, so she was perfectly matched — hair bows to patent leathers. As for me, a minor miracle had occurred: as of yet, there were no runs in my hose. However, in this rare moment of near perfection less than an hour from the opening of the service, one aspect of the morning was glaringly imperfect: less than an hour before the opening of the service, I had no idea what I was to say!

As the service began, I was in the front row. The music began and it was extra-phenomenal. The crowd looked good and they *were* extra-friendly (and as a bonus, extra-large!). The district superintendent and his wife were in the next section over — smiling! I was smiling, too, but inside I was shaking — the second song was beginning, and I had less than five minutes to come up with something brilliant to say. The music minister began to close his second song, and gave me a wink to let me know that it was almost my turn. Suddenly expecting that my part in the service would be the beginning of the end, I thought to myself, "Well, at least the music was great today..."

Taking the stairs and taking the microphone, Psalm 118:23-24 came to my mind. I was positive that it was just me, because there seemingly isn't anything extra-impressive or especially brilliant about those verses. What child ever came out of Vacation Bible School without learning "this is the day that the Lord has made"? As I smiled and welcomed this group of people, I was multi-tasking: quick thinking an argument with the Lord. How was this the verse I was to share on today of all days? District superintendent here and I open the service with "this is the day that the Lord has made"? All chairs full and I open the service with "this is the day that the Lord has made"? No, I had become convinced inside myself that the verse that I was going to share today would be something obscure — preferably from Leviticus, or better yet: Nahum! Certainly not "this is the day that the Lord has made"!

Running out of words of welcome, and running out of time, the argument ended. The Lord won. I looked out across the congregation and realized that Psalm 118:23-24 was brilliant, and it was perfect for this occasion. Three years previous to this date, our church began with 12 people (5 of whom were in my family) in a school cafeteria, and look how far we had come. With my free hand uplifted to God and with tears in my eyes, I shared the verse that the Lord had laid on my heart: "**This** was the LORD's doing; It is marvelous in our eyes. **This** is the day the LORD has made; We will rejoice and be glad in it." Yes — Psalm 118:23-24! This day, this group of people, this church — it was all the Lord's doing, and we rejoiced together in His goodness. The day was just right, the verse was just right, and it was all Him — especially considering that I had been frantically searching through Nahum during the opening songs for something appropriate, I couldn't take any credit.

The congregation smiled back. They looked at each other, and I could see that they knew this celebration was a result of "the Lord's doing", and that this was truly a day to "rejoice and be glad" together. Because they know me as well, I decided to confess: I told them that I had wanted to be extra-impressive today, and I told them all about my searching for some obscure reference that would cause all of them, including the illustrious district superintendent, to be astonished at my great and vast knowledge of the Bible. So I came clean, and we shared a laugh. I laughed at my own silliness, worrying so much and trying so hard to impress everyone. The kind, generous district superintendent and his precious wife laughed because they remembered being young pastors, and possibly they could identify with wanting to be impressive. The congregation laughed at the idea that I would consider myself capable of impressing anyone, and probably because they remember the Sunday when I sprayed my hair with Lysol instead of hair spray because I forgot to put all my cleaning supplies away after cleaning my bathroom and grabbed the wrong bottle. It becomes increasingly more difficult to impress people after coming to church with a fresh pine scent!

As it turned out that day, it was the Lord that impressed the people. Truth be known, I would not want it any other way. If I am ever thought of at all, I hope that people remember that they saw Jesus in me — in spite of the runs in my hose and the fresh pine scent in my hair. Though sharing Psalm 118:23-24 was a complete surprise to me, the Lord knew exactly what He was doing. It was "the day that the Lord had made", and I was glad that I had obeyed His leading.

In my life, God moves in ways that I do not expect. Often, almost daily, things happen to me that I find surprising or unpredictable. For example, marrying a police officer and ending up as a pastor's wife. (That may classify as more of a shock than a surprise!) Moving from a small town in the foothills of the North Georgia mountains to the bustling and vibrant city of Miami, Florida was unexpected as well. I remember finding out six months into my first pregnancy that we would have twins. I could never forget how I learned on our sons' first birthday that I was expecting another baby. These were three wonderful and overwhelming surprises! In every day, however, the expected and unexpected, I realize nothing is a surprise to our Lord. I am encouraged by Jeremiah 29:11 in learning that God has an "expected end" (KJV) for me. The very events that catch me "off guard" are all part of the Lord's master plan for me. Realizing the depth of His concern, the detail of His plan, and the inexplicable strength of His love, I am free to rejoice in these "surprises".

I find encouragement in the book of Esther. Esther lived a life that was in itself unexpected. A Jew choosing to remain in Persia years after the captivity had been ended? An orphan becoming a queen? A single person rescuing an entire nation from utter annihilation? Esther's response to the situations facing her is extraordinary, influential and pure. She consistently displays a constant and deliberate devotion to God.

As we spend the next few weeks getting to know her, I pray that you will be inspired, encouraged, strengthened, and blessed. I pray that you will come to a fresh knowledge of the God who truly does have an expected end for you, and learn to praise and serve Him through your own unexpected moments. God is no respecter of persons: He can do in you a work as powerful as what He did in Esther. Perhaps more encouraging than the fact of God's ability is the fact of God's *desire* to work through you!

Another aspect of our study together will be recognizing the power of God's love in our lives if we allow Him to do His work in us. Through examples found in the book of Esther — positive and negative examples alike — we will discover that God's love is able to liberate us. God's love will not only give you freedom *from* hindrances that attempt to keep you from living the full, successful life that He intends; God's love is able to give you freedom *to* serve Him and others with peace and joy. At the close of each chapter, we will focus on an aspect of God's love. If His love is accepted into your heart and life, it will enable you to achieve the very things that God means for you to accomplish! Touching on themes and emotions that we all have experienced, we will learn how God's love can release us from fear and free us to bring about change — in our own lives and in the lives of others.

I open this book much the same way that I might open a conversation with you or a service at my church: with a prayer that the Lord could use these words to encourage or uplift the people He puts in my path. If anything impressive happens, it does not have anything to do with the person that I am on the outside — it all has to do with the Person that I have on the inside, and He always knows just what to say. This is what you are holding in your hands: my little offering, my reminders, my encouragement, my lessons from the Lord.

God's plan is for you to be successful and vibrant for Him. The Lord desires to use you to minister and radiate His goodness to everyone He puts in your path. I believe that you have the capability to achieve greatness as Esther did! Throughout this study, we will look to God as the author and finisher of our faith, and we will look to Esther as a great example of what is possible as we submit ourselves to His plan. As you find and submit to God's plan for your life, you can rise above your own expectations. Through the power of His love, you can have a powerful impact on your world. You may find the strength you need in what you may consider to be the most unexpected place of all: in yourself!

Perhaps Esther isn't the only new friend you will find in this book — if you ever pass a woman in the grocery store whose hair has a fresh pine scent, I hope that you'll introduce yourself to me. We'll rejoice in the unexpected together!

Blessings,
Jennifer

INTRODUCTION

I had been mistaken about several things, but today one mistake stood out: I thought that I would feel relief when the end came, but the feeling that I experienced was not relief. The storm was over, and I felt older. The feeling of being older was unexpected, but of course, the trial had been unexpected as well.

Older. Not wiser, just older. Ashamed to admit it now, but the truth was that I had not asked for wisdom. Nor was I more mature — I had not asked for maturity. My prayer throughout the trial was mostly that it would end. Realizing now that an end would have come whether or not I prayed, I looked back at my lack of faith with great regret. I hoped that in spite of my weakness, perhaps God would see fit to give me the wisdom and maturity that I lacked. I longed to hear Jesus speak to my spirit as He had spoken to Paul so long ago, "My grace is sufficient for you, for My strength is made perfect in weakness" (2 Corinthians 12:9).

Quiet. Not only older, I felt quiet, too. Quiet on the inside, and I needed time to remember. I needed to remember victories given to me by the Lord, and be encouraged inside myself that Jesus had come to my rescue this time as He had so many countless times before today. Infinitely more important than reliving old victories, I needed to read again the promises that God gave to me through His word — the ones that He gave to all of us — and be led back to the path I was on before the struggle came. Experience was one thing, I knew, but the power is in the Word of God, not in my experience. I knew that, if I turned to the Lord, "times of refreshing" would come from His presence (Acts 3:19). I needed the refreshing, and I needed His presence.

In this quiet, I felt a desperate need to be alone with the Lord. Was it the quiet that made me desire the Lord, or was it the feeling of being older? Suddenly I remembered that God also promises to renew our youth, and I smiled as if an old friend had gently teased me... Actually, an old Friend had. With a thankfulness in my heart for a smile that only could come from the Lord at a moment such as this, I decided to listen.

The spirit of the Lord did speak in the quiet. His words strengthened me, and I could sense His peace as I repeated them to myself: "*Certain circumstances drove you into the prayer closet; do not allow the easing of the circumstances to drive you back out*". Was it possible that I was not only older, but wiser after all? Was it possible that the quiet I felt was actually a drawing closer to the God Who had drawn near to me through my struggles? Perhaps His strength had been made perfect in my weakness. Perhaps this promise was mine to claim already.

Good days had come as bad days had come. Through both, the Lord had been faithful. This trial had come and I had come out with the Lord's help. Now I knew that I could face any trial, so long as I kept myself close to the Lord. Another promise came to mind, and this promise Jesus had made to His disciples was even sweeter to me now that I had experienced it again firsthand: "I will pray the Father, and He will give you another Helper, that He may abide with you forever – the Spirit of truth, whom the world cannot receive, because it neither sees Him nor knows Him; but you know Him, for He dwells with you and will be in you. I will not leave you orphans; I will come to you" (John 14:16-18). The trial had come but, even more importantly, Jesus had come!

In my remembering, I began to read again a favorite story. In my desire to learn again of victories that the Lord had given to His people in the past, I turned to the story of another woman who came through a trial. These pages were well worn, as I had read her history over and over again. From the first words, her story started with a hope that was encouragement and healing to my storm battered soul: "*Now it came to pass*". It came to pass! This season, this struggle, this series of circumstances had come to pass, not to stay. There was a joyous expectation in these words: the trial that would be described in the coming pages had come to *pass*!

Easy to find, as my fingers had found it so many times before, was the story of a young Jewish girl destined for greatness. Years before her birth, her people had been taken into captivity. Though that captivity had ended, this orphaned girl had stayed in the city of their bondage with a cousin who raised her with as much care and attention as he would have shown to his own child. Through an unlikely series of events, this girl was promoted to a position of great honor, and eventually became the vessel that God used to rescue an entire race.

Through Queen Esther, the course of history was changed. It is nearly impossible to imagine our world today had Haman been successful in his attempt to wipe out the Jews altogether. Esther made her mark on the world, and her struggle had made its mark on her.

Using an orphaned Jewish woman, God carefully and purposefully orchestrated events (both ordinary and extraordinary) to rescue His people. In this powerful and exciting book, we will study the life of a courageous and godly young woman who not only rose to the high standard that God had placed inside her, but also rose to the challenge that God placed before her. Esther is the true story of a woman who became queen and who used her influence to save her people. We will also see how Esther's influence went far beyond her years at the palace. As with every person in whom God has placed greatness, Esther lived a life that continues to inspire and challenge those who come after her.

Her story is, in the easiest terms and by the most convenient definition, an historical account of how God delivered the Jews from total destruction at the hands of an evil man. However, to describe Esther's story as a mere historical account does not do justice to this powerful and dramatic life. Esther's life was, in every way, *unexpected*. The untrained observer looking at this young Jewish woman may not have thought much of her at all. Certainly there was nothing extraordinary about where she lived, when she lived, how she lived, or even who she was.

I wonder how Esther felt prior to becoming queen. I wonder how she felt during her preparations in the palace, not knowing what would happen from day to day. Did she feel ordinary? Too ordinary to be in the home of a king? Do you ever feel as if you are ordinary? I feel as if there is nothing extraordinary about me. I am a mother of three, a driver of an SUV, cooker of dinners and cleaner of bathrooms, lover of Jesus, regular church attendee, I drink diet soda and I spend more time curled up with a good book than on the elliptical trainer (let me be honest: yesterday I used the elliptical trainer to hang my husband's ironing!). How many thousands of women did I just describe? Are you one of them?

Considering how average I feel, I am awed that God even knows my name, and that He can distinguish me from the masses. That's enough for me! That is not enough for the Lord, however; He means for you and me to live extraordinary lives, and be brilliant for Him. Though I cannot relate personally to Esther's greatness (I just don't sense greatness in myself), I am inspired by her. I think, "If God could accomplish such amazing feats through Esther, maybe He could do something wonderful in me..." When I dare to dream like that, I realize something pretty exciting: that the same greatness that was in Esther is in me! After all, that greatness isn't me at all, just like it wasn't Esther: "it is the same God who works all in all" (1 Corinthians 12:6).

Mercifully, my trial (at least this one — as it was not the first, it would not be the last) was over. Over time, the wounds would heal, and I would not bear any outward marks or scars. Inside, though, I would not be the same again. Not worse off — the Lord is too generous for that. Even in the worst of times, He can create beauty and stability. Now I carried something from this struggle inside myself, and I pray that I will never let it be forgotten: the knowledge gained from experience. The promises that the Lord had spoken fresh to me today were spoken to me every day, and I realized that I had never been left alone.

Esther had never been left alone, either. Certainly there was honor in having been chosen to be queen, but it was not easy. Esther would not ever be the same again. Taken, likely against her will, she lost more than her home and family on that day. Esther lost her own dreams. Esther had to trade in her own personal hopes for a greater vision that would exceed her expectations. At a young age,

Esther had to display wisdom and maturity beyond her years: she had to make this trade without truly knowing the end result. Esther could not have done this without at least one assurance inside her: she would not be alone.

In this book, we will come to know several important people: *Esther*, the Jewess still living in the city of her captivity, even though the captivity has been over for many years; *Mordecai*, Esther's guardian and cousin; *Ahasuerus*, king of Persia; and *Haman*, the evil man using his influential position with the king to plot and against the Jews. We will also come to know a few others who have smaller roles in this story, but are equally significant: *Vashti*, the dethroned queen; *Memucan*, one of Ahasuerus' many advisors; and *Zeresh*, Haman's wife who unwittingly encourages her husband to his own tragic end. Whether good or bad, each of these people have something to teach us in their examples.

One item that makes the book of Esther so unusual is that this is the only book of the Bible that does not mention the name of God. Throughout the entire book, there is no written reference to God or to the Holy Spirit at all. Matthew Henry wrote: "though the name of God be not in it, the finger of God is, directing many minute events for the bringing about of His people's deliverance."[1] While God's name is not mentioned, He is obviously at work. God's *actions* are key — these "minute events" are of the utmost importance. If we do not search carefully for the evidence of His handiwork, we could miss Him entirely!

Isn't it the same for us, friend? God is always with us, but we can become so overwhelmed with our circumstances that we forget to search for our source of solace and rescue. Our lives could be a little like the book of Esther: His name may not be revealed to us in flashing neon lights, but that does not mean He is absent or separate from us. In the story of Esther, God's name may not be mentioned, but God was there. Guiding the hand of the historian writing the history, God was there. We need to look for Him. We need to turn our face to Him and realize that God is not seeking glory, He is seeking YOU and ME.

The author of the book of Esther is not known. He never names himself, but in reading the book it is apparent that he is a man familiar with both Jewish and Persian customs. Nearing the end of the book of Esther, we read that Mordecai, Esther's cousin, "wrote these things and sent letters to all the Jews, near and far".[2] This statement leads many Bible scholars to believe that Mordecai may have written the entire book. However, he does not name himself or take credit for the work. Another possibility is that a Persian historian wrote the book of Esther. The fact that God's name is not mentioned could indicate that the history was copied from Persian records. Being godless people, no Persian historian would have mentioned God. In Esther 6:1, King Ahasuerus calls for the chronicles of his reign to be read to him during a night of restlessness. Perhaps it was from these books that we get Esther's story. In either case, the book is remarkable. Regardless of who wrote this book, God is clearly the author. He is glorified!

For our purposes, it is not really crucial to know who wrote the book. We will refer to the writer of Esther from here on as our " historian." What is crucial, however, is that we receive the truth of this book: it is not just a story, it is a *history*! Exciting, passionate, surprising, miraculous... the best part is that this book is true! I love a true story! It makes me think that if God could do it years ago, then surely He can do it today. If He can work through Esther or any other person, than maybe He can work through me and you!

How will studying the life of Esther benefit you? Perhaps like your life, initially Esther's life seemed ordinary. Perhaps like your life, Esther's life took an unexpected turn. Dealing with unexpected events is one thing that we can completely identify with — you and I deal with surprises daily! (Trust me, there's never a dull moment with twin boys in my house!) Perhaps just as the Lord's direction may surprise you at times, Esther herself may have been surprised at the ways the Lord moved in her life. Through all the events that may have caught her unaware, she handled every turn with grace and integrity. Esther's one constant in her ever changing life was her faithfulness to God, and she depended on Him continually.

Wherever you are on the journey of your life, your ability (or inability) to gracefully deal with the challenges that life presents to you daily will define you. Consistently and deliberately maintaining your faith and letting God be your ever present help and guide will enable you to successfully handle life's twists and turns. In this, Esther is a wonderful example!

Throughout the study of her life, we will touch on many issues that will help you be the successful woman that God intends for you to be. Like Esther's path to becoming queen may not have been her original dream for her life, the road He leads you on may or may not be the one you expected to travel. As you put your trust in God's love for you and His wisdom, you will find success. As you learn these lessons from Esther's life, you may not always be able to predict your destination, but you will be able to take confidence in this: that what may be surprising to you is no surprise to the Lord.

As I become excited by the possibilities of what God could do (and desires to do and will do!) in my life and your life today, a favorite verse flashes through my mind: "Jesus Christ is the same yesterday, today, and forever"![3] God is still powerful, still able, and still willing! Every day of your life, the extra-special days and the extra-common days, God is moving. As you are faithful, He is preparing you for the greater purpose that He has for your life. As you read Esther's story, be inspired to read into the details of your own life as well — God is always working in the life of a faithful believer!

In these details, one is never to be forgotten: GOD LOVES YOU! God's great investment of time *in* you is a natural outcome of His great love *for* you. Behind every challenge and in every triumph is your Heavenly Father: spurring you on to greatness, encouraging you to expand your horizons, teaching you to hear His voice and giving you the boldness to obey... In His love, the believer can find peace, contentment, freedom and more — learning to rely on His love and trust His heart will empower you and enable you to achieve success in Him!

This study will be divided into ten weeks, each week divided into five days of "mini lessons". Each lesson begins with an illustration that will introduce the idea of the personal application for the day before getting into the Word. Each lesson may take you about ten to twelve minutes, so you can easily add this to your daily quiet time. If you do not currently have a daily quiet time, this little study may serve as a great tool to help you develop that important discipline. As you read the Word, you will find that you will develop a hunger for more! Also, after reading through Esther and studying this book together, we will see that it is not at all just dry history: it is a powerful and timeless example to what God can do with a person completely submitted to Him, regardless of personal cost.

As we begin, pray that God will open your eyes to the greater purpose that He has for your life. Open your heart to the story of Esther — and open your heart to what God would unfold in YOUR story as you submit your life to Him! Just as the Lord had a great purpose in His heart for Esther, He has a great purpose in His heart for you. Throughout the study, you will recognize that Esther was not only committed to the *purpose* that God had for her; she was committed to the *process* that it required. God's purpose for you also requires a process. As we study Esther together, pray that God would reveal His vision to you, and also pray for the strength it will take to embrace the process that will get that vision accomplished in your life. Whatever your role is: daughter, sister, wife, mother, career woman, or friend; God desires to use you to make an impact in your community and in your world!

Older? Yes. Quiet? Yes. Wiser? Well, maybe it's too early to tell. More mature? I don't know if I am that yet, either. I know what I am: "confident of this very thing, that He who has begun a good work in you will complete it until the day of Jesus Christ" (Philippians 1:6). God will continue to work on me, just as He will continue to work on you. In that knowledge, I can find peace in the midst of the storm. You can, too.

Are you ready? Say a prayer, grab your favorite Bible and a pencil (Who knows? God might begin speaking to you today — take time to record what He says to you!). Find a quiet place, a quiet time, and get comfortable. At your favorite table or your favorite chair, invite God to meet with you. No "multi-tasking" this morning — your deadlines, dishes and laundry will keep! You are about to discover a new friend: an orphaned Jewess, living in a godless community. Her name is Esther, and she is preparing to be a queen. Surprisingly, you might find that the two of you have quite a bit in common!

And wouldn't that be unexpected?

ESTHER: CHAPTER 1
King Ahasuerus dethrones Queen Vashti

This week as you study, keep one word in the back of your mind: **providence.** This is an important word in our first chapter, but also important throughout the entire book of Esther. Defined in *Systematic Theology* by Dr. Augustus Hopkins Strong, providence is "that continuous agency of God by which He makes all the events of the physical and moral universe fulfill the original design with which they were created".[4] In other words, God is in complete control of His creation. He is continuously working to see His purposes come to pass. Even behind the scenes, sometimes seemingly hidden from human eyes, God is in control. His providence — His ACTION — is especially important to search for His providence and action during the book of Esther, as His name is never mentioned.

While you are seeking for God's handiwork in Esther's story, begin to seek for His handiwork in *your* story! In every detail, in every moment, God is there loving you, encouraging you, rejoicing with you, grieving with you... The Word tells us that apart from Him, we can do nothing.[5] Invite Him to be a part of every aspect of your life this week!

DAY ONE: KING AHASUERUS

Selected Reading

As you open the word of God today, open your heart to what God has to say to you this week. Just as God was working "behind the scenes" in Persia so many years ago, He is working in your life today — whether you recognize it or not is up to you!

FRIEND TO FRIEND...

Expected or unexpected — expectations can get us into trouble sometimes. We will focus today on Ahasuerus and his expectations as he ascends to his throne. When we meet Esther, we will see that she had a set of her own expectations.

One sort of expectation, like hope, is wonderful. This is the type of expectation that keeps us connected to the vision that God has placed inside us. Jeremiah 29:11 is certainly familiar to all of us, and in this passage God promises to give us "a future and a *hope*". In Hebrews 11:1, faith is described as "the substance of things *hoped* for". This hope and expectation draw us to the Lord, like a cord in our spirit pulling us toward God as we strive to be close to Him. Keeping a tight hold on that cord can be a wonderful asset to us on our journey home. It is in the Lord that we find our freedom, and keeping this hope in our hearts will keep us free to worship and serve Him without fear.

Of course, another kind of expectation can be binding to us rather than freeing. When we look to people or even to ourselves rather than the Lord, we will find another kind of expectation. I remember allowing myself to be impacted by this type of expectation as a young pastor's wife. You see, I had developed this picture in my mind of the perfect pastor's wife — my own expectation of what success in my new role would look like. Unfortunately, the expectation I had created in my mind looked absolutely NOTHING like me. In my mind, a pastor's wife was quiet, beautiful, spiritual, a Bible scholar, a wonderful mother, had no need of friendship outside of her husband and Jesus, and always perfect in every word and action. (If you knew how chatty and clumsy I am, you would know this is not only impossible for me, it is laughable to expect that I could ever even come close!) This expectation also seemed to be supported by people in the church where I was raised, making it all the more believable. The more I dwelled on these unrealistic and unscriptural expectations (and the more I dwelled on my inability to achieve them), the more worried and withdrawn I became.

Fortunately, the Lord worked on me — and in a different way than I expected. I expected that becoming a pastor's wife would magically make me all the things that I thought I should be in this role. Instead, I learned that marrying Michael did not turn me into another person any more than standing in an orchard would have made me an orange. Gently, and over time, the Lord revealed to me His expectation for my role. I was not to become another person at all — I was to continue growing in Him and doing my best to fulfill His expectations of me which I could find in His Word. God saw me where I was, and He was interested in drawing me closer to Him (which would inevitably produce change). He had created me. God knew, as I did not yet know, that my personality was a part of His creation. Somehow, even chatty and clumsy and laughably imperfect, God would be able to use me. The wrong expectation had created anxiety . The right expectation had created peace.

James 1:23-24 teaches us, "For if anyone is a hearer of the word and not a doer, he is like a man observing his natural face in a mirror; for he observes himself, goes away, and immediately forgets what kind of man he was." James compares the Word of God to a mirror, showing us what we are and who we are. The wrong kind of expectation can turn our focus away from the Lord, and make us forget what we are supposed to look like: we will "immediately forget what kind of man" or woman we are. James warns us not to allow that to happen. We find the promise to go along with the instruction in verse 25: "But he who looks into the perfect law of liberty and continues in it, and is not a forgetful hearer but a doer of the work, this one will be blessed in what he does." Look into the Word and find out who you are to become. Strive daily to fulfill the expectations that the Lord has for you and you will be blessed in what you do! As God did not expect me to turn into someone else on my first day as a pastor's wife, He does not expect you to turn into someone else in order to achieve your goals: you will find your success in being yourself serving the Lord!

God's providential power is working in your life today. He has created you with your specific personality traits and your specific family relationships to be successful in your specific location and occupation. No need to worry that you are the wrong person in the wrong place (as I did!): you were created with a destiny and a purpose. You were given a future and a hope. Even before the moment you were born, God had already invested too much time in you to let you wander without a course or direction. He means for you to be successful. As you follow Him closely, you are sure to find that success! If you find your personal expectations or the expectation of those around you to be a hindrance, let them go! Look to the "mirror" of the word of God to find out who you are: a royal priesthood, a member of a chosen generation, the apple of God's eye, a joint heir with Christ, a daughter... And thank Him for creating the wonderful person that you are! In His providence, you were created with a specific purpose. In His love, you will find the tools you need to fulfill that purpose.

Where will Ahasuerus and Esther find themselves? As he comes into power, Ahasuerus has an expectation for his life — will his expectation be fulfilled? Esther, living quietly with her cousin Mordecai, has an altogether different expectation for her life — will her expectation be fulfilled? As we get to know them better, we will find out.

> *Now it came to pass in the days of Ahasuerus (this was the Ahasuerus who reigned over one hundred and twenty-seven provinces, from India to Ethiopia)* Esther 1:1

Our story begins with: "Now it came to pass in the days of Ahasuerus". Are you a little disappointed? I was! To be honest, this phrase was not the "catchy" beginning that we may have expected from a story as powerful and exciting as Esther's story! Stay with me — there's nowhere to go but up from here!

Esther is not mentioned in this chapter. The first person to whom we are initially introduced is King Ahasuerus. As this book may have been copied from Persian records, the king is referred to by his Persian name. However, Ahasuerus is generally believed to be Xerxes I, and he is referred to as Xerxes in other books of the Bible. Let us "back up" a little bit to find out who this man is and what has gone on in the years before he became king. Understanding his history will help us to better understand his state of mind. Understanding his history will also help us to better understand his importance to Esther's story — and ours.

Chronologically, the events recorded in the book of Esther happen in between the events recorded in the books of Ezra and Nehemiah. While Ezra and Nehemiah deal with the activity of the Jews who *left* Persia once their captivity had ended, Esther is the history of the Jews who *remained* in Persia once the captivity had ended.

Ahasuerus' grandfather is King Cyrus, who ruled Persia from around 538 B.C. to 530 B.C. At the time when Cyrus (Ahasuerus' grandfather) became king, the Jews had already been in captivity in Babylon for almost seventy years. Perhaps the Jews were feeling discouraged or forgotten by their God, but remember our word: **providence**! God has not forgotten His chosen people, and He is constantly working on their behalf!

It is interesting to look into the reign of King Cyrus, King Ahasuerus' grandfather. In his relatively short time on the throne, he was a successful and savvy leader. One accomplishment in particular would become important in Esther's history: Cyrus led a successful attack against Babylon, putting Babylon under Persia's control. Therefore, when the Jews (Esther's ancestors) were taken into captivity, they were brought into a country ruled by Persia (Ahasuerus' ancestors). Years before their appointed time in history, we can see that God was ordering specific events to determine their course. Years before Ahasuerus and eventually Esther came into power, God was carefully orchestrating events to create the atmosphere in which Esther would be successful in her purpose.

Isaiah prophesied regarding Cyrus' reign years before he was to come into power:

Who says of Cyrus, 'He is My shepherd,
And he shall perform all My pleasure,
Saying to Jerusalem,"You shall be built,"
And to the temple, "Your foundation shall be laid."'
"Thus says the LORD to His anointed,
To Cyrus, whose right hand I have held -
To subdue nations before him
And loose the armor of kings,
To open before him the double doors,
So that the gates will not be shut
Isaiah 44:28-45:1

Toward the end of the time when the Jews' captivity should be over, Cyrus (Ahasuerus' grandfather) comes into power. Almost two hundred years previous to Cyrus' reign, Isaiah had prophesied concerning the rebuilding of the temple. Cyrus was mentioned *by name*! (It is possible that Daniel, who had come to Babylon at the time of the Jewish captivity, was the prophet who showed Cyrus the record of this very prophecy!) Cyrus must have felt pretty important to see his name in such a record, especially considering it was in a prophecy by a God whom he did not even serve. To appease the Jews, and most likely help his own political career, Cyrus fulfills this prophecy. In his first years as king, (and remember — we are still years away from Ahasuerus' reign) , Cyrus ends the Babylonian captivity, and begins the process to rebuild Jerusalem.

In his account of this history, Ezra describes Cyrus' role in the end of the captivity.

> *Now in the first year of Cyrus king of Persia, that the word of the LORD by the mouth of Jeremiah might be fulfilled, the LORD stirred up the spirit of Cyrus king of Persia, so that he made a proclamation throughout all his kingdom, and also put it in writing, saying, Thus says Cyrus king of Persia: All the kingdoms of the earth the LORD God of heaven has given me. And He has commanded me to build Him a house at Jerusalem which is in Judah. Who is among you of all His people? May his God be with him, and let him go up to Jerusalem which is in Judah, and build the house of the LORD God of Israel (He is God), which is in Jerusalem. And whoever is left in any place where he dwells, let the men of his place help him with silver and gold, with goods and livestock, besides the freewill offerings for the house of God which is in Jerusalem. Ezra 1:1-4*

The Lord "stirred up the spirit of Cyrus" so that His purposes would be fulfilled. In this decree, Cyrus releases the Jews from their captivity in Babylon and gives them leave to return to Jerusalem if they wish to do so. Furthermore, Cyrus commands the rebuilding of the "house of God" in Jerusalem, the temple which had been destroyed years before. Reading further in the same passage in Ezra, we learn that Cyrus even returned articles that had been taken from the temple during Nebuchadnezzar's reign.

In spite of Cyrus' decree, it seems that he started strong on behalf of the Jews, but did not finish. Possibly, his intentions toward the Jews were good and he did became busy with other matters. It may be more likely to assume that Cyrus "did his good deed", helped his political image, and lost interest in the project once his own selfish purposes were fulfilled. Whatever the case, Cyrus' help to the Jews did not continue and the rebuilding of the temple came to a stop. A change came for the Jews when Cyrus' son, Darius, came into power.

Cyrus' son, Darius, was a powerful man as well. During the rebuilding of the temple, the Jews ran into some problems with the Samaritans. Although Cyrus did end the captivity and ordered the rebuilding of the temple, he apparently did not do much to continue his help to them and the construction was delayed for many years. King Darius coming into power gave the Jews renewed hope that the temple work could begin again, and they were not disappointed. Please continue to remember that all this is leading to Ahasuerus: Cyrus is his grandfather, and Darius is his father.

Now that Darius is in power, he has some decrees of his own to make. Again, Ezra writes of one important decree.

> Moreover I issue a decree as to what you shall do for the elders of these Jews, for the building of this house of God: Let the cost be paid at the king's expense from taxes on the region beyond the River; this is to be given immediately to these men, so that they are not hindered. And whatever they need -- young bulls, rams, and lambs for the burnt offerings of the God of heaven, wheat, salt, wine, and oil, according to the request of the priests who are in Jerusalem -- let it be given them day by day without fail, that they may offer sacrifices of sweet aroma to the God of heaven, and pray for the life of the king and his sons. Also I issue a decree that whoever alters this edict, let a timber be pulled from his house and erected, and let him be hanged on it; and let his house be made a refuse heap because of this. And may the God who causes His name to dwell there destroy any king or people who put their hand to alter it, or to destroy this house of God which is in Jerusalem. I Darius issue a decree; let it be done diligently.
> Ezra 6:8-12

In Ezra 6, we read that Darius commanded that the decree that Cyrus given concerning the house of God in Jerusalem be carried out, and that the work continue unhindered. Beyond that, the work would be completed "at the king's expense". Darius was not only making sure that the work would be continued, but he was paying for it himself! Darius also commands a heavy penalty to anyone who tried to prevent the Jews from rebuilding their temple: death by hanging.

Both Cyrus and Darius had selfish motives — their decision to help the Jews was most likely motivated by political ambition — but "the king's heart is in the hand of the LORD, Like the rivers of water; He turns it wherever He wishes"![6] God was working through these men of power, but God's chosen were never forgotten or abandoned for a moment. He was speaking to the Jews in their captivity and in their newfound freedom.

During the years of captivity, the Lord had offered encouragement and direction to his people through many sources, including the prophet Jeremiah:

Thus says the LORD of hosts, the God of Israel, to all who were carried away captive, whom I have caused to be carried away from Jerusalem to Babylon: Build houses and dwell in them; plant gardens and eat their fruit. Take wives and beget sons and daughters; and take wives for your sons and give your daughters to husbands, so that they may bear sons and daughters — that you may be increased there, and not diminished. And seek the peace of the city where I have caused you to be carried away captive, and pray to the LORD for it; for in its peace you will have peace. For thus says the LORD of hosts, the God of Israel: Do not let your prophets and your diviners who are in your midst deceive you, nor listen to your dreams which you cause to be dreamed. For they prophesy falsely to you in My name; I have not sent them, says the LORD. Jeremiah 29:4-9*

What does God say about the captivity of the Jews in Babylon? God, through the prophet Jeremiah, encourages His people that He not only knows where they are, but that He is the one that caused them to be carried away captive. God had a plan and He reminded His people that they were continually in His hands. What a tremendous example of providence!

In addition to encouragement, God gives some instruction as well. God's instructions to the Jews in captivity are specific and each requires a process. Each direction requires time, and each represents the process that will bring about His purposes. First, He instructs them to build houses, but beyond that to *dwell* in those houses. My young daughter loves a "sleepover." She loves to have guests in our home and she loves to be the guest in a friend's home. A sleepover is fun, but it is a *visit* — it is not *living* somewhere. To dwell or to live somewhere indicates that a significant amount of time will be spent in a designated location. The Jews were not to treat their captivity as a visit to Babylon — they were to live there until the Lord ended their captivity.

Another instruction to the Jews: they were to have children, let those children marry and have children themselves... Again, to produce children and grandchildren requires a certain amount of time. Yet another instruction that required an investment on the part of the Jews: they were to plant gardens, and wait so that they could be fed from those gardens... we could not put a seed in the ground and expect to immediately eat an apple from the same seed.

The Jews were instructed to "seek the peace of the city where I have caused you to be carried away captive, and pray to the LORD for it; for in its peace you will have peace" (Jeremiah 29:7). God was instructing and encouraging them. Notice

His words: "the city where *I have caused you to be carried away* captive". God was telling His people, "I not only know where you are; I am the reason that you are there! Even in your hardship, I am with you and I am in control!" The Lord wanted them to focus on the NOW of the situation, and not be consumed with the sadness and fear that might overtake them during the captivity. To give them a hope that would enable them to overcome, the Lord also gave them a promise: that at the appointed time, He would return to them and bring them back from their captivity. Jesus gave us a similar promise, didn't He? See John 14:18.

One more before we close for today.

> *So the elders of the Jews built, and they prospered through the prophesying of Haggai the prophet and Zechariah the son of Iddo. And they built and finished it, according to the commandment of the God of Israel, and according to the command of Cyrus, Darius, and Artaxerxes king of Persia.* Ezra 6:14

Whose command made it possible for the temple to be completed? The temple was completed "at the command of the God of Israel, and according to the command of Cyrus, Darius, and Artaxerxes, king of Persia" (v. 14). The men mentioned are Ahasuerus' grandfather (Cyrus), his father (Darius) and his son (Artaxerxes — remember Babylonian records refer to Ahasuerus as Xerxes, and his son is referred to as Artaxerxes). Did you notice one name that is not mentioned on this list? Ahasuerus himself! As you can see, Ahasuerus comes from a powerful family, and most likely has high expectations for his own reign.

Will his expectations be right or wrong? Fulfilled or unfulfilled?

Before you close for today, ask the Lord to reveal to you His expectations for your life. As you begin the process of learning what He intends for you and from you, release yourself from any current expectation that may be causing you anxiety — God means for YOU to be a success!

શ્ર

DAY TWO: ESTHER 1:1-9

Now we are "getting down to business" as they say! Esther is not mentioned in this chapter, but you are about to see how God is moving on her behalf. God is moving on your behalf as well! Praise God for His providence!

FRIEND TO FRIEND...

Have you ever felt as if you go unnoticed? Have you ever felt that you were not valued by the people around you? I wonder if Ahasuerus felt this way. If he ever did, he is about to change all of that: he is going to throw a party in his own honor. Today, we are going to continue along the same lines as yesterday, but change the focus from our personal expectations to the expectations we have of the people around us. We are going to think about changing the way we value the opinions of people in our lives.

In Colossians 3:23, Paul encourages believers: "whatever you do, do it heartily, as to the Lord and not to men." In the New Living translation, the same verse and the one following are written this way: "Work hard and cheerfully at whatever you do, as though you were working for the Lord rather than for people. Remember that the Lord will give you an inheritance as your reward, and the Master you are serving is Christ." Whether or not you are noticed by people, be encouraged that you are noticed by God! Confidence in His love for you will free you from the opinions of people around you.

While it is nice to be recognized, recognition from people should not be a desire or motivator in our lives. While praise from people may feel good, it does not last. Eventually, people will disappoint you or become disappointed in you. Well meaning, kind people are still people, just like you, capable of making mistakes or saying hurtful words. If praise from people can build you up, then disapproval from those same people can tear you down.

Years ago, I taught music in an elementary school. I will never forget a story that a friend once told me about his childhood music teacher. When he was in the 3rd grade, his class was practicing for the school musical. My friend remembered how excited he was; dancing with all his joy, singing with all his heart at the top of his lungs during rehearsals. As the performance drew closer, his anticipation drew stronger, as did his pride in his performance. One day, his teacher singled him out and called him over. My friend remembers thinking, "I bet I'll get a solo!" When he rushed to her side to hear the great news, she proceeded to tell him that during the performance he should move his mouth along with the words but not make any sound.

He laughed as he told the story, but I felt sad. My friend decided at that time he had no talent for singing or performing, and never attempted anything of this sort again. (Bless his heart!) I won't dramatize it — at eight years old, he was probably not on the road to becoming a major music superstar, and his life now is happy and full. However, at the moment of those words from his teacher: "You don't have to make any sound", he determined that he would not make any sound, and hasn't sung a note outside of his shower since. His teacher's words had power over him, and he always remembered them.

At the time that my friend told me his story, more than ten years had passed since he was in the 3rd grade. He had not forgotten. Now it has been more than ten years since I heard the story, and I have never forgotten. The more I thought about it, the more I became convinced of these two things: first, I never wanted to allow a person's words that kind of power in my life. Second, if my words could have that kind of power in the life of anyone else, I would try to choose my words carefully. (A challenge I find difficult to maintain at times — it isn't easy, is it?) The Bible says that the power of life and death are in the tongue (Proverbs 18:21). It is so true. Please, friend, do not allow your life to be held captive by someone else's words: find your life in what the Lord has to say about you!

If you can allow God's love to do its complete work in you, you will not need the approval of those around you. The wonderful thing about being released from the need of man's approval is that simultaneously you will be released from concern when people disapprove of you. Just as a negative response from man could stop your progress by creating fear, a positive response from man could stop your progress by creating complacency. God loves you! God sees you! God is smiling on you as you serve Him, and that is enough.

However, as with every area of our lives, there is a balance to be found. It is possible to go so far beyond caring about the opinions of people that you become callous to the needs and feelings of those around you. It is also possible to go so far beyond caring about the opinions of people that you become unteachable. The Bible encourages us to seek wisdom. Proverbs 16:16 tells us it is "much better to get wisdom than gold". Wisdom can be found in a close, vibrant, growing relationship with the Lord, but a great support to godly wisdom can be found in the godly people around you. Proverbs 24:6 teaches us that "there is safety in a multitude of counselors". There are people in your life whom God has placed near you to help you on your journey. (Providence!) Here is a personal challenge, and one that only you can determine how it will be achieved in your life: you must strive to strike a healthy balance between allowing the right people to help you and not allowing the wrong people to hinder you.

Now let's find out where Ahasuerus finds his self-worth; whether from his own opinions or those of the people around him.

> Now it came to pass in the days of Ahasuerus (this was the Ahasuerus who reigned over one hundred and twenty-seven provinces, from India to Ethiopia), in those days when King Ahasuerus sat on the throne of his kingdom, which was in Shushan the citadel, that in the third year of his reign he made a feast for all his officials and servants — the powers of Persia and Media, the nobles, and the princes of the provinces being before him --when he showed the riches of his

glorious kingdom and the splendor of his excellent majesty for many
days, one hundred and eighty days in all. Esther 1:1-4

As we learned yesterday, the men who ruled before Ahasuerus came into power were very successful kings. His grandfather, Cyrus, had united the two powerful kingdoms, Persia and Media, during his reign. Furthermore, Ahasuerus' father, Darius, had established Shushan (Susa) as the capital. When Ahasuerus ascends to the throne, Persia is a "force to be reckoned with"! Living in this capital city developed by his father and surrounded by evidence of his predecessors' greatness, Ahasuerus now rules over 127 provinces. Though he is only three years into his reign, Ahasuerus is feeling one of two emotions: either he is very proud of himself, or he is very disappointed in himself.

Reflecting on his family history, Ahasuerus must have come into his reign with truly high expectations. The expectations on Ahasuerus from his own family as well as the inhabitants of Persia had to have been huge. The pressure on him to live up to and possibly surpass the success of his predecessors must have been great. Ahasuerus must have come into his reign with his own expectations as well, but what his personal expectations were, we cannot know.

I wonder: did Ahasuerus know himself? Discouraged rather than inspired by the success of his predecessors, had he given up before he even began? Did he determine before ascending to the throne of Persia that there was no way for him to achieve the level of success enjoyed by his father or grandfather? Was he nervous?

On the other hand, was Ahasuerus ultra-confident? Was he so certain of his ability to rule that he failed to prepare? Was he spoiled? Whatever his state of mind upon beginning his rule of Persia, I believe that Ahasuerus has come to an accurate understanding of his position now. Perhaps he is thinking to himself, "Three years in this chair, and what have I done?"

Whatever the case, Ahasuerus throws himself a great party. Ahasuerus either feels that there is much to be celebrated already during his short reign, or he feels that a party will mask the fact that his reign has been less than illustrious. Hoping to boost his own self esteem and boost his image among his subjects, he decides to celebrate... well, something.

It is significant to notice what the historian noticed: three years into Ahasuerus' reign, and the most noteworthy item to record is this party.

In Persia, King Ahasuerus is working hard. Ahasuerus throws this party for the officials in his kingdom to show off his power, to show off his possessions and declare himself the king of the world. Ahasuerus is spinning his wheels to receive adulation from his people. Six months is a long time to entertain company, even if it is a great celebration! At my house, we enjoy having guests, but sometimes it is hard work! Cleaning before they arrive (and after they depart!), stocking the fridge before they arrive (and, again, after they depart!)... being a host can be a joy, but after six months even the best host could be weary of company. Apparently, Ahasuerus did not feel quite done yet (well, maybe he has someone else to do the cooking and cleaning!).

> *And when these days were completed, the king made a feast lasting*
> *seven days for all the people who were present in Shushan the citadel,*
> *from great to small, in the court of the garden of the king's palace.*
> Esther 1:5

As if six months was not quite enough, he continues this for one more week to give EVERYONE, not only the officials in his kingdom, an opportunity to see his "great power". Ahasuerus wanted to make sure that people in his kingdom were completely and totally convinced that he was the greatest. The wine was free-flowing, the food was delicious, the palace was beautiful, and King Ahasuerus was doing his best to present a perfect tribute to his power. Of course, in convincing others of his greatness, Ahasuerus may be attempting to convince himself as well.

However misguided his motives are, Ahasuerus is (at least by his "job description") in a position where he should be serving his people. His throne should have given him an attitude of concern for the well-being of his subjects. Here is one area where women can identify with him: we are caretakers as well. On your job, perhaps you are looking out for the needs of your company and your superiors. In your home, perhaps you are looking out for the best needs of your family. If you are a wife or mother, perhaps you are continually taking care of your husband or children. These can be "thankless" roles at times, can't they?

Ahasuerus, in throwing this party, may be thinking to himself that he has gone unnoticed. He obviously wants to draw attention to himself, and he desires a specific result: that people would see his "great power". Ahasuerus is looking for commendation from man. Considering the great lengths he is going to with this audacious party, we might say that he is desperate for it. Do you ever find yourself seeking the good opinion of people around you? Unfortunately for Ahasuerus, he does not have our advantage: you and I are children of God! Our first concern should be pleasing Him.

Ahasuerus' main concern is pleasing people, and you and I probably agree: pleasing people can be hard work.

> *There were white and blue linen curtains fastened with cords of fine*
> *linen and purple on silver rods and marble pillars; and the couches*
> *were of gold and silver on a mosaic pavement of alabaster, turquoise,*
> *and white and black marble. And they served drinks in golden ves-*
> *sels, each vessel being different from the other, with royal wine in*
> *abundance, according to the generosity of the king. In accordance*

with the law, the drinking was not compulsory; for so the king had
ordered all the officers of his household, that they should do accord-
ing to each man's pleasure. Esther 1:6-8

The palace of King Ahasuerus is described as very ornate and colorful. In these few verses, several different elements are mentioned: white and blue curtains fastened to silver rods with purple and linen cords, marble pillars, mosaic tiled floors made out of alabaster, turquoise, white and black marble.... The drinks were served in golden cups (vessels), and no two cups were alike! A great deal of planning and preparation went into this celebration. One more time, let's look into a little bit of history here.

In Exodus 20, we find the Ten Commandments. In the third commandment, God declares that "You shall not make for yourself a carved image" (Exodus 20:4). Perhaps because of a desire to stay obedient to this commandment, the Hebrew people (Jewish people) during Bible times may not have been very artistic. Also, because of their time in slavery, they may not have had the outlet or opportunity for much artistic creativity. Just put this little tidbit in the back of your mind for now — we'll get back to it later!

During this time, another "party" is going on: Queen Vashti is hostess to a banquet for the wives of all these men coming to the palace.

Queen Vashti also made a feast for the women in the royal palace
which belonged to King Ahasuerus. Esther 1:9

Notice it took our historian 8 verses to describe Ahasuerus' party, but one verse was sufficient for Queen Vashti's banquet. While the king was celebrating his excess, the queen was having a beautiful yet modest feast for the women of the kingdom. Though her celebrations were much smaller, Vashti was fulfilling her role as a support and complement to her husband.

For Vashti, her modest celebration was enough. She was not necessarily seeking the good opinion of man — she was steadily and modestly doing the work that was appropriate for her to do. Vashti was confident in her role, and was satisfied with a quiet gathering in her quarters. Even though the difference between them was great, her gathering did not represent any criticism of her husband — her role was one of support and complement to Ahasuerus. In contrast to the king, Vashti was not seeking praise or attention from Ahasuerus or any of his many guests.

The contrast between Vashti and Ahasuerus is sharp, and it is not only revealed in their style of entertaining guests. Ahasuerus is desperately seeking approval from the people in his kingdom. Near and far, he has invited everyone. His party was for "officials and servants" (Esther 1:3), and the "great and small" (Esther 1:5). Ahasuerus could not have possibly known all of these people personally, yet apparently he has put great stock in what they have to say about him, having gone to such extreme lengths to impress this mass of people.

Vashti, on the other hand, does not find it necessary to seek out the spotlight. In her quarters, Vashti's party is intimate and quiet. Being in the background is fine with her: she does not draw her confidence from a crowd. She knows herself, and she sees the value in a job well done, regardless of popular opinion.

Of course, she is not to stay in the background for long.

As Queen Vashti entertains the women, she is also looking out for the needs of her household by fulfilling her role and reflecting the best of her husband — be encouraged today that what you do (whether it be as a woman, sister, professional, wife, or mother) is ordained by the Lord. You are a valued treasure, woman of God!

ॐ

DAY THREE: ESTHER 1:10-12

As we are in the hands of a providential God, sometimes a decision that we consider small could become a turning point for us or for those around us. Pray that God would show you the importance of daily bathing our lives with prayer and thanksgiving — even in the small things!

FRIEND TO FRIEND...

I would like to think of myself as efficient and organized. However, the people closest to me would probably use stronger words. Words like obsessive, compulsive or even ridiculous! I have to admit: my organized personality versus my husband's "rolling with it" attitude makes for some funny stories during his sermons! I have a schedule and routine for almost everything. I enjoy having a to-do list and a plan, and I feel great when my day goes according to my schedule. But even with the best laid plans (and trust me, I almost always have a plan!), I am never immune to the unexpected!

In every day, whether the day is good or not so good, God is good. When I go to bed at night, I might reflect on my day. I will judge it to have been a good or bad day based on events, people that I saw or spoke with, or what I was or was not able to accomplish. I'll have to be honest — sometimes I look at my to-do list in the morning, and judge my day to be good or bad before it even starts. On those days deemed to be bad before they begin, the "snooze" button on my alarm clock gets a workout!

In the Word, we are reminded of how limited our judgement is, and simultaneously encouraged of how perfect and complete God's judgement is. In the familiar passage Isaiah 55:8, the Lord tells us His thoughts are "not our thoughts" and His ways are "not His ways". His thoughts and ways are so much higher than ours. He has a complete view! Sometimes "backing up" can give you a much clearer picture. For example, if I wanted to see my entire hometown, it might be easier to see by helicopter above the city than in my car driving through it. Even in emotional situations, getting some distance may mean gaining some perspective: stepping away for a period of time can make all the difference in the world.

Praising God on good days is easy, isn't it? My son, Jacob, is a cheerful kid. His personality is pure sunshine! If there is a positive side to be found, Jacob does not have to look hard. Finding the good comes naturally to him. He is quick to smile and quick to laugh. He loves being outside, so a warm, sunny day is his ideal! However, rain is a different story for this happy little guy. For Jake, rain may mean a cancelled ball game. Rain means an afternoon inside when he would rather be outside riding his bike, walking his dog, or dribbling his basketball. I find myself to be the same way: when the "sun" is on my face (things are going well, everyone is happy and healthy, etc.), praise flows easily. When "rain" comes (trials, financial struggles, sickness), I have to lift up an "in spite of" praise, which does not come naturally to me!

Through the prophet Isaiah, the Lord says that "the rain comes down, and the snow from heaven, and do not return there" (Isaiah 55:10). We know that the rain will come, but let's not stop with the rain: God, in His providence, has a reason! The rest of this verse in Isaiah encourages us that the rain came to "water the earth, and make it bring forth and bud, that it may give seed to the sower and bread to the eater". The rain may disappoint us initially, but our disappointment truly comes from our limited knowledge. While my Jacob is disappointed over his soggy afternoon, the reason for his disappointment is not truly the rain: the true reason for his disappointment is his lack of information. If Jacob knew the entire picture as God knows the entire picture, a cancelled ball game would seem minor in light of the farmer who is rejoicing over the first rain ending months of drought. If Jacob knew the entire picture, my sunshine boy would rejoice with the farmer rather than mourn for his "ruined" afternoon!

It is the same with us. Sometimes I think to myself, "Maybe this would be easier if I only understood *why...*" Every day we see or we experience personally situations which we cannot explain. When I married Michael , I prayed for success in our ministry. When we moved to Miami, it was to a rental house without air conditioning (in MIAMI), to a job where the salary represented a cut of more than $25,000 per year from our previous positions, and to a youth group of 6 that met in a children's church room. Believe me, after our first youth service, we were asking God for the *why* of our call to Miami. Had we missed His leading? I was so homesick and so short sighted that I cried nearly every day. I thought my heart would break under the pressure and disappointment that I felt in our first ministry job.

This initial heart-wrenching time led to a heartbreak of another kind. Four years after accepting this position, Michael came home and shared with me that he felt as if the Lord was calling us away from Miami. By this time, the youth group had grown to around 150 teenagers who had become part of our lives. Success was not to be measured by salaries or properties or even by numbers: God had been good and kind and generous, and we would never be the same again. We had formed close relationships, and we had seen the Lord change lives. Where I had once felt heartbreak over coming to Miami, I was now feeling heartbreak over leaving this place I had come to love so dearly. I realized that what I had prayed for years before had come: we *had* experienced success in our ministry time there.

When my grandmother fell sick a few years ago, I prayed for a miracle. When she passed away, I had to recognize through my heartbreak that I had received a miracle, just not the one I had asked for: my precious grandmother had gone home. There are so many other examples of difficult times that cannot be explained even with the benefit of hindsight. You have experiences such as this: a miscarriage, a rebellious son or daughter, a lost job, a sickness that did not heal... If we could sit down with the Lord and have Him explain to us, "My daughter, don't worry. You see, I have a plan and here are the specific reasons that these things that are happening to you, and here are the blessings that will come as a result of this temporary pain..." Even though we might wish for more at times, He does just that through His word: "I know that plans I have for you... plans for a future and a hope" (Jeremiah 29:11).

God, in His generous wisdom, never leaves us only with the "rain." He always offers us a reason to praise, even in our ignorance. The rain did not come to ruin Jacob's afternoon — it came to "water the earth, and make it bring forth and bud, that it may give seed to the sower and bread to the eater" (Isaiah 55:10). We might be ignorant of many things. We might not be able to understand or explain everything that happens in our lives, but we can be confident of this: the Father loves us and intends the best for us.

In the practical application, there is a spiritual application as well: just like the rain and snow that comes from heaven to fulfill a specific purpose, "So shall My word be that goes forth from My mouth; It shall not return to Me void, But it shall accomplish what I please, And it shall prosper in the thing for which I sent it." (Isaiah 55:11). Nothing that God does is without purpose. In Romans 8:28, Paul writes, "we know that all things work together for good to those who love God, to those who are the called according to His purpose." *All* things work together for *good*, and that is a reason to praise even when we do not understand!

Our God is sovereign. By definition, sovereign means supreme ruler, possessing ultimate power, able to act independently and without support or clearance form an outside source. That definition describes God, surely. While He does possess ultimate power, His greatest concern is you and me. He desires for us to be in relationship with Him. Seeing and knowing so much more than we do, His knowledge cannot be measured or even reasonably compared to anything that we can comprehend. God uses His sovereignty, His wisdom, His power to enable us to be close to Him.

Once we realize that God is sovereign, we must leave our lives in His hands. I have experienced victories in my personal life, but sometimes the trials that preceded these victories were "doozies"! If I had known beforehand what I would have had to walk through to receive the victory, I might have said, "NO THANKS!" and merely walked away, but God is more generous than to allow that. Sometimes, in this way, I can view my lack of information (lack of ability to judge my situation rightly) as a blessing in disguise... of course, there are times (more often than I would like to admit!) when I allow that same lack of information to become a source of frustration.

Paul writes in Romans 11:33, "Oh, the depth of the riches both of the wisdom and knowledge of God! How unsearchable are His judgments and His ways past finding out!"

The mind of God is unsearchable! His thoughts are higher than our thoughts, and His ways higher than our ways. In times of great tragedy and times of great triumph, God is in control. In the heartwarming times and the heartbreaking times, God is constantly at work in the lives of His people.

Even though I may have judged the day before it even started, I have to raise my hands in surrender and say, "this is the day that the Lord has made and I will rejoice and be glad in it..." I have to recognize that God is love and God is good all the time — and maybe, just maybe, I'll feel less inclined to hit the "snooze" button before my day begins!

Vashti and Ahasuerus did not know they were being held in God's mighty hands. They did not have the privilege that we have: we are in relationship with Him. We can experience daily that God is good and His mercy does indeed endure forever.

To remember where we were...

"Now it came to pass in the days of Ahasuerus (this was the Ahasuerus who reigned over one hundred and twenty-seven provinces, from India to Ethiopia), in those days when King Ahasuerus sat on the throne of his kingdom, which was in Shushan the citadel, that in

the third year of his reign he made a feast for all his officials and ser-
vants — the powers of Persia and Media, the nobles, and the princes
of the provinces being before him -- when he showed the riches of his
glorious kingdom and the splendor of his excellent majesty for many
days, one hundred and eighty days in all." Esther 1:1-4

Ahasuerus' celebration is starting to wind down, and he has exhausted all of his material possessions to show off to his guests. Perhaps he senses that his guests' interest is waning, or perhaps he is becoming bored himself. Ahasuerus must have begun to wonder inside himself : what else can he show his guests that may improve their opinion of him? The guests have seen his ornate, breath-takingly beautiful palace... they have filled themselves with his delectable foods and perfectly aged wines... surely they have been privileged to hear the best musicians and see the best dancers... no expense has been spared at this extravaganza, but maybe Ahasuerus (six months later) is looking for a new novelty to show off in front of his guests.

Ahasuerus is — if you will pardon the vernacular — drunk. No surprise there! The party has lasted for six months, and Ahasuerus has been the center of attention. Most likely, the officials and princes in the kingdom have been rotated through the palace as guests. To have all of his "leadership" there at once may have made the kingdom weak — and six months is a long time! Of course, being a good host — and one very proud of himself at that — Ahasuerus has been fully present the entire time. He doesn't want to miss a moment of his people celebrating his greatness!

"On the seventh day, when the heart of the king was merry with wine,
he commanded Mehuman, Biztha, Harbona, Bigtha, Abagtha,
Zethar, and Carcas, seven eunuchs who served in the presence of
King Ahasuerus, to bring Queen Vashti before the king, wearing
her royal crown, in order to show her beauty to the people and the
officials, for she was beautiful to behold." Esther 1:10-11

These seven men listed in verse 10 are close servants to Ahasuerus, and they probably have been with him throughout these six months as well. (No doubt can be left in anyone's mind as to what his closest servants have been doing — certainly they were indulging along with Ahasuerus in his excess!) Being eunuchs, these seven men were also allowed contact with the queen. This privilege had come to them at considerable personal sacrifice. Through different duties that these men had been assigned to perform, they had opportunities to be in Vashti's quarters at times. Afforded this relatively close connection to Vashti, they also probably had some idea or understanding of her personality.

Any prior experience with the queen, if there was any, did not factor in to anyone's thinking at this moment. When Ahasuerus decides to bring in Queen

Vashti, not a single one of these men suggests that this may not be a welcome idea to the queen. After six months of partying, six months of drinking, six months of revelry, things are bound to get out of control at some point. Ahasuerus is about to find out that, as far as his queen is concerned, he has just "crossed the line".

At the moment unaware of her husband's command, Queen Vashti is having her own modest, tasteful celebration in another part of the palace for the wives of the officials who have come to feast with the king. Now, she has received a request to parade herself in front of her drunk husband as well as his drunk friends. As she contemplated refusing the king's request, she may have been under the impression that, if she refused, he would forgive her later. Vashti may not have realized that this one decision could mean the loss of her crown.

But Queen Vashti refused to come at the king's command brought by his eunuchs Esther 1:12

Whether or not Vashti was completely understanding of this moment is a side issue to what is really going on here — **providence**. Even though God is not mentioned, He is beginning to shake things up, and Vashti is the first person that has to be moved in order to make room for another. Like Ahasuerus, Vashti is not a believer. Unlike Ahasuerus, Vashti does not require man's approval at any price. She knows her own mind, and she understands her own important position. The queen makes a decision that the people around her would consider to be a grave error: Vashti refuses to honor the king's request.

Without realizing it, Vashti is in the hands of a God that she does not even know, and He is at work in Persia. If she had been allowed the privilege of knowing the far reaching consequences of this decision (beyond the loss of her crown, to the rescuing of an entire race), would she have made the same decision? This lack of information on Vashti's part is fulfilling God's greater purpose.

Queen Vashti and King Ahasuerus are great examples of God's power and (here it is again) His **providence** at work. A request comes, and decision is made. A door is closed, and a door is opened...

Before you close today, think about situations in your own life where the providence of God was at work. Can you think of a specific time? Pray that God would help you to recognize His work in your life, and exercise your faith to trust His heart before you understand His reason!

❧

DAY FOUR: ESTHER 1:13-19

This is picking up a little, huh? I thought that you might be worried after all the history in the beginning that this might be somewhat... well, dry! A woman that I knew a long time ago used to say, "There's never a dull moment in the kingdom!" Thank God for every day — the seemingly common and the extra-exciting! He is working through both!

FRIEND TO FRIEND...

Mistake number one today: looking for encouragement from the apostle Paul! J.B. Phillips translates Romans 9:20-21 this way: "The potter, for instance, has complete control over the clay, making with one part of the lump a lovely vase, and with another a pipe for sewage." Today was not my day. I already felt like that "pipe for sewage"; what I wanted was a promise about becoming the "lovely vase"! Hopeful that Paul might offer a few inspirational words about how the vase and the sewage pipe both being valuable and important in their service, I read on. I was to have no such luck! Paul continues in Romans 9:31-32 that certain people (specifically in this passage, Israel) had "failed to reach their goal. And why? Because their minds were fixed on what they achieved instead of what they believed."

Okay, so it wasn't encouraging, but it was true. Truth was exactly what I needed today, like a splash of cold water in my face. Having their minds fixed on their achievements, rather than their beliefs, was what caused these people to fail years ago, and it was what could cause me to fail today. Being more concerned with *accomplishment* rather than *relationship* could mean the difference between success in my calling and failure to recognize what is of true importance.

When Michael brought our family to his hometown to plant this church, I had no idea how attached we would become to our congregation. Michael's style is highly relational. Where some pastors might be "above" their church members, Michael was right there with them. From the very beginning, he was living life with them, becoming a part of their lives and letting them be a part of our lives. Just being around Michael, people can sense his genuine love and compassionate spirit. He is someone with whom people feel an instant connection and friendship. From his pulpit, he is open and engaging. The children and I never mind that our family's stories regularly become sermon illustrations. Even when the children come to the sanctuary rather than the children's service (they like to hear Dad preach every once in a while), they laugh along with everyone else when Michael tells our stories. Through Michael's honesty and self-effacing style, our family becomes our congregation's family, and we love the feeling of being connected in our church.

We had always decided that we would open our hearts and lives to the people who came to our church. We had the idea that if we kept ourselves behind walls with people, somehow we would be keeping ourselves behind walls with the Lord. We knew that people would come and go as people always do, but we were determined that this knowledge would not cause us to become hard or distant. We would bless them when they came, and we would bless them if they left. If a family was to leave and our children asked questions (of course, they would ask questions as they had become attached as well), we would be generous in our compliments and vague in our heartbreak. We would take the opportunity to pray with them and teach them how to love and how to let go in our example. We came into the ministry with one goal: to see people successful in Christ. If they found the tools they needed in our church, then praise God. If they found what they needed elsewhere, we would praise God for their success. As time progressed and the church grew, we realized that, in allowing this transparency between us, we were afforded more opportunities to minister more effectively to the people in our church.

Of course, in opening my heart for the possibility of joy, I had opened my heart for the possibility of pain. Along with the greater opportunities to minister, there were greater opportunities for personal heartbreak when people found a new church home, or left for some other reason. This is a fact of life that pastors have to face. Every time, I am tempted to close my heart and "never let it happen again". I know, however, that if I allowed that hardness to come into my heart, I would be going against my own calling and I would lose the effectiveness that God meant for Michael's ministry and mine.

Today was a day to face that very temptation. A family who had become dear friends had left the church with no warning or explanation. Not even good bye. When they were missing on that first Sunday, we didn't realize that they had removed themselves from our church. We thought maybe someone was sick or an alarm clock didn't go off or something simple. If it had been something serious, they would have called us, of course. We had done so much for them and with them. We rejoiced when they rejoiced, we cried when they cried, we prayed with them, we prayed for them, we loved them and felt as if they loved us in return.

Of course, one Sunday turned to two, and then three. I mentioned to Michael that I had called and left a message. He told me that he had the same thought as well. He had left a message and sent a card. We felt sad as the realization sank in: they had left the church.

People don't know how to leave a church, and many pastors don't take such a loss graciously. In all our determinations about pastoring, we had considered the possibility of losing members, but this family was the first. It was time for a lesson for all of us, and I felt the Lord tugging at my spirit. I was to take the first step. Sunday afternoon, Michael taking a nap, kids playing games in their room... Now was as good a time as any. I got into my car and headed toward their house.

Suddenly nervous, I sat in the driveway for a minute at first. What was I doing here again? Pastor's wives don't do this. I had been around pastor's wives all my life. Since sensing my call to full time ministry at eighteen, I had been paying close attention to them, and I had never seen one of them do this. I got my words together. I needed an eloquent prayer for such a moment as this one: "Lord, help" (okay, so it wasn't eloquent). I remembered a verse in Jeremiah: "I, the LORD, search the heart, I test the mind, Even to give every man according to his ways, According to the fruit of his doings" (17:10). The Lord knew my heart, and He understood. In this situation, I knew that I had opened myself up to Him. In this situation, I knew that my heart was pure before Him. All of a sudden, my courage returned. I opened the car door and willed myself toward the front porch.

As I walked up the driveway, I also thought about Paul's warning which I had read earlier that morning: "they failed to reach their goal... because their minds were fixed on what they achieved instead of what they believed" (Romans 9:31-32). This family was not my achievement; they were the Lord's creation. What I believed was that I had been right in opening my heart to them. What I believed was that Michael and I had been faithful to the Lord and that we had helped this family while they were in our flock. I had not failed to reach my goal thus far, and I felt determined not to fail now.

This front porch was not unfamiliar to me. I had been here before on many occasions, with my husband and children. Happy times: dinners, cook-outs, birthdays, engagement announcements, births.... Sad times as well: teenaged child rebelling, financial struggles, hospital stays or even death .... We had been invited to share heartache and joy alike. No, "invited" is the wrong word. We were needed. We were family, and family comes together at such times.

This afternoon, however, was different. I was standing on this familiar front porch for a reason that had never brought me here before: I came to say good bye.

On this front porch, I knocked on the door. This family had been with us for years, and we had been with them. Remembering how this family had helped and blessed our congregation, I quietly smiled. Remembering how they had enriched our personal lives with their friendship and encouragement, I could feel the tears burning behind my eyes. We would miss them. Remembering all that we had done for them, I wondered how they could leave with no word or even warning. Just stopped coming. Just stopped answering our phone calls or cards. Apparently they could leave it like that. I could not.

The doorknob turned, and the butterflies in my stomach flew away as I heard the words of Jesus come in a rush to my spirit: "Assuredly, I say to you, inasmuch as you did it to one of the least of these My brethren, you did it to Me" (Matthew 25:40). I wasn't serving them; I as serving Him. Everything Michael and I did for them, sacrificing family time, finances, giving of ourselves and resources... We had done all those things as unto the Lord, and He would heal our broken hearts.

The door opened. I smiled and did what I came to do: "We love you very much. We understand that you have left our church, but I didn't want you to leave without hearing me say goodbye. It would make me feel just awful if someone could leave our church and think that no one had noticed. I hope it won't be awkward if ever you need us or if ever we see each other out somewhere, it's small town, of course..." I did not need their reason for leaving. At this point, that didn't matter.

I left as quick as I came. My mission was accomplished. If I ran into them now, there would be no need for awkwardness, as I had given all of us closure. I felt the beginning of the Lord's healing at work in my life. Tomorrow would be a new day, and my heart would be ready to receive the next family that God would place in our path. Maybe the next time that this family left a church, they would remember this day. Maybe next time, they would offer a kind word and a goodbye to their pastor on their way out.

Of course, that would not be my responsibility. My responsibility would be to continue serving the Lord and our church with an open heart and open arms. My responsibility would be to continue daily placing myself in the hands of the Master Potter, and allowing Him to mold me and shape me into what He willed for me. Through heartbreaking times and heartwarming times alike, I would have to stay pliable an malleable in His hands. "The potter, for instance, has complete control over the clay, making with one part of the lump a lovely vase, and with another a pipe for sewage" (Romans 9:20-21).

Even though I had felt like the sewage pipe this morning (I do hate to say good bye!), I felt confident that I would be made over again in the hands of the potter. This sweet family was still in His hands as well, and there was comfort to be found in that knowledge. Tomorrow would be a better day. Actually, today hadn't turned out so bad after all. Paul's words were more encouraging now than they had been earlier, and sensing the truth working in my spirit was soothing.

I realized it was my position as "the pastor's wife" that made this family leaving harder to take. I also knew that my response would be noticed by othe ple in my life, making it all the more important for me to get it right. Righ my response would be criticized, so I had to follow the Lord's leadi the results to Him.

In Persia, Vashti has a decision to make, and her decision is made more difficult because of her position. In another time or place, refusing a husband's request may have been merely a domestic argument, easily resolved and forgotten once tempers were settled. However, this husband was Ahasuerus, the self proclaimed "king of all kings". This wife was Vashti, his queen. Both had an example to set, and both were surrounded by people to impress. Ahasuerus wanted to impress by showing off his possessions and seeking the adulation of his subjects. Vashti placed the value of leading by example high over the passing praise of men.

People were watching to see Vashti's response to what they must have recognized as a vulgar request. Unfortunately, people were also watching Ahasuerus to see his response to Vashti's refusal. Vashti must have felt compelled to act in the way that she felt was right, regardless of Ahasuerus' reaction, or she might have chosen an easier road.

Let's return to Vashti and Ahasuerus now.

But Queen Vashti refused to come at the king's command...
Esther 1:12a

Ahasuerus is stunned. After consulting (well, if you can call the exchange between Ahasuerus and the eunuchs a consultation) with his seven closest servants, he decides to request that the queen come to him. He sends the eunuchs to his queen to request her presence. To his complete astonishment, she has refused. This may have been the first time that he has been refused anything, especially something so seemingly simple as asking his own wife to come to him.

...therefore the king was furious, and his anger burned within him.
Esther 1:12b

His "anger burned within him." Ahasuerus is beyond angry — he's burning! (I won't ask you to own it, but maybe you know that feeling!) Ahasuerus wanted his wife to come to him. Wherever you stand on being submissive to a husband (we'll get to that one later!), this probably seems like a small request. As a result, the denial seems equally small: "He wanted her to come, but she was busy and she'll come later.. .What's the big deal?" In our society, this request and this denial may seem like a detail not worth our time, but please consider: you are in Persia now, more than 400 years before the birth of Christ. That is a LONG time ago, and you know how things change!

When the king's eunuchs come into deliver the king's request, Vashti is also entertaining guests. She is holding a banquet for the wives of the officials in another part of the palace. The request to appear before the men probably comes as great shock to the queen. The eunuchs may have issued this command in front 'ashti's guests. In that case, it may have come as a great shock to the women around her. After all, they know the customs of the kingdom as well as the queen does. Vashti is being asked to parade herself in front of King Ahasuerus' friends… She is being asked to appear before the husbands of the very women that are in her quarters.

Vashti is put in a difficult position: honoring her husband's requests would mean going against the traditions that had been instilled in her for many years. Of course, not honoring her husband's request would also mean going against what she has been taught as far as submission to her husband. At this moment, Vashti determined that upholding Persian customs was more important than honoring her drunken husband's request.

God is at work — in what seems like a bad day for Vashti, His purposes are being fulfilled.

Matthew Henry writes that it "was against the custom of the Persians for the women to appear in public" and that King Ahasuerus "put a great hardship upon her when he did not court, but command her to … make her a show".[8] Vashti had probably been groomed to be queen for the better part of her life. She must have been well acquainted with all Persian customs, and surely took her role as queen very seriously. Not only was Vashti supposed to be a support and comple-ment to her husband, she was also expected to set an example for the women in the kingdom. At this moment, she is surrounded by the very women for whom she is supposed to be setting an example . For her to leave these women and ap-pear in front of all these men may have been unthinkable to her.

> *Then the king said to the wise men who understood the times (for this was the king's manner toward all who knew law and justice, those closest to him being Carshena, Shethar, Admatha, Tarshish, Meres, Marsena, and Memucan, the seven princes of Persia and Media, who had access to the king's presence, and who ranked high-est in the kingdom): "What shall we do to Queen Vashti, according to law, because she did not obey the command of King Ahasuerus brought to her by the eunuchs?"* Esther 1:13-15

When Ahasuerus finds himself in a situation that he feels requires immediate action — this refusal from his queen — he turns to his seven advisors. These are different men than the seven servants. The historian names all of them so we will not confuse these two groups. (The servants are named in verse 10; the princes are named in verse 14). According to the verse, these men were familiar with "law and justice", had "access to the king's presence", and ranked "highest in the kingdom".

These seven men are also described as men "who understood the times". The phrase "understood the times" may have suggested that they used astrology or divination to determine the best course of action. Continue to remember that Persia is not a God-fearing nation, and these are not God-fearing people. Even though Ahasuerus is certainly aware of his own father's and grandfather's help to the Jewish people, it does not necessarily follow that Ahasuerus is knowledgeable of or even sympathetic to the customs of the Jews and their God.

While King Ahasuerus has been rotating his guests during these six months, these seven princes have most likely been with him the whole time as well. To Ahasuerus, it may have seemed that these were the right men to go to for advice, but Ahasuerus is not at his sharpest after these six months of celebrating. We can only imagine that these advisors are as bored and as drunk as King Ahasuerus, even though earlier in this chapter (verse 8) the historian makes a point of telling us that the guests were not required to drink. These men may have been "partying" right along with Ahasuerus for these six months, and their judgement may be hindered by the atmosphere as much as the king's judgement has been hindered.

On a more personal note, can you think of any time when you sought out the wrong person for advice or counsel? I sure can! You would not seek advice on your finances from someone who filed bankruptcy yesterday, nor would you seek advice on marriage from a child. When you need wise counsel, you need to find someone who has experienced victory in the same situation in which you are experiencing difficulty.

Of course, when I catch myself looking to the wrong people for advice, many times I realize something: I am not really looking for advice, I am looking for support. Sometimes we seek out people that we expect will be sympathetic to our cause. Ahasuerus may have done this very thing in choosing these men. Maybe Ahasuerus has already determined what he wants to do with Vashti, and now he is looking for validation. Big mistake! Here is a lesson we can take from Ahasuerus: there are situations in our lives when we should seek an opinion from an objective party. The Bible encourages us to seek wise counsel. We should use wisdom and choose someone with more experience and wisdom than we have ourselves.

If Ahasuerus wanted approval, he found it in these seven advisors. If he merely wanted a decisive opinion on what course of action to take, he has found that.

> And Memucan answered before the king and the princes: "Queen Vashti has not only wronged the king, but also all the princes, and all the people who are in all the provinces of King Ahasuerus. For the queen's behavior will become known to all women, so that they will despise their husbands in their eyes, when they report, 'King Ahasuerus commanded Queen Vashti to be brought in before him, but she did not come.' Esther 1:16-17

When Ahasuerus asks for advice, one of the advisors speaks out quickly. Memucan answers Ahasuerus, and apparently he has taken Vashti's refusal pretty personally himself. Perhaps Memucan's wife is among those women that Vashti is entertaining. Memucan exaggerates this situation to make it seem like a very serious infraction indeed, and he wants the king to see it his way. Memucan says, "Queen Vashti has not only wronged the king, but also **all** the princes, and **all** the people who are in **all** the provinces" (v. 16). He suggests that the queen's refusal will make **all** women despise their husbands (v. 17). ... Is Memucan taking this situation a little far?

> *This very day the noble ladies of Persia and Media will say to all the king's officials that they have heard of the behavior of the queen. Thus there will be excessive contempt and wrath.*
>
> *If it pleases the king, let a royal decree go out from him, and let it be recorded in the laws of the Persians and the Medes, so that it will not be altered, that Vashti shall come no more before King Ahasuerus; and let the king give her royal position to another who is better than she.*
>
> Esther 1:18-19

Memucan strongly suggests a new law — a decree — to be sent out from Ahasuerus. (As upset as he is about what he considers a grave error on the part of the queen, Memucan does not want his name connected with this decision). Beyond that, he suggests that this be written into the laws of the Persians AND the Medes. Translation: this law can never be reversed. What is this decree? That, as an example to all the women in the combined kingdoms of Persia and Media, Vashti should lose her crown and be banished from the king forever. Memucan communicates to Ahasuerus that another woman should take her place in the palace. He tells the king, "let the king give her position to one who is better than she" v. 19. This is all pretty bold on the part of Memucan, especially considering that he is talking about Ahasuerus' wife.

Memucan seems pretty emotional about this issue, and he's not the only one acting out of his emotions. Tomorrow we will learn Ahasuerus' decision, and Vashti's fate.

Before we close our lesson today, thank God that those "emotional moments" in your own life have not also been your defining moments. Remember that your salvation isn't a decision — it's a lifestyle! God is daily working out the best on your behalf as you are daily faithful to Him!

DAY FIVE: ESTHER 1:20-22

At the end of the week, remember that God is still present — but beyond His presence, He is active and working in your life! Trust Him with the details of your day today!

FRIEND TO FRIEND...

In Daniel chapter 3, we have a wonderful history about three determined young men and an equally determined king. Shadrach, Meshach and Abednego were Jews in Babylon, serving under the heathen King Nebuchadnezzar. One day, Nebuchanezzar commissions a statue to be built and worshiped by the inhabitants of the city. He gives an order that everyone is to bow down and worship this statue at the sound of an orchestra, threatening death by fire for those who do not bow.

The account of Shadrach, Meshach and Abednego does not suggest that there was any conflict in these young men's minds. In obeying Nebuchadnezzar, they would be disobeying their true King. They would be breaking one of the Ten Commandments: ""You shall not make for yourself a carved image...you shall not bow down to them nor serve them" (Exodus 20:4,5). This was unimaginable. They would refuse to bow, and in doing so, they would trust the Lord in whatever consequences would follow their obedience to His commandments.

When Nebuchadnezzar is informed of their refusal to bow, he has the young men brought to him. The king reminds them of his order, and the consequence of not obeying the order: they will be burned alive in a fiery furnace. Even finding themselves faced with dire consequences, these three young men remain determined to serve God and fulfill His purposes. They are prepared with an answer for him: "O Nebuchadnezzar, we have no need to answer you in this matter. If that is the case, our God whom we serve is able to deliver us from the burning fiery furnace, and He will deliver us from your hand, O king" (Daniel 3:17). Shadrach, Meshach, and Abednego acknowledge that they are not bowing as Nebuchadnezzar wants them to, but they do not try to defend themselves. There was no need to get into an argument when their minds were already made up.

My favorite part of this response, however, comes next: "*But if not*, let it be known to you, O king, that we do not serve your gods, nor will we worship the gold image which you have set up" (Daniel 3:18). In other words, "Even if our God decides NOT to rescue us, we still will not serve your idol." That's determination!

Truly, Shadrach, Meshach and Abednego had made their minds up long before Nebuchanzzar even had his idol commissioned. The true reason they were able to face such a threat with such tenacity was that they had long ago decided to follow the Lord with their whole heart. The decision of this day was not whether to begin serving the Lord and refusing to bow; these young people already knew what they stood for, and they remained steadfast in their faithfulness to the Lord. Whether the Lord came to their rescue on this day was of little matter to them. They intended to serve the Lord.

In order for you to fulfill the call that God has placed on your life, you will have to find yourself DETERMINED and TENACIOUS in following that call. On terrific days, you must be faithful. On terrible days, you must be faithful. When you display this kind of determination, you can be confident that God will show up every day.

In Daniel 3:19-25, the history continues. At the close of this conversation with Nebuchadnezzar, things did not seem to go in Shadrach, Meshach and Abednego's favor. As the king had threatened, these three were in fact thrown in the fire. What Nebuchadnezzar did not yet realize was that they would not go into the fire alone. Who was there in the midst of them? Three were thrown into the fire, but when Nebuchadnezzar looked into the furnace, he told his guards, "I see four men loose, walking in the midst of the fire; and they are not hurt, and the form of the fourth is like the Son of God" (Daniel 3:25). The Son of God was in the furnace with them! Shadrach, Meshach and Abednego were confident that their faith would see them through, and determined to remain true to their God. They were not disappointed!

Once you are determined to serve the Lord, and you begin to allow that determination to guide you in every decision, there is one more thing that you must continually release to the Lord: the *outcome* of your faith walk. Shadrach, Meshach and Abednego completely left the outcome of their decision in Babylon on that day to the Lord. Whether or not He came to their rescue in the way that they may have hoped, they would trust Him enough to go into the fire with or without any assurance that they would come out on this side of heaven.

Every decision you make has a consequence. In determining to walk in faith, you must also determine to leave the consequences in the hands of the Lord. He loves you so much, and that perfect love can release you from the fear of the unknown *if you allow it*. Trust Him enough to serve Him, and trust Him enough to take care of the consequences of your acts of obedience.

In Persia, Queen Vashti is determined. Like these three young men we just read about, she is determined to do what she feels is the right course of action, regardless of the personal consequences. Of course, she does not yet know what those consequences are going to involve, but I have a suspicion that, even if she had known, her decision would have been the same. God, in His providence, had placed a woman strong enough to stand up to a king on the throne in Persia, in order that one day soon the door would be opened for another strong woman to assume that same throne. Individuals may not be aware of outcomes, but the Lord knows the beginning from the end.

Vashti's decision is made. Now it is time for Ahasuerus to react. The outcome will affect Ahasuerus and his kingdom in ways that he cannot even begin to imagine. He is angry, but how will he ultimately respond to what he considers Queen Vashti's public display of rebellion against him?

Let's return to Esther chapter one.

> *"...Vashti shall come no more before King Ahasuerus; and let the king give her royal position to another who is better than she. When the king's decree which he will make is proclaimed throughout all his empire (for it is great), all wives will honor their husbands, both great and small."* Esther 1:19-20

Memucan says one more thing to "seal the deal" and sway King Ahasuerus to agree with him: he compliments the king. He takes this opportunity to compliment the king on how great the kingdom is, Memucan says that this decree will be proclaimed through ALL the kingdom. Memucan also predicts that ALL wives will honor their husbands because of the king's wisdom in this matter. This is a very high expectation — with one decree, Ahasuerus will erase domestic struggles between husbands and wives. Wow — what a decree!

King Ahasuerus is only thinking of one thing at this moment: his hurt ego. In his mind, he has suffered tremendous embarrassment at the hands of his own wife. To make it worse, this happened at a party celebrating how great he is, in front of all the people in the kingdom that he most wants to impress! Had he not been drunk, he might have been angry at himself for making such a vulgar request of his wife. However, encouraged on in this course of action by his advisors, his anger at this moment is directed at Vashti, and Ahasuerus reacts.

> *And the reply pleased the king and the princes, and the king did according to the word of Memucan. Then he sent letters to all the king's provinces, to each province in its own script, and to every people in their own language, that each man should be master in his own house, and speak in the language of his own people.*
> Esther 1:21-22

The king is pleased by the advice, and the historian tells us that his princes are pleased also. With his princes at his side, Ahasuerus has letters sent out to all the provinces, each in their own languages, that "each man should be master in his own house". Though we do not know exactly what the letter contained, most likely this communication further explained Queen Vashti's "shameful" behavior, and also praised King Ahasuerus' swift and decisive action. (I wonder: did that letter contain the specifics of what Vashti was refusing?)

King Ahasuerus is talking to a lot of people — his seven closest servants, his seven closest advisors, and now letters explaining the situation to all the people in all the provinces. From Vashti, we are only certain of one word from her mouth: *no*. There is no record of any communication between her and anyone. No advisors, no friends, no servants — Vashti communicates her refusal of Ahasuerus' request apparently without comment. Imagine Vashti's situation. She has done nothing wrong or even inappropriate. While Ahasuerus seems determined to shout his side of the story to anyone who will listen, Vashti is just as determined to maintain her dignity. She is seemingly silent. She does not even try to defend herself.

In this situation, Vashti could have responded. While she may not have had the ability to send out her own letter to the provinces, at the minimum she could have told the women in her chambers how very wrong Ahasuerus was. That would have spread the word around! However, there was no way to defend herself without embarrassing the king even further, and this would have gone against her training for the throne as much as refusing him did. Some might criticize her for not being submissive. It seems to me, however, that she handled this situation with more grace and aplomb than Ahasuerus deserved from her. Vashti had reason to talk; she was the one being wronged. Ahasuerus did more than embarrass her with a ridiculous request, he humiliated her publicly. Vashti's only recorded response through it all was her initial refusal. That simple "no" speaks volumes about this queen.

God is still at work. Ahasuerus thinks he is getting rid of Vashti because of her refusal to honor his request. What he does not know is that GOD is arranging all these events to clear the way for Esther to become queen.

God was busy at work in Persia, but His work is not complete: He is still making a tremendous investment in you! Every day, remind yourself that you have a Father in heaven who is generous, wise and loving. In Jude 20-21, we are encouraged to maintain our walk with the Lord: "beloved, building yourselves up on your most holy faith, praying in the Holy Spirit, keep yourselves in the love of God, looking for the mercy of our Lord Jesus Christ unto eternal life". Keeping your walk with the Lord fresh will keep you connected to the hope that He means for you to have: the *right* kind of expectation!

Remember that your hope is in the Lord, and not in the opinions of others. Release yourself from the need to please people, and commit yourself completely to pleasing God. Psalm 146 instructs the believer to put their hope and trust in God rather than in man. Man is described so often in the word as temporal — in Psalm 146:3-4, the psalmist tells us that there is "no help" in man. Always, hand in hand with a warning is the encouragement. The next verse, Psalm 146:5, states, "Happy is he who has the God of Jacob for his help, whose hope is in the LORD his God". Our hope rests in the eternal, far reaching plan of a God who knows the beginning from the end. Please the Lord, and do not be afraid if people are not pleased with you. Please Him, and let it be a "bonus" when people are pleased with you. Do not allow either situation to stop your progress: God sees you, and that is enough!

Understand that our judgement is limited, and look to Jesus, "the author and finisher of our faith" (Hebrews 12:2). God knows the beginning from the end. If you are in a season of bounty and blessings, praise God *and grow*! If you are in a season of famine and struggle, praise God *and grow*! The season has come to pass, good or bad, and you can feel confident that God is working through both.

One more: "In Him also we have obtained an inheritance, being predestined according to the purpose of Him who works *all things* according to the counsel of His will, that we who first trusted in Christ should be to the praise of His glory" (Ephesians 1:1-2). Isn't that a comfort? That is a verse that covers like a blanket, providing warmth and protection to every area: God works all things according to the counsel of His will. We have obtained (past tense: you already have everything you need in order to be a success in Him!) an inheritance from the Lord, and He has a purpose and a plan for you! God is so good!

Why does God offer this protection to us? Why does He offer these precious promises? Why does God never leave us alone? What attracts Him to us so much that He ordained a purpose and plan for us before we even existed? Love! He loves us more than we could ever know or even understand. His love can cast out our fears (1 John 4:18), and it is because of love that we can feel confident as we serve Him. The Word of God encourages us to "know that the LORD your God, He is God, the faithful God who keeps covenant and mercy for a thousand generations with those who love Him and keep His commandments" (Deuteronomy 7:9).

Bask in that love for a few minutes as we close this first week . God sees you, loves you, and will never leave you alone — let that give you confidence to go out and change your world!

Our "background work" is finished! Now that we understand how it was that King Ahasuerus found himself in need of a queen, we are ready to meet our heroine: Esther!

Just as God was working on Esther's behalf a long time before anyone knew anything about her, God is working on your behalf right now — and He values you even on days when you do not feel valued by anyone! As you continue your journey with the Lord, look to Him for approval — not to the people around you!

≫≪

"Then she called the name of the LORD who spoke to her, You-Are-the-God-Who-Sees; for she said, 'Have I also here seen Him who sees me?'"
Genesis 16:13

Father, You truly are the God who sees me!
If I allow it to, Your love will free me.
Your love will free me from being bound or motivated
by the opinions of the people around me...
Your love will free me from quick judgements
(my own or those of people around me)...
Your love will free me to grow confident in the knowledge that in You I am safe.
Your love will free me from worrying about consequences of my obedience to You.
Your love will free me to truly become the woman of God
that I know You are calling me to be —
passionate, purposeful, pure...
Jesus, thank You that He who the Son has set free is free indeed...
You are the God who sees me, and I love You!

≫≪

---

1.   Matthew Henry, Matthew Henry's Commentary on the Whole Bible, Volume Two (USA: Hendrickson Publishers, 1996), p. 866.

2.   Esther 9:30

3.   Hebrews 13:8

4.   Dr. Augustus Hopkins Strong, Systematic Theology, p. 420.

5.   John 15:5

6.   Proverbs 21:1

7.   Matthew Henry, Matthew Henry's Commentary on The Whole Bible, Volume Two (USA: Hendrickson Publishers, 1996), p. 868.

ESTHER: CHAPTER 2

Esther becomes Queen; Mordecai Saves the King

As we saw in Esther chapter 1, God had been at work on behalf of His people years before Esther and Mordecai came to Persia. Through the captivity and through the relief, God was working behind the scenes to bring us to this exact point in history. Through observing the impulsive and emotional manner in which Ahasuerus conducts his life, we can clearly see that God does not require our help in order to bring His plans to pass. His providence is continuing along in spite of the series of "damage control" challenges that Ahasuerus presents. While Ahasuerus can be an example of what not to do, this week we will meet someone whose example we *can* follow: Esther. In Esther's example, we will see that tremendous feats can be accomplished as we partner with the Lord, following Him in faithfulness and obedience.

During this week, we are continuing with our look at God's providence in the life of Esther. Pray as you begin your moments of study this week that you will be able to recognize the truths revealed in this history. Also, pray that God will help you to apply these truths to your own life. Remember, the providence of God was at work in the life of Esther just as it is at work in your life today! God began His work on behalf of Esther years and years before she was even born. For Esther and for the Jews who would come after her, a series of events was carefully and purposefully orchestrated by the God Who knew the beginning from the end.

In addition to providence, preparation and obedience are big themes in chapter 2. During this chapter, Ahasuerus is preparing for a new wife, Mordecai is preparing Esther for whatever the Lord may do in her life, and Esther is preparing to be queen.

Be encouraged that this is the same love God has for you today! His care is personal and powerful in your life. It is a huge and truly amazing thought: God loves *you*! For some of us, "Jesus loves me" has been drilled into us since we were children in Sunday School, and it is an accepted comfort. For others, that love is hard to believe. In Jeremiah 31:3, the Bible says, "The LORD has appeared of old to me, saying: 'Yes, I have loved you with an everlasting love' ". Ageless, timeless, and continually drawing you toward the eventual goal that God has for your life... Words are simply not enough for His great love!

Beyond the fact that God's love is constantly drawing you toward achieving the goal He has for your life, God's love is also providing everything you need to be successful. There are "firsts" that we all experience in our lives, and along with the unknown often comes a little worry. I remember the night before my first day of teaching. I could hardly sleep for the constant concern that I might not do well enough. 1,000-plus children would come through the doors of the music room every week; would I have the words they needed to hear? Would I be able to impart my knowledge to them? You probably felt the same way on one of your first days! I also remember being pregnant with my first child (and as it turned out, first *two* children!): would I be a good mother? How would I know what to do with a baby, then a two year old, then a five year old, and so on?

Life is full of first times and unfamiliar circumstances. Life is unpredictable. Even our best attempts at planning and preparing and organizing sometimes can come up short in many situations. We have to remember that we are serving a providential God, and that none of these "firsts" are firsts to the Lord. Nothing that is a surprise to us is ever a surprise to Him. Rest in His love this week, and find confidence in the knowledge that whatever it is you need, God has already provided it. Whether the need is spiritual, financial, emotional, or physical, nothing escapes God's notice, and nothing is too small for His attention. Jesus Himself encourages us, "I tell you, do not worry about your life.... For your Heavenly Father knows that you *need*" (Matthew 6:25, 32 emphasis mine). God's love is able to free you from the worry that you will not have what you need as you need it. Release yourself this week to that freedom, and rejoice in it! Your Heavenly Father loves you, and He knows what you need. He has already provided it, so you have no reason to worry!

Last week we met Queen Vashti and King Ahasuerus. This week we meet Esther and her cousin Mordecai. Exciting events take place in Persia this week! Are you ready?

❦

DAY ONE: ESTHER 2:1-4

Patience is a fruit of the Spirit — pray that the Lord would help you to develop and demonstrate patience in your life!

FRIEND TO FRIEND...

Before I close my eyes at night, I usually read or watch a little television. Taking a risk here on a supernaturally boring beginning to this story, I am asking you to stay with me: last night I was watching a program on a health channel about head injuries. The program documented several people who had been in varying types of accidents or illnesses that resulted in severe head trauma, and discussed the challenges that each one of these people and their families faced since the incident. Each story began with videos, pictures and family testimony about the victim before the trauma; then the cameras would follow these people from the doctor's office and into their homes.

Of course, not all cases were the same, but I began to notice one striking similarity. Almost all of these people displayed a major change in personality since they had met with their tragedy. Once gentle and loving, they were now angry and irritable. Who wouldn't become frustrated after such a horrible, life-altering event? Their frustration was understandable, of course, but it was something else that caught my attention. In addition to their anger, the victims were also inappropriate or even vulgar in their speech. It seemed as if they were somehow unable to control what came out of their mouths.

Finally, an explanation: in several of these cases, a specific area of the brain, the frontal lobes, had been damaged or destroyed. The frontal lobes are responsible for processing experience into memory, and serve as a kind of "control center" for the brain. Among the many responsibilities of the frontal lobes is a type of censorship action. Apparently our brains have a sort of a "filter" that prevents us from saying everything we think the minute we think it. For these cases, one of the myriad results of their tragedies was that the "censor" in their brain had been destroyed, sadly explaining their inability to control their words.

Isn't our creator God amazing? In His providence, He knew such a mechanism in our brains would be necessary. Of course, there have been times when I wished that my "filter" worked a little better... don't we all have those "did I actually say *that* out loud" moments? However, I find with maturity and experience, I do improve. Recognizing my body as a temple of the Holy Spirit and allowing Him to put to best use the functions He placed in me from birth represents a great partnership. God has given us specific tools and "checks" that help us to be successful in life. Now it is up to us to take every opportunity to use those tools to our benefit.

As the Word warns us, we have an enemy "seeking whom he may devour" (1 Peter 5:8). One area where we can be vulnerable to attack is through our emotions. Your emotions can drive you to greatness, but they can also drive you to destruction if left unchecked. Like fire and water can be useful when in control, they can destroy when out of control. Your emotions have the same power: able to be used to our benefit or our detriment.

Many of us may be able to recall times when acting out of an immediate emotion, rather than waiting on the Lord, got us into trouble. Even as we strive daily to seek and achieve God's will for our lives, emotions can become stumbling blocks. The Word is always true — God truly can work all things together for our good (see Romans 8:28), but we need to operate in wisdom. Our emotions can easily get us into situations with less than desirable results.

Isaiah 40:28-31 is a very familiar passage:

> *Have you not known? Have you not heard? The everlasting God, the LORD, The Creator of the ends of the earth, Neither faints nor is weary. His understanding is unsearchable. He gives power to the weak, And to those who have no might He increases strength. Even the youths shall faint and be weary, And the young men shall utterly fall, But those who wait on the LORD Shall renew their strength; They shall mount up with wings like eagles, They shall run and not be weary, They shall walk and not faint.*

Who will have their strength renewed? "Those who *wait* upon the Lord". Waiting could signify passivity: being still. Waiting could also indicate action: serving. Waiting — either kind — can be nearly impossible while we are being run by our emotions. In learning to balance your emotions with wisdom, learning to wait upon the Lord in both senses of the word, you will find that your strength is renewed every day in every situation. On the other hand, operating out of emotions can be exhausting.

In your Christian walk, the ability to discern seasons is vital. There are times in your life where immediate action is not only unnecessary, it can be damaging. There are situations in which your best course of action is to "be still and know that He is God" (Psalm 46:10). Allowing Him to speak to you in the midst of your storm, finding your peace in Christ when your life seems upside down may be exactly what is needed. There are times when patience is the order of the day, and waiting on the Lord to move or instruct you in the way you are to move is exactly what is needed. Sometimes the most difficult course to take is to *wait* and allow the Lord to direct your heart "into the love of God and the patience of Christ" (2 Thessalonians3:5). However difficult it may be, practicing *waiting* will serve you well.

"Waiting" can also signify an *action*. A waitress will *wait* on you in your favorite restaurant. You may *wait on*, or *serve*, your family. In being able to discern the seasons of waiting passively, we must also be able to discern the seasons of waiting *actively*. Even in times when you might feel unsure of the next step, there are continually ways for you to serve the Lord: prayer, study, service to others being a few examples. In times when everything is going along smoothly, waiting actively on the Lord is always in order. Paul encourages young Timothy to "be diligent to show yourself approved" (2 Timothy 2:15). In learning to wait actively on the Lord, it is good advice for us as well. Applying ourselves to faithful service to the Lord (active waiting) will sustain us through times when the waiting requires patience and stillness. In our Christian walk, both kinds of "waiting" are needed: an active waiting on or serving the Lord, and likewise a passive waiting for the Lord to move on your behalf.

As everything in our relationship with the Lord is a partnership or covenant, this waiting is a "two way street". As we serve the Lord, He is moved to action on our behalf. Psalm 37:3-7 speaks to both kinds of waiting (parentheses mine): "Trust in the LORD (*passive*), and do good (*active*); Dwell in the land (*passive*), and feed on His faithfulness (*active*). Delight yourself also in the LORD, And He shall give you the desires of your heart. Commit your way to the LORD (*active*), Trust also in Him (*passive*), And He shall bring it to pass (*the Lord's action*). He shall bring forth your righteousness as the light, And your justice as the noonday (*the Lord's action*). Rest in the LORD (*passive*), and wait patiently for Him (*passive*)".

Tremendous and amazing results can come from this kind of waiting. Of course, the Lord in His generous and kind manner will send you opportunities to practice if you want to learn to wait! In His providence, those opportunities are already provided — it is for you to take advantage of them. Will you?

Unfortunately, patience is not one of Ahasuerus' virtues. He is motivated by his emotions, and seems to rush right into whatever comes into his mind without much forethought. Let's return to Persia, and find out what Ahasuerus is rushing into today.

> *After these things, when the wrath of King Ahasuerus subsided,*
> *he remembered...* Esther 2:1

"After these things".... By the beginning of chapter two, four years have passed since King Ahasuerus dethroned Queen Vashti. God was working through this Persian chronicler as he wrote this history and perhaps spared us these four possibly tedious years. During chapter one, Ahasuerus is either so proud of himself that he throws himself a huge party or so disappointed in his own reign that he throws a party to divert attention from the fact that his time on the throne has been rather dismal.

Now Ahasuerus is feeling sad, quiet, pensive. "After these things", he remembers and reflects on the events on the past four years.

> *After these things, when the wrath of King Ahasuerus subsided,*
> *he remembered Vashti, what she had done, and what had been de-*
> *creed against her.* Esther 2:1

When we left King Ahasuerus last week, he was "burning" with anger. He no longer feels that anger, and though the Scriptures do not tells us what he is feeling now, he may feel regret over his actions, or even loneliness for his former wife. However, it is important to notice what the historian *does* tell us. It is written that Ahasuerus remembers two things: first, he remembers Vashti; and second, he remembers "what had been decreed against her".

Notice how the historian phrases Ahasuerus' action: "what had been decreed against her". Knowing that Ahasuerus will surely read the records, it is almost as if he does not want to offend Ahasuerus by connecting the king's actions too closely with Vashti's removal from the throne. He writes what Ahasuerus wants to remember, and leaves it to us to "read between the lines". Regardless of the manner in which the historian chose to record this event, Ahasuerus' actions can not be separated from what had happened to Vashti. Ahasuerus remembers what Vashti had done; not what *he* himself had done. He remembers "what had been decreed against her"; not what *he* had decreed against her. In his mind, Ahasuerus twisted this situation and made himself the victim somehow.

After six months of celebration and declaring himself the greatest and most powerful king in the world, Ahasuerus' celebration ends in a failed attempt to show off his most beautiful "trophy": his wife, Vashti. Remember: the law that dethroned Queen Vashti had been written into Persian and Median law. Even the king himself could never reverse it. If Ahasuerus had been regretting what he had done to Vashti, or even missing her, there was absolutely nothing that he could do to restore her to her previous position.

Ahasuerus' feelings are vastly different than the anger that he was feeling before, and the people closest to him are beginning to take notice. They conclude that he must be lonely for a wife.

> *Then the king's servants who attended him said: "Let beautiful young virgins be sought for the king; and let the king appoint officers in all the provinces of his kingdom, that they may gather all the beautiful young virgins to Shushan the citadel, into the women's quarters, under the custody of Hegai the king's eunuch, custodian of the women. And let beauty preparations be given them. Then let the young woman who pleases the king be queen instead of Vashti." Esther 2:2-4*

They decide to begin a search for the most beautiful women in the kingdom — the entire kingdom, which included all 127 provinces. They further determine that once these women are brought to the palace, beauty preparations should be given to them under the supervision of the king's own eunuch in charge of women.

When his servants suggest that he look for a new wife, Ahasuerus wholeheartedly agrees. If he cannot have Vashti back, he might as well get on with the business of finding "another one better than she" (Esther 1:19), right?

Ahasuerus may be depressed, but probably not entirely for the reason his servants think. In chapter one, we read about Ahasuerus and his party. Three years into his already disappointing reign, Ahasuerus planned this grand event in order to divert his attention from his lack of accomplishment. As the party dwindled and came to a close, Ahasuerus' attempts to impress his guests spiraled downward; leading to bad judgement on Ahasuerus' part and ultimately Vashti's removal. Losing his queen could not have been one of Ahasuerus' desired results.

His servants are not altogether wrong: Ahasuerus may be depressed over Vashti's removal from the throne, but there may be another reason. Remember: Ahasuerus is reflecting on four years worth of actions. Today, his former queen may be foremost in his mind, but her removal is not the only event of importance during these last four years. It is merely the only memory that Ahasuerus wants to have connected with his history.

We learned earlier about the expectations Ahasuerus might have had for his reign considering the accomplishments of his father and grandfather. Ahasuerus' father, Darius, led at least two attacks against Greece during his reign. Both were miserable failures. At the time of his death, Darius was planning still another attack. Darius may have considered these failures black marks on an otherwise successful rule.

Histories generally agree that Ahasuerus also led an attack against Greece. This attack was launched between 482 B.C. and 479 B.C. This time frame puts us in between chapters one and two of Esther. A possible explanation for Ahasuerus' attack against Greece is Ahasuerus' need to feel successful. Succeeding where a king as great as his father had failed would have been a tremendous (and public) victory. Unfortunately, Ahasuerus' attack against Greece was a humiliating failure. As a victory, an attack on Greece would have been a huge boost to Ahasuerus. However, the failure must have been as public as a victory would have been, and now that Ahasuerus is back at the palace, he is lonely for the comfort and companionship that a wife could have provided for him at such a time. "After these things" (Esther 2:1) could possibly refer to his failed attempt to take over Greece, as well as the loss of his wife four years ago.

Whatever reason (or reasons) Ahasuerus has for his present mood, his servants seek out a remedy for their king's feelings. They come up with a plan, and present their idea to Ahasuerus. The plan is to go into all the provinces, find the most beautiful young women, parade them before Ahasuerus in some sort of demented beauty pageant fashion, culminating in Ahasuerus choosing a new wife.

Ahasuerus is about to stage a tremendous beauty pageant to find a replacement for his proud first wife. (Ahasuerus apparently does not understand women!) After these failures, after these actions and reactions, after this time of reflection and quiet, it seems that during these four years, this king has not learned very much.

For the time being, the most important thing to Ahasuerus is *Ahasuerus*, and his response to the servants' suggestion comes as no surprise.

This thing pleased the king, and he did so. Esther 2:4

Ahasuerus is making an emotional decision once again. He *is* lonely, he *is* depressed, and a search for a new wife (and all the women that will come along while trying to find his new wife) seems like a good idea. In this decision, much like the decisions that led up to Vashti's removal, the king could have benefitted from the ability to wait.

It is important to realize that the way you prepare is just as important as the situation for which you are preparing. Ahasuerus is preparing for a wife, and generally that is a good thing. Marriage can be a blessing. We are barely two chapters into the Bible before God says, "It is not good for man to be alone" (Genesis 2:18). Did you ever notice that Adam's lonely state was the first thing during creation that God did not consider good? There is nothing wrong with Ahasuerus wanting a wife. However, there is something wrong with the way he is preparing for marriage: staging a beauty pageant and treating these women as objects. A pattern is revealed in Ahasuerus. After treating his first wife as an object, he lost her. Without the advantage of the Holy Spirit to keep him in check, Ahasuerus is out of balance. Fortunately for him, God has a better plan working; and in spite of his mistakes, Ahasuerus will benefit from God's providence.

In spite of Ahasuerus' rush into every decision that strikes him in the moment, God is busy "behind the scenes". Even this situation is going to work out for the benefit of God's people, the Jews. All is in His providence!

Let's offer up a quick prayer as we close: "Lord, teach me to wait and to wait — I need both to serve You actively and wait expectantly on Your perfect timing. Help me to discern a 'time for action' and a 'time to be still', and help me to operate in Your wisdom (and not my emotion) during both times."

※

DAY TWO: ESTHER 2:5-10

Today we meet Esther, and there's a lot of talk about beauty. Father, show us the right way to be beautiful in your sight — help us to seek approval from You, not from man.

FRIEND TO FRIEND...

In 1 Samuel 16:7, the Lord speaks to Samuel the prophet. He tells him, "the

LORD does not see as man sees; for man looks at the outward appearance, but the LORD looks at the heart." As He is the same yesterday, today and forever (Hebrews 13:8), I find great comfort in knowing He does not judge me by my outward appearance.

Of course, the flip side is that He is continually searching my heart. To be honest, there are days when I think that having good looking hair might be more easily achieved than a pure heart or right attitude! Most days, common sense wins out. I remember that what is more difficult to attain is often times more valuable, so I put in a ponytail and spend a few extra minutes in prayer rather than in front of the mirror!

As with everything in life, there is a balance to be found between these two. There is nothing wrong with being outwardly beautiful, of course. In and of itself, wearing nice clothes, make-up or jewelry is absolutely fine. The Lord wants you to feel good about yourself, and these outward things may help you in that. The Lord also wants you to present your best as His representative here on earth, and you might find that outward attentions help a little bit in that way. However, outward appearance is not enough to sustain. A healthy relationship, with the Lord and with people, must be built on inner qualities, and developing an inward beauty must not be ignored for the sake of the outward.

In 1 Peter 3:3-4, we are admonished in this way: "Do not let your adornment be merely outward -- arranging the hair, wearing gold, or putting on fine apparel -- rather let it be the hidden person of the heart, with the incorruptible beauty of a gentle and quiet spirit, which is very precious in the sight of God." There is no instruction against "outward adornment", only a warning against letting our concern for beauty end with what is on the outside. Easier said than done? Maybe, but a healthy balance can be found in practicing!

You are already the apple of God's eye — you are already beautiful to Him.... but a quiet and gentle spirit is very precious in the eyes of the Lord. Precious means: "having great value, greatly loved or treasured, considerable".[1] Precious means something rare. If a quiet and gentle spirit truly is rare, then it is something you must work at (not everyone wants to work), something that is harder to come by... something that is prepared.

We can tell by the means Ahasuerus chooses to select a new wife that his expectations are very low; he is only looking at outward beauty. In our own lives today, the world sets such low standards for us. God expects more, and it is the inward beauty — the hidden man of the heart — that is important to Him. Measuring yourself against His standards for you, rather than those we might find in magazines or television, you will find that His love is easily attainable. Basking in the warmth and comfort of His love, you will find that His approval is more than enough to sustain and satisfy you. Precious daughter of the Most High, you are the apple of His eye already!

When we left Ahasuerus yesterday, his servants had just made a suggestion that, not surprisingly, the king finds most agreeable: a nationwide search for a new queen. The servants explain their idea to Ahasuerus. The historian tells us, "this thing pleased the king, and he did so." The search is on! King Ahasuerus has agreed to gathering all of the most beautiful young women in the kingdom to come and "audition" for the role of his queen. A beauty pageant of this grand scale will take place right in his livingroom, and the winner wins... well, HIM. Even better than that, these women will have to go through a period of beautification: "let's make them even more beautiful before they get the great honor of meeting YOU, your royal highness!" Ahasuerus thinks this is a great idea, and God's *providence* continues to roll right along.

> *In Shushan the citadel there was a certain Jew whose name was Mordecai the son of Jair, the son of Shimei, the son of Kish, a Benjamite. Kish had been carried away from Jerusalem with the captives who had been captured with Jeconiah king of Judah, whom Nebuchadnezzar the king of Babylon had carried away.*
> Esther 2:5-6

Mordecai is a Jew living in Shushan (remember from last week — this is the city that Darius established as the capital). His great-grandfather is Kish the Benjamite, who was brought to Persia / Babylon during the Babylonian captivity. Even though King Cyrus ended the captivity many years ago, many Jews have remained in Persia. Mordecai's family was among them.

Mordecai's heritage is an vital part of God's plan, so let's be careful not to over look this important detail. God always has a remnant of people. Even though Mordecai is no longer captive to the will of man keeping him in exile, he is still captive to the will of God. As a result of his obedience to God, Mordecai remained in Persia even after he was free to leave. God has promised to protect His people, and His plan is in action. Mordecai is an important part of that plan!

Also important to note is that this the historian's first mention of Jews living in Persia. Mordecai descending from Kish the Benjamite is interesting, because another important biblical figure also descended from Kish: Israel's first king, Saul. Saul was Kish's son (1 Samuel 9:1). While this point may not seem important in a history of Ahasuerus, the ancestry of this Jew is very important in the history of Persia. Mordecai's most important connection is about to be introduced to us: his cousin, Esther.

"And Mordecai had brought up Hadassah, that is, Esther, his uncle's daughter, for she had neither father nor mother. The young woman was lovely and beautiful. When her father and mother died, Mordecai took her as his own daughter." Esther 2:7

Ahasuerus is not the only one in Persia busy preparing; Mordecai is preparing as well. For many years now, he has been preparing Esther, raising her for the future that God intended for her.

As you prepare, consider that you might be preparing for a future you do not know anything about; and that you may be preparing someone other than yourself. Mordecai's first step was to obey God. Certainly it was God who told him to stay with Esther in Persia, even after her parents had died. We are never told that Mordecai had married; what reason was there for him to stay in Persia? Even so, Mordecai stayed in Persia with Esther and raised her as his own daughter. Raising her was a process, and he had to depend on the Lord to know the right thing to do. He had no way of predicting what would happen in her life or his, but he was obedient during the process (remember Jeremiah 29?). Mordecai was preparing Esther for a future he did not know anything about yet, but Mordecai knew something that we need to keep in our hearts as well: serving God every day will develop qualities in us that will serve us well, whatever the future may hold. Mordecai was preparing Esther to be faithful to God, knowing that quality could only help her in her life.

Mordecai did not know what God had in store for Esther — but he did know that God had a plan for her, just as He has a plan for all of us. Mordecai poured his life into her. Is there someone that you are supposed to be pouring your life into? Perhaps while reading this history, you are identifying with Esther. Maybe you are an "Esther", but consider that you may be a "Mordecai". It is likely you will identify with both of them at different seasons in your life. Pray that you will be able to discern those seasons.

Mordecai and Esther are cousins. Sometime after the Jews were carried away to Persia, Esther's parents died. Out of the heartbreaking tragedy of losing her parents, God's providence was still at work. His word promises that in the hands of the Lord, "all things work together for good to those who love God, to those who are the called according to His purpose" (Romans 8:28). This promise surely applied to Esther. Now Mordecai, the perfect person to groom this young girl, anointed and providentially chosen for this task, is raising Esther as his own daughter.

The Bible tells us, "the young woman was lovely and beautiful…." Not just lovely, not just beautiful, but lovely AND beautiful — that's Esther. In the King James translation, she is described as "fair and beautiful". The word "fair" comes from the word "to'ar". This word, when literally translated, means *lovely on the outside*. Esther's outward appearance was very pleasing.[2] The word "beautiful" comes from the word "tobe". This word, literally translated, goes far beyond external beauty. It means "good in the widest sense, used as a noun.... also as an adverb: beautiful, cheerful, at ease, fair, in favor, glad, good..... gracious, joyful, kindly.... loving, merry, most pleasant, precious, prosperity, ready, sweet, well."[3] These words give us a much more accurate view of Esther: she is more than beautiful!

Please take note that Esther's *circumstance* did not dictate her *attitude*. Esther's life does not sound easy by any means. First, she is living in a city that has not been entirely friendly to Jewish people, even though the captivity is over. On top of that, she has lost her parents and any other family other than Mordecai. In spite of these hardships, she is described as lovely and beautiful — inside and out! Esther has not allowed herself to become bitter over circumstances that were out of her control.

This is a wonderful example for us to follow: as we are faithful to God, He is faithful to us. Rather than allowing situations to make us disagreeable, we need to keep our focus on the Lord. Allow Him to move through everything that comes to you, both good and bad. In the end, you are a child of the true King! Though great times and hard times, God is working out a perfect plan for you!

These inner strengths and qualities in Esther are about to become necessary for her very survival. If the hardships of life in Persia could not make Esther bitter, another test of her character is about to come: Ahasuerus' servants are out collecting young women as potential candidates to be queen. At first, such an opportunity may seem exciting, but consider that these young women are being given no choice in the matter. Possibly afraid, definitely alone, each were taken from their homes and families by force.

> *So it was, when the king's command and decree were heard, and when many young women were gathered at Shushan the citadel, under the custody of Hegai, that Esther also was taken to the king's palace, into the care of Hegai the custodian of the women.*
> Esther 2:8 NKJV

After the virgins in the kingdom are gathered, they are taken to Hegai "the custodian of the women". Hegai is going to "weed out" any women whom he thinks will not be suitable for the king. He will look them over and if they are pretty enough to keep around, he orders their beauty preparations. What will Hegai think when he meets Esther?

> *Now the young woman pleased him, and she obtained his favor;*
> *so he readily gave beauty preparations to her, besides her allowance.*

> *Then seven choice maidservants were provided for her from the king's palace, and he moved her and her maidservants to the best place in the house of the women.* Esther 2:9

Esther impressed Hegai from the first, and he immediately agreed to begin her beauty preparations as well as her diet ("her allowance"). Esther is going on to "round two" in this "pageant"! Initially this may sound glamorous, but this is truly a "fish out of water" situation for Esther. Remember the description of the palace in chapter 1? Esther has never seen anything like the excess in Ahasuerus' palace and, considering her background, is probably very uncomfortable. She has been raised to have a simple faith in God, and this palace may feel to her like one huge tribute to a man: Ahasuerus (and knowing him, it probably is!). Add this to her already isolated and lonely feeling that must have resulted from being removed from her home with Mordecai, and we can easily imagine the difficulty that Esther is experiencing.

Hegai is not the only person with instructions for Esther. Upon being taken to the palace, Mordecai had directions for her as well.

> *"Esther had not revealed her people or family, for Mordecai had charged her not to reveal it."* Esther 2:10 NJKV

Esther may have had an even harder time in the palace due to the fact that so far her background has been kept a secret. It is difficult enough being some place where you do not fit in, but for Esther to have to keep her true identity a secret as well must have been very hard. A lonely year will pass before she is ready to be received by the king.

Even though it may have been hard to keep her religions identity secret, Esther obeyed. Many times, not telling the entire truth is a mistake. However, given Esther's situation, this secret-keeping is not to be considered a lie. Matthew Henry wrote, "All truths are not to be spoken at all times, though an untruth is never to be spoken".[4] Esther's obedience to Mordecai reveals a very important aspect of her inner beauty: Esther is submissive to authority.

Esther possessed outward beauty, but she has inward beauty as well. This was important to God back in Persia, and it is important to God today.

As you close the Bible on this lesson today, thank God for the wonderful qualities He has placed in You so that you will be effective and successful in your calling. If you don't know what those qualities are, ask God to reveal them to you throughout this week - you are a treasure, and God has placed a treasure inside you!

❧

DAY THREE: ESTHER 2:11-15

Before starting any new venture, it is important to seek the counsel of the Lord, and to be willing to seek the counsel of others. In chapter 1, we found King Ahasuerus seeking advice from a wrong source. Esther will provide a better example for us today! Ask the Father how and in what situations you can apply this lesson to your own life!

FRIEND TO FRIEND...

When someone new visits our church, Michael makes an effort to make contact with that person sometime through the next week. This contact might be a phone call, a letter, or a visit to their home. In the very beginning, Michael's favorite way to make contact was to go to their home with a little "thank you for taking the time to worship with us" gift: a homemade treat from my kitchen to theirs. The response was generally very pleasant, and people were surprised and glad that a pastor would make such a gesture. Every visit was different. At one location, Michael might not be invited past the front porch. At another, Michael might be ushered right into the kitchen to share a glass of their sweet tea along with the homemade treat. Inevitably, such an invitation included happy conversation and lots of "let's get to know each other, my new friend".

During one of the visits, Michael was especially enjoying himself. He could tell right away that this couple was "just good folk", as we might say in Georgia. Of course, Michael is such a lover of people and so enjoys getting to know people, it's never a surprise when he immediately makes himself and his new acquaintances comfortable. Just as Michael was getting ready to say goodbye (he never wants to overstay his welcome), the husband stopped him. He said, "Pastor, I have to tell you something about myself. Once you hear it, you may not want me at your church — some pastors don't."

What could be so disturbing that a pastor wouldn't want this sweet couple among their congregation? (Shouldn't pastors love everybody?) Michael was interested enough to stay and listen. "Well, pastor, here it is: I am an ordained minister through the Assemblies of God. Though I am in a secular job now, I have been in full time ministry in the past. I have also served several churches as interim pastor while maintaining a secular job. Thought you should know that up front — some pastors would prefer knowing that, and many would prefer if I went somewhere else. If you are among them, my wife and I will understand."

Michael was shocked to learn that this man had felt unwelcome in any church. Fortunately, his shock did not render him speechless. His reply was immediate:

"Wow — I don't feel as if I wouldn't want you in my church because you are an ordained minister. Of course, you have a decision to make now, too — after hearing me preach, you might not want to be in my church! I'd feel honored if you decide to come and make this church your home. I'd consider it a blessing if someone of your stature, experience, and dedication to the Lord's work wanted to come and serve Him with me. Brother, you are welcome; and whether or not you decide to attend this church, I hope you'll become a friend."

Many years later, this couple is still with us. As Michael had hoped, they have become close friends. They have also become our most trusted counselors, and we have turned to them countless times for advice. Because of their experience, they are able to identify with us and understand the difficulties or heartbreak of pastoring. There is also no one who understands our joys and triumphs more than they do. They can keep a confidence. They can also tell us if we seem to be heading in a wrong direction. Looking back on that first confession: "Pastor, I am an ordained minister", we realize what a treasure we could have missed had we been threatened by another man's gifts. Michael embraced him where other pastors were afraid to have someone wiser or more anointed close by.

Proverbs 11:14 declares, "in the multitude of counselors there is safety." There are times when you need only to ask the Lord, and discern for yourself what is the best course of action in a given situation. However, there are also times when it is important to allow God to use the people around you to help you. I think that is why the Lord sent this precious couple to us: He knew that even though Michael is a pastor, he still needs a pastor. Imagine the loss if we hadn't taken advantage of that gift. There is no other appropriate response but to receive this present with gratitude: "Thank you, Lord, for knowing in Your providence what we needed; and thank you, dear friend, for sharing your life with us."

In Romans 12:4-8, Paul writes about gifts: "For as we have many members in one body, but all the members do not have the same function, so we, being many, are one body in Christ, and individually members of one another. Having then gifts differing according to the grace that is given to us, let us use them: if prophecy, let us prophesy in proportion to our faith; or ministry, let us use it in our ministering; he who teaches, in teaching; he who exhorts, in exhortation; he who gives, with liberality; he who leads, with diligence; he who shows mercy, with cheerfulness."

"Having then gifts differing according to the grace that is given to us, *let us use them*." Recognize that the gifts inside you are not only for you; just as the gifts inside other people around you are not only for them. We are meant to help each other. God designed us this way on purpose! All being members of one body, our successes are shared — there is no need to be threatened by another person's gift.

Use your gifts, and encourage the people in your life to use their gifts as well. You will be blessed as a result!

Unfortunately, one thing that keeps us from asking for help or taking advantage of the talents in people around us is pride. Never allow pride to keep you from asking for counsel when it is needed! 1 Corinthians 12:20 is another passage about gifts: "now indeed there are many members, yet one body. And the eye cannot say to the hand, 'I have no need of you'; nor again the head to the feet, 'I have no need of you.' " We need each other, and joining our gifts together will result in a much stronger body. If you have time, read 1 Corinthians 12:4-20. Reflect on how there can be unity in the diversity of gifts if we use our different gifts properly. Determine that you will not be threatened by anyone else's gifts!

Esther was not afraid of the gifts in the people around her. Let's see how she responds to the wisdom of others today.

> *And every day Mordecai paced in front of the court of the women's quarters, to learn of Esther's welfare and what was happening to her.*
> Esther 2:11

Every day, Mordecai goes to the palace gates to inquire after Esther and learn of what was happening to her. He goes to the palace gates with purpose. He paces in front of the women's court until he has learns the day's news about Esther. Even though she is no longer under his roof, he stills feels a strong responsibility toward her, and acts accordingly. He is a faithful man, and has set a great example before Esther. The news that he hears concerning Esther daily must be good: her inward beauty and submission to authority are two of the many wonderful traits that God placed in her so that she will be effective in Persia.

Even though Esther is in an unfamiliar place and experiencing "firsts" every day in the palace, God is making sure she has what she needs. Esther did not need to feel nervous! She needed wise counsel; it has been provided for her in Mordecai and Hegai. She needs a pleasant and patient personality; that has been being developed in her by the Lord for many years. In your own life, you are constantly undergoing change and growth as you are submitting to the Lord. Whether or not you can see it, God is continually preparing you for what lies ahead so that *you will have what you need when you need it.* The God who loves you so much knows your future, and He is preparing you today for what you will experience tomorrow.

Esther is receiving what she needs as well. She is in the palace undergoing her beauty preparations — a twelve month process! Even through this extended period of time, Mordecai is still at the palace gates every day (the Bible does not say that he stopped his concern for her at any point). It is an entire year before she goes into the king, and Esther submits to the preparations without ever turning her back on the other more important authority in her life: Mordecai. She has continued to keep her heritage a secret. This secrecy is probably a matter of protection for her and for Mordecai.

As Ahasuerus is preparing for a new wife, as Mordecai is preparing Esther for a new life, Esther is preparing to be come a queen. It is important to notice that Esther is obedient and faithful without being certain of the outcome of this year. She has no guarantee of ever returning to her own life, she has no guarantee that she will become queen, so we must assume that she is not motivated by results in her service to the Lord. Esther is obedient without any promise other than the knowledge inside her that she will not be abandoned by the Lord at any time. She will be faithful regardless of foreseeable consequences, and the example that this kind of faithfulness sets for us is fantastic.

Once evaluated by Hegai worthy of the expense of the preparations, each young woman must undergo Ahasuerus' scrutiny as well. After a year, Esther is prepared to face the king, and is now awaiting her turn to enter his chambers.

> *Each young woman's turn came to go in to King Ahasuerus after she had completed twelve months' preparation, according to the regulations for the women, for thus were the days of their preparation apportioned: six months with oil of myrrh, and six months with perfumes and preparations for beautifying women. Thus prepared, each young woman went to the king, and she was given whatever she desired to take with her from the women's quarters to the king's palace. In the evening she went, and in the morning she returned to the second house of the women, to the custody of Shaashgaz, the king's eunuch who kept the concubines.* Esther 2:12-13

After their period of preparation, the women go, one at a time, in to the king's palace. They leave the women's quarters in the evening and return in the morning… and their life's course is determined within a period of 24 hours or less. Imagine the scene: these women were taken from their families and everything familiar to them a year or so before they are sent into the king. For a year, they are in the custody of Hegai the custodian of the women. Each step that these women take toward the palace is a step toward one of two things: either the beginning of a new life or the death of every possible dream that each one might have had for her life. A step toward becoming Ahasuerus' wife and queen of Persia — tremendous honor and riches; or a step toward becoming one of the king's concubines — a life devoid of true love or passion.

Each candidate completed these twelve months and went into the king as a potential queen. The next morning, each woman left the king's chambers as one of a countless number of mistresses in his harem. The history does not indicate that they were rejected and returned to their own homes. They were returned to Shaashgaz, the keeper of the king's concubines. The finality and sadness of the conclusion of this year must have been excruciating.

> *"She would not go into the king again unless the king delighted in her and called for her by name."* Esther 2:14

Like a splash of ice water, that sentence feels cold. A rush of emptiness and loneliness all of a sudden, they have been used and, for all practical purposes, thrown away. When they returned the next morning, they did not even go to the court that has been their home for the past year. These women went into the custody of Shaashgaz, the eunuch custodian of the concubines. That is quite a demotion for these young women — their future has just been decided, and they had no say in it. Hopes of marriage to anyone for one of these rejected women is completely over. "She would not go into the king again..."

These women must have felt a tremendous loss and sorrow. Whether or not they had actually wanted to be queen (remember that they had no choice in the matter — they had to come to the palace either way), they had been preparing for this moment for a year. Perhaps they had waited even longer for their turn to see the king. All this anticipation for one evening, and before they know it, it is over. Even if becoming the queen had not been a desire for some of them, becoming a concubine surely was not in any of their plans. What a crushing heartbreak it must have been.

Is the word providence still in the back of your mind? God is about to "shake things up" even more! When Esther's year of preparations is complete, she is told that it is at last her turn to see the king — rather, for the king to see her.

> *Now when the turn came for Esther the daughter of Abihail the uncle of Mordecai, who had taken her as his daughter, to go in to the king, she requested nothing but what Hegai the king's eunuch, the custodian of the women, advised.* Esther 2:15

In addition to beauty preparations and diet, surely Esther has received instruction concerning protocol as well. She is aware of the fact that she will be allowed to carry one small item with her when she is received by the king. Remember, Esther has continued throughout this year to be faithful to Mordecai's instructions and careful upbringing as well as submitting herself to Hegai's authority. Esther is a young woman who is accustomed to being under authority; she recognizes the importance of sound advice. Esther receives counsel from Hegai, and takes with her only what he suggests to her. Who would be better than Hegai to advise her in how to make a pleasing first impression with King Ahasuerus? Hegai was in charge in preparing these women; he must have had a good idea of Ahasuerus' likes and dislikes.

During this year of preparation, Esther has most likely recognized Hegai's important role. She goes to him for advice as to what to take with her, and it serves her well. It is not recorded that any other woman sought Hegai's advice — perhaps it was mentioned because it was peculiar only to Esther. This shows us one more aspect of Esther's personality: she is not threatened by the gifts in other people. Esther has submitted herself to God's will, and recognizes that God is placing people around her who are potentially a help to her, if she is humble enough to recognize and receive advice from someone else. She recognizes that Hegai's knowledge can help her.

One more thought for today: do not over look the important difference between Esther's asking for advice, and King Ahasuerus' asking for advice. Remember in chapter one, when Ahasuerus sought after advice, he went to people in a very similar situation or even beneath him. Remember Memucan and the other princes? How could men who did not even live with the queen or know her well have *any* idea how to handle her? In Esther 2:15, we have an example of Esther being able to discern wisely her situation — there were times to keep to herself, and also times to ask for help. When Esther sought advice, she sought it from a good source. Just as it made all the difference in the world for Esther, it will make all the difference in the world for you.

Take a moment to thank God for the people in your life whose advice and character are an encouragement and help to you. Pray that He will cause you to be someone whose encouragement will be a blessing to others this week!

❧

DAY FOUR: ESTHER 2:15-18

"You never get a second chance to make a first impression".... well, that's not exactly from the Bible (okay — not at all from the Bible!), but it's still true! What is the first impression that people get from you?

FRIEND TO FRIEND...

Joanie is absolutely beautiful. It's an opinion, I suppose, but I have never met anyone who didn't agree wholeheartedly. She possesses an outward beauty, to be sure, but there is something more: she seems to get prettier every time you hear her.

That sentence does not seem to make sense, I know. Shouldn't it read "every time you see her"? Maybe. Maybe, but the truth is that she does get more and more beautiful through every conversation. Proverbs 25:11-12 often comes to my mind when I am around her. These verses say that a "word fitly spoken is like... an ornament of fine gold". With all of her "words fitly spoken", she has a collection of these fine gold ornaments about her spirit, and they cause her to, well, to sparkle in a way. Every time she speaks a word another "ornament" is collected. It's too simple, isn't it? Possibly a more adept explanation could come from a more adept mind, but I'm a little simple myself, and sometimes I find the simplest explanations work best.

An outward beauty ("passing" the Bible calls it in Proverbs 31:30), is a gift, of course. However, it is the inner beauty that Joanie possesses that I so admire in her. The gift God placed inside her did not come prepared as her outward beauty did. Her outward beauty comes altogether naturally. The beauty inside her, incorruptible and precious as described in 1 Peter 3:4, came to her as a seed. Everything that Joanie needed to achieve this inner beauty was there, but it needed to be developed. It needed to be *prepared*. As a result of Joanie's dedication to the Lord and to developing the most valuable gifts given to her, everyone who knows her is blessed. Even people who do not recognize that these attractive qualities are a result of time spent with the Lord love her and desire to be close to her. This way, she has found "favor and high esteem in the sight of God and man" (Proverbs 3:4).

Sometimes, in observing Joanie and having the privilege of being around her, I am most encouraged that this kind of beauty is possible. If the Lord was able to develop it in her, could He develop the same in me? Well, with God all things shall be possible, right? (I have quite a long way to go!) Most times, I smile when I think of Joanie, and feel blessed that she is among my acquaintances. Her kind words collected about her like ornaments of gold; and her quiet and gentle spirit, which are precious in the sight of the Lord and in the sight of everyone around her, make her an absolute joy. Highly favored. To make it simple: you can tell that Joanie is everyone's favorite, and with good reason!

In "You've Got Mail" (a remake of a charming old movie "The Shop Around The Corner"), two characters are corresponding by email, and have never met. Without names or specifics, they write to each other. At times, advise each other. In one scene, they are discussing their decidedly different reactions to people in varying situations. One can never find the right response at the right moment; while the other boasts of an ability to have a smart, though not always generous, response to every comment. Joe Fox, the character with the smart 'come-backs' ("zingers", he called them), offers a piece of advice to Kathleen Kelly regarding her complaints of never knowing what to say. He says to her, "let me warn you: when you finally have the pleasure of being able to say exactly what you mean to say the moment that you mean to say it, remorse inevitably follows."

Isn't that the truth? When in an argument or faced with a critical person, all of us have had moments on either end of the spectrum. Without fail, every time I have taken the opportunity to "answer back" or defend myself, I have come to regret it deeply. When I have found myself at a complete loss for words, I have been thankful because I imagine whatever I might have come up with in the heat of the moment would not have graced me or the hearer. The best times are those, when faced with a criticism or argument, I have had no desire to have any answer at all — that's when I know that the Holy Spirit is working in me.

In Ephesians 4:29-32, the apostle Paul had a similar (but better!) piece of advice, "Let no corrupt word proceed out of your mouth, but what is good for necessary edification, that it may impart grace to the hearers. And do not grieve the Holy Spirit of God, by whom you were sealed for the day of redemption. Let all bitterness, wrath, anger, clamor, and evil speaking be put away from you, with all malice. And be kind to one another, tenderhearted, forgiving one another, even as God in Christ forgave you." Kind to one another, tender, forgiving...that's truly beautiful!

I wonder if Joanie struggles with words as sometimes I do. Listening to her beauty (because now you understand that beauty can be *heard* as well as *seen*), I can't imagine that she does, but I do understand that we are all a work in progress. Esther had opportunity for bitterness, surely. After a year in the palace, there were many opportunities for her to display what was on the inside. Taken by force from her home, having to give up all plans and dreams she may have had for her life, moving to a strange place and being surrounded by strange people... After a year in the palace, Esther passed any opportunity to demonstrate bitterness. She displayed her inner beauty every day, and obtained favor from all who saw her.

Let's return to Persia, and see the result of this favor on her life.

Esther obtained favor in the sight of all who saw her. Esther 2:15b

Esther's turn finally comes, and she has spent a year preparing to see the king. Esther most likely has spent this year watching, observing, and learning. Perhaps she has also been building relationships with the women around her. This moment is pivotal in her life, and Esther recognizes the importance of making wise decisions. In similar moments, others have gone to the king and never come back to the quarters that Esther has shared with them over the past months. Judging by the response that Esther receives from the people around her, it is apparent that she has spent this year well.

"Favor" is defined in the Strong's Concordance as "graciousness, pleasant, and precious, well-favored".[5] Just as the historian only records Esther asking for advice before seeing the king, he only mentions Esther obtaining favor from all who saw her. The others did not receive this favor, this immediate appreciation from "all who saw" them! This special favor was reserved for Esther.

Now it is time for Esther to leave the custody of Hegai. By tomorrow morning, she will find out what her future holds: a place in the throne room, or a place in the harem. Will Ahasuerus view Esther in the same way as the others in the palace have? Will she receive favor from the king as well?

> *So Esther was taken to King Ahasuerus, into his royal palace, in the tenth month, which is the month of Tebeth, in the seventh year of his reign. The king loved Esther more than all the other women, and she obtained grace and favor in his sight more than all the virgins; so he set the royal crown upon her head and made her queen instead of Vashti.* Esther 2:16-17

After finding favor with all the people that saw her on the way into the king, Esther finds favor with the king himself. The first reaction that our historian records is that "the king loved Esther". Following that initial reaction, we are told in verse 17 that she "obtained grace and favor" with the king.

Here in verse 17, the word "favor" is just a little bit different than the word "favor" in verse 15 when translated back to the original language. The favor Esther found with the king is defined in the Strong's concordance as feeling "*courtesy to an equal,* kindness, mercy". 6 It's interesting to notice that the king felt all the things that everyone else felt when he saw Esther. Ahasuerus found her pleasing, precious, beautiful... Then Ahasuerus takes that feeling a step further: he recognized her as his equal. That is rather extraordinary if you take a moment to consider the source of this high compliment. King Ahasuerus: the self-proclaimed "greatest king of the world" feels as if he has met his equal in an orphaned Jewess? That is truly the favor of God on Esther's life!

And Ahasuerus placed "the royal crown on [Esther's] head and made her queen instead of Vashti" (2:17).

> *Then the king made a great feast, the Feast of Esther, for all his officials and servants; and he proclaimed a holiday in the provinces and gave gifts according to the generosity of a king.* Esther 2:18

After the king decides Esther will be his queen, he throws a party. You might remember that this guy is famous for his parties! He proclaims the day he met Esther as a holiday: "The Feast of Esther". Ahasuerus celebrates with all his servants and all his officials, and the news of the new queen is spread to all the provinces.

Ahasuerus also gives Esther gifts "according to the generosity of a king"... that must have really been something! I love that little phrase... "gave gifts according to the generosity of a king". It is another little parallel to make between you and

Esther: your King — the Lord of Lords — gives to you gifts according to His generosity as well, doesn't He? Every day is something new!

Esther prepared and gave her best to King Ahasuerus, and the response from him was tremendous. Imagine if you prepared your heart daily to give God your very best — wow! The Lord cannot resist that! Open yourself up to your King and expect great things!

Before you close the word today, consider that phrase again: "gifts according to the generosity of a king". You have a king celebrating you today — the King of Kings, truly the greatest King... He desires to give you gifts according to His generosity!

❦

DAY FIVE: ESTHER 2:19-23

Are you still thinking about yesterday? Don't let today go by without thanking God for the treasure inside you! It is His good pleasure to give you the kingdom today!

FRIEND TO FRIEND...

My oldest son, Tyler, is a treasure. In addition to being hard working and pleasant, he is one of the kindest children that I know. In observing Tyler, it is apparent he has a strong desire to do well, and (most of the time!) he puts forth his best effort. It is also important to Tyler to know that we think he is doing well. It is my sincere prayer that one day he will "work heartily as unto the Lord and not unto men" (Colossians 3:23), but as he is growing into that relationship with the Lord, our praise strengthens and encourages him. Knowing also that Tyler will learn about a relationship with his Heavenly Father by his relationship with his father and with me, we don't hold back our praise. Besides, we're crazy about this kid! As sweet as Tyler is, we never have to look hard to find reasons to tell him how proud we are of him.

I remember one specific day being a day to tell Tyler that we were proud: his first report card had just come home. It was no surprise to us that he had done well; Tyler always was a smart child. Considering also his desire to please, we had anticipated Tyler would love school, and that his teachers would love him. We were right on both counts. Still hardly able to believe he and his twin brother had been in kindergarten nine weeks already (time had flown by), I had Tyler sitting in my lap while I looked over his report card. Looking at his face, I noticed his eyebrows were crossed and his usually cheerful countenance seemed to have turned dark with worry. As I read, he had been waiting for me to interpret the words on this page for him. Though I tried to respond quickly to his obvious concern, Tyler beat me to it and spoke first. "Mommy, did I do good?"

Putting down the report card, I held him and smiled at him and assured him that he had done "very good". I told him in as many different ways as I could think of at the moment that his Daddy and I were so proud of him. As quickly as the shadow across his face had come, it was gone. All smiles again, he wanted to tell his Daddy himself that he had had a good day. Tyler bounced off, and the report card was left alone on the end table, already forgotten.

A good report card was the result of wise choices through the grading period. It was really the series of good choices on Tyler's part that Michael and I were proud of, not the report card itself. The good report was an affirmation of his previous hard work. In life, Tyler will have to understand that the end result is not always the most important thing, but the choices that he made in getting to the end result are. Simple enough to understand: good choices will end in good results, and bad choices will end in bad results. A good lesson for anyone to learn, right?

I learned on that day what was important to my son. Two things were of primary importance: the knowledge inside himself that he had done well, and the knowledge that we thought he had done well. Tyler didn't need a report card to know that. Since that day, he has never seen another report card. Actually, none of my three children have. When other moms mention the stress of waiting for the report card, or talk about how their child is upset or worried about report cards coming, I stay quiet. Michael and I try to teach our children to do their best every day and to work hard every day. The result of this discipline generally ends in a good report. As a result, the one day that report cards come home is not a source of stress. We are not merely surviving from nine weeks to nine weeks, and my children are confident and happy. When report cards do come, they have one question: "Mom, did I do good?"

Yes, Tyler, you did "very good". With your faithful and generous manner, I suspect that you always will.

In Psalm 119:57-58, the psalmist writes, "You are my portion, O LORD; I have said that I would keep Your words. I entreated Your *favor* with my whole heart; Be merciful to me according to Your word". Proverbs 3:3-4 says, "Let not mercy and truth forsake you; Bind them around your neck, Write them on the tablet of your heart, And so find favor and high esteem in the sight of God and man". In Proverbs 3:34, we read God "gives grace to the humble". "Grace" and "favor" are words that can be used interchangeably here. Both of these verses use the same word for "favor" as we read in Esther 2:15. The similarity in the language is not the only item to notice here: both of these verses contain a cause and effect. The psalmist sought the favor of the Lord. He desired to hear the Lord tell him he had done well.

You will notice in these verses, they give an instruction, then says you will receive favor as a result of following those directions. In Psalm 119:57, the instruction is to keep God's word and ask for His favor. In Proverbs 3:3-4, the Word says to keep mercy and truth written on the tablet of your heart. In Proverbs 3:34, we are encouraged that favor will be given to us as we stay humble in the sight of the Lord. Wise choices have to be made and instructions have to be followed to experience the Lord's favor and sense His pleasure in us.

We have to remember that ultimately favor will come to you as a natural outcome of your faithfulness to the Lord. It comes back to what we spoke about last week: being motivated and driven by God's opinion of you rather than the opinions of man. Your aim should be to live up to God's standards for you, rather than standards that the world may have for you. In striving to meet God's standards, you will surely surpass the standards of men. You will receive your praise from the right source — your Heavenly Father — and you will find it to be more than enough.

Looking at the story of Esther on the surface, it may seem that she has been singled out for her outward beauty. However, as we have seen over the past couple of days, she has many inner qualities that are shining through. Her submission to authority, her ability to discern her situation, her ability to recognize and not be threatened by the talents of others, her faithfulness to her people (by not revealing her heritage).... God has placed so many important qualities inside her that her outward beauty is just a little bonus!

It is the same for you — *you are beautiful* — (you truly are, woman of God!), but what makes you special, what makes you valuable, what makes you worthy is the treasure *inside* you! Just as God placed these specific treasures inside Esther to make it possible for her to fulfill her purpose, God placed specific treasures inside you to make it possible for you to fulfill your purpose. Learn to recognize and embrace the qualities that make you the woman God created you to be. You will soon discover that you are able to walk in favor of the Lord as Esther did.

Earlier in the week, we touched on how pride might prevent you from accepting or asking for help. That is not the only caution you should be aware of as you prepare for and progress on your journey with the Lord. Let's look at one more verse before we return to Esther and close out chapter two.

Colossians 3:22-24 states, "Bondservants, obey in all things your masters according to the flesh, not with eyeservice, as men-pleasers, but in sincerity of heart, fearing God. And whatever you do, do it heartily, as to the Lord and not to men, knowing that from the Lord you will receive the reward of the inheritance; for you serve the Lord Christ." *Work* — and don't be deceived into thinking that achieving your goals in Christ will be easy — as if the only person watching you is the Lord. Sometimes people will recognize your gifts and offer their praise. Stay humble, and do not allow that praise to be a motivator. Other times, people will fail to recognize your gifts and they'll offer criticism, or not notice you at all. Stay humble and do not allow the lack of praise to be a hindrance. Becoming content with the praise of men will stop your progress as much as becoming discouraged by their criticism. Find your contentment in the Lord. As Christians, we do not have to depend on people to make us feel good or to let us feel bad!

Proverbs 18:16 says that a man's gift will bring him before "great men" — your translation may say before "kings". Where do those gifts ultimately come from? Our Father, of course! God is working through you to achieve a specific purpose, and God must have all the glory. Good opinions or bad opinions, our concern has to be for the things of the Lord. As we are striving to live up to HIS standards and being who HE created us to be, let us work "heartily for the Lord and not unto men"!

For Esther, it seems as if everyone surrounding her is dedicated to her success. It will not always be that way, however, and the manner in which Esther has remained faithful to the Lord through the process will serve her well. As she has allowed the Lord's faithfulness to sustain her through easier times, she will allow Him to sustain her through difficult times. She has received praise from men (favor from all who see her, remember?), but she has remained humble and that praise has not become what motivates her.

This final section of chapter 2 is about Mordecai. We have been able to gather a little bit about him by considering Esther's character. We can assume he was a very devout and faithful man by looking at Esther. Mordecai, after all, was the one who had raised Esther — something of him must have come through in her. Even though Mordecai is mentioned at the beginning of this chapter, we are getting ready to see him "in action".

> *When virgins were gathered together a second time, Mordecai sat within the king's gate. Now Esther had not revealed her family and her people, just as Mordecai had charged her, for Esther obeyed the command of Mordecai as when she was brought up by him.*
> Esther 2:19-20

Just as he did during Esther's preparations, Mordecai comes to the king's gate daily to inquire after her. Even the fact that Esther has become queen has not kept him from his concern for her. The historian mentions again that, Esther has continued to submit to Mordecai's authority and has not yet revealed her heritage. A change in circumstances has not produced a change in character in Esther and Mordecai. They are as faithful to the Lord as they ever have been. As hard times drove them to their faith, relief has not driven them away from it.

On this particular day at the palace gate, Mordecai learns about Esther, and learns something else as well.

> *In those days, while Mordecai sat within the king's gate, two of the king's eunuchs, Bigthan and Teresh, doorkeepers, became furious and sought to lay hands on King Ahasuerus.* Esther 2:21

Mordecai overhears two of the king's eunuchs, Bigthan and Teresh, talking. He learns they are planning to "lay hands" on King Ahasuerus. To make it plain, they are plotting an assassination, and King Ahasuerus is the target. The fact that they were eunuchs tells us they were Babylonian officials; they were close to the king and his affairs. It is quite possible that these two were not only *talking* about an assassination attempt, they could be the ones to carry it out.

Mordecai had spent many days at the king's gate. He had been there every day since Esther moved to the palace over a year ago. During this time, Mordecai had also become familiar with those who were around the gate. He knew who Bigthan and Teresh were, and he discerned that they were serious about this plan. Mordecai recognizes this as a serious threat to King Ahasuerus.

> *So the matter became known to Mordecai, who told Queen Esther,*
> *and Esther informed the king in Mordecai's name.*
> Esther 2:22

When Mordecai comes to realize these men are serious, he makes Esther aware of the situation quickly. Mordecai tells Queen Esther, who in turn makes the matter known to the king. Consider that it would have been very easy for Mordecai to keep silent and keep this information to himself.

Also, do not let it escape your attention that Queen Esther tells the king about the assassination plot *in Mordecai's name.* Just as it would have been easy for Mordecai to keep silent, it would have been easy for Esther to accept the credit for diverting this crisis. What a great boost it would have been for her new role as queen, if Esther had made one of her first actions to be saving the life of her husband. Such an act would have surely endeared her to the hearts of the Babylonian people. Ahasuerus would have been sure to sing her praises as well. (Imagine -Ahasuerus congratulating himself on choosing such a fine queen... you have not forgotten, have you? All of this is in God's providence!) A few more things that we love about our heroine, Esther: she is humble, she is patient, and she waits for her promotion to come from the Lord. This was Mordecai's discovery, and she gives him the credit.

King Ahasuerus could have been killed, but remember our theme here: **providence!** God is constantly moving! Why would he go to such measures to save the life of a king who does not even serve Him? Because His providence is in action, and He is orchestrating events that may seem unimportant to us. His ways are not our ways, right? Our Father sees EVERYTHING: our sight is so limited in comparison.

Romans 8:28 is true — God **can** work out everything for the good of those who love him and are called according to His purpose. However, this verse is certainly not a license for us to place ourselves in wrong circumstances, and then expect God to work it out for our good. The important difference between King Ahasuerus' life situation and yours is that you have the great advantage of serving God *right now*. Ahasuerus makes a mistake, the Lord rearranges things to make it work out for the best. Ahasuerus gets drunk and makes a rash decision, the Lord moves the right people into his path to make it right. Ahasuerus wants a new wife? God had that one covered years ago when the Jews were moved to Babylon for the captivity. We will witness God's providential power over and over again.

Your life is not that way. Thankfully we are not going through life merely hoping for the best. God is working on our behalf, and you have an active part in seeking out His will for your life. Like He did for Esther, God has been planning and providing for you long before you had knowledge of your need. He covered you before you were born (Psalm 138), and brought you to this time for a specific purpose. In His love, there is no fear of failure. In His love, there is no fear of lack. Your God is a God of provision, and as you submit and prepare, you can feel confident in His love.

> *And when an inquiry was made into the matter, it was confirmed,*
> *and both were hanged on a gallows; and it was written in the book*
> *of the chronicles in the presence of the king.* Esther 2:23

Ahasuerus, after confirming that this story is true, finds Bigthan and Teresh, and rather than them "executing" the king, the king executes them. These events are recorded in the king's chronicles in his presence.

Much preparation is going on during this week. Esther is going to need all this preparation for what is coming next. Though he is still completely in the dark concerning everything that is going on around him, Ahasuerus needs it as well. Mordecai is about to uncover a plot against the king that will reveal something even darker than an assassination plan. Bigthan and Teresh were just two "bugs" that happened to crawl out when Mordecai "lifted the log" and exposed their plan. This was just the beginning. All sorts of creepy crawlies are going to come out in chapter 3!

Pray that God would help you daily walk in the truth that He is orchestrating your life — "be anxious for nothing"! Just as the work is His, so must the glory be! Praise God for His hand on your life — and rest in the knowledge that you are not unnoticed by your Father!

⊱

Do not fear, little flock, for it is the Father's good pleasure to give you the kingdom.
Luke 12:32

Father, Your love is amazing!
If I allow it to, Your love will free me.
Your love will free me
from fear of lack in any area of my life —
spiritual, emotional, physical, financial...
Your love will free me from worry
and let me rest safely in Your strong arms.
As I partner with You and add my faithfulness to Your providence,
You are not only able to give me good gifts,
it is Your pleasure to bless me!
You are generous, kind, compassionate...
You are a good shepherd,
and I am so thankful to be one of Your flock!

⊱

1.   Concise Oxford English Dictionary, Eleventh Edition, (USA: Oxford university Press, Inc. New York 2006), p.1129.

2.   James Strong, The Exhaustive Concordance of the Bible, (Peabody, Massachusetts: Hendrickson Publishers.) # 3303, #8389.

3.   James Strong, The Exhaustive Concordance of the Bible, (Peabody, Massachusetts: Hendrickson Publishers.), # 2896, #4758.

4.   Matthew Henry, Matthew Henry's Commentary on the Whole Bible, (USA: Hendrickson Publishers, 1996), p.870.

5.   James Strong, The Exhaustive Concordance of the Bible, (Peabody, Massachusetts: Hendrickson Publishers, 1996), #2580.

6.   Biblesoft's New Exhaustive Strong's Numbers and Concordance with Expanded Greek-Hebrew Dictionary. Copyright (c) 1994, Biblesoft and International Bible Translators, Inc.

ESTHER: CHAPTER 3
Haman's Plot Against the Jews

We meet the last of our "major players" this week. Having met already Ahasuerus, Vashti, Esther, and Mordecai; it's time to meet one more person: Haman. I would like to describe Haman as a *little* man with a *big* position (a potentially dangerous combination).

This week, we will see how easily a disaster can be created by a person who is driven by emotions. We will also discuss how sometimes this type of person may even appear to succeed. We will remember no matter what man may do, God is still in control. Be thankful this week that even though evil people may come into power (and fall from power) your fate is not controlled by such people. Your fate is continually controlled by your Heavenly Father. Put yourself wholly into His hands — He takes such good care of you!

As you allow yourself to experience the freedom that can be achieved through God's love for you, you can be freed from being emotion-driven in your life. Your emotions are a gift from the Lord. Emotions are an important part of your personality. Your emotions can reveal what your anointing is. What are you passionate about? Perhaps your emotions are pointing you toward the work God has for you.

However, if we allow our emotions to control us, we can quickly become *out* of control. For example, let us consider the emotion of anger. The Bible encourages us to "be angry and do not sin" (Psalm 4:4). We are not to deny our emotions, but we are not to be controlled by them, as we have witnessed Ahasuerus to be at times. Sound difficult? It can be — but as a result of living in God's love, you can experience peace and freedom from emotional living!

Just as we began our first two weeks together, find a quiet corner and get comfortable....and don't forget the power of God's love and His PROVIDENCE!

℞

DAY ONE: ESTHER 3:1

An important part of recognizing God's providential power in your life is obedience to Him. In order to see His plans come to pass in our lives, obedience is key. Logical or not, we must obey our Father — He sees so much that we do not see!

FRIEND TO FRIEND...

I do not hire babysitters very often, but my children enjoy it when I do. They have a few favorite teenagers who always think of fun things to do. They also know the evening will most likely include a pizza delivery, a video rental, special snacks and drinks and the best childhood splurge: no bed time!

When the babysitter comes, the children know that I need a few minutes with her before the "party" starts; there are instructions that we need to go over. A list of emergency numbers will be posted on the front of the refrigerator, and everyone's favorite treats will be inside the refrigerator. I will talk to her about the children's likes and dislikes, and what is allowed and what is not allowed while I am out of the house. When I am finished with my directions, I will ask if she has any questions or if there is anything she needs to know that I failed to address with her. Any manner of question might be perfectly acceptable, but if she were to say, "Mrs. Spivey, which of these instructions do I actually have to follow, and which ones can I completely ignore?", my "evening out" would immediately become an "evening in"! My plans would be cancelled, and the babysitter would be driven home to determine "which ones" on her own time. As I am entrusting her with the safety and well-being of my children, I expect her to follow *all* my instructions.

Fortunately for us, Jesus does not act as hastily when He gives instructions. Jesus is a wonderful teacher, gentle and patient. Through His time here on earth, even though people did not always agree with Him, He always made a powerful impression. No one, having obeyed and worshiped, left His presence unchanged or disappointed. However, it was a different story for those who chose not to follow Him. His teaching, like His entire life, is a gift to us: it is *free*, but it must be *accepted*.

Once, Jesus crossed paths with a rich young ruler. This young man approached Jesus with a simple yet important question, recorded in Matthew 19:16: "Good Teacher, what good thing shall I do that I may have eternal life?" Jesus never spoke down to anyone, and in this instance, made an effort to put this young man at ease. His answer began, "Why do you call me good? No one is good but one, that is, God" (Matthew 19:17a). For Jesus, God's only Son, become flesh and dwelling among men, to put Himself on the same level with this young man should have served as a source of great encouragement. In essence, Jesus says, "Don't worry — I know your feelings and have experienced your trials. No one is good but God, but that will not stop you from inheriting eternal life. Let me tell you how you will achieve it." Immediately following this sweet encouragement, Jesus gives the answer to the young man's question. Jesus tells him, "... if you want to enter into life, keep the commandments" (Matthew 19:17b).

So far, so great! A question and an answer. The conversation turns sour at the young man's next query. After Jesus tells him that in order to receive eternal life, he must keep the commandments, the young man asks: "Which ones?" (Matthew 19:18).

"Which ones?"

At the risk of revealing a certain impatient aspect of my personality, I have to admit that this question irritates me so much. Jesus is more patient than I am, and He gently offers a wise answer. However, it takes me a while to get past the question. Which ones? It seems to me that the young man is asking Jesus not only which commandments must be followed, but also which commandments can be completely ignored. Jesus had great compassion on this young man, and continued the conversation. I think that once I heard, "Which ones?", the next words out of my mouth would have been "good bye".

Not our loving Father. God is not "slack concerning His promise, as some count slackness, but is longsuffering toward us, not willing that any should perish but that all should come to repentance" (2 Peter 3:9). Jesus knew the importance of this young man's question. The most intense desire of His heart was that this young man accept the truth, and follow Jesus' commands leading to eternal life. Patiently and gently, Jesus spells out the commandments that this young man would need to follow. Sadly, the rich young ruler found the commandments too difficult, and the Word tells us "when the young man heard that saying, he went away sorrowful" (Matthew 19:22). He *went away* from Jesus, having made the choice against total submission and obedience.

When the Lord gives an instruction, His intention is that we will obey it completely. Consider that wherever you are in your walk with the Lord, whether you are new to your faith or have served the Lord many years, you are still His *child*. God knows the beginning from the end; no matter how much we may think that we know, He knows more. The Word reminds us that our knowledge is limited. Job 26:14 states, "Indeed these are the mere edges of His ways, and how small a whisper we hear of Him." Paul writes in 1 Corinthians 13:9, "we know *in part* and we prophesy *in part*" (emphasis mine).

Our knowledge will not always be limited in this way. Paul encourages us that "when that which is perfect has come, then that which is in part will be done away" (1 Corinthians 13:10). Until that day, we must find contentment and satisfaction in the exchange the Lord offers to us today: trade your judgement for His. Obey His word fully. Do not pick and choose for yourself "which ones". Find confidence in the knowledge that all of the Lord's words are for your benefit and prosperity in this life. The Lord means for you to be successful and fulfilled, but this happiness will be impossible to achieve without complete obedience.

There will be times in your life when you feel blind to the future. You will have times when you cannot imagine the reason why God is asking something from you. In those times, you must trust that the Lord will make perfect everything that concerns you (Psalm 138:8). In those times, you must trust that God in His vast knowledge knows the beginning from the end. If you feel blind to what lies ahead, then operate in blind obedience. Submit to the Lord. Say to Him, "I don't know why You require this of me, but I will obey You and trust in Your plan." Exchange your judgement for His. In that trust and in His love for you, you will find peace.

We will see today in Persia how failure to obey had disastrous and far-reaching results.

After these things... Esther 3:1

"After these things..." apparently a favorite phrase of our historian, but somehow this does not seem like an adequate description for the events that have passed since the end of chapter two. As chapter two comes to a close, we learn that Mordecai has rescued Ahasuerus from an assassination attempt. How exciting! Mordecai saved the life of a king who loves to throw a party, so chapter three should begin with a celebration in Mordecai's honor, right?

Well, maybe not.

> *After these things King Ahasuerus promoted Haman, the son of Hammedatha the Agagite, and advanced him and set his seat above all the princes who were with him.* Esther 3:1

King Ahasuerus promotes Haman. After Mordecai saves the king's life, he is seemingly forgotten. He will not stay out of the picture for long. God is still working.

Haman seems to have come out of nowhere; until now, his name has never been mentioned. However, he is very important to our story. While his introduction here may have seemed rather abrupt, there is information within this verse that is not be missed. Haman is the son of "Hammedatha the Agagite". The term "Agagite" does not refer to a place; this term refers to a person. The reference is to King Agag of the Amalekites. Haman's father was a subject of King Agag.

You may be wondering: what is the significance?

Genealogies in the Bible may seem random at times, but with a little study, the importance becomes very clear. You will remember last week when we learned Mordecai's background in chapter 2. In Mordecai's genealogy, we learned that he is descended from Kish the Benjamite. Another important biblical figure descended from Kish as well: Saul. Saul was Israel's first king, and Kish's son. Saul (whose descendant here is Mordecai) and Agag (whose descendant here is Haman) share a history.

Agag was king of the Amalekites. The Amalekites were a known and constant enemy to the nation of Israel, and the animosity between these two groups of people was strong. Though there are many examples of this tension in the Word, we will focus on one instance in particular: between King Saul and King Agag. As we explore the relationship between these two men, keep in mind that these represent the families of Mordecai and Haman.

Samuel also said to Saul,

> *The LORD sent me to anoint you king over His people, over Israel.*
> *Now therefore, heed the voice of the words of the LORD. Thus says*
> *the LORD of hosts: 'I will punish Amalek for what he did to Israel,*
> *how he ambushed him on the way when he came up from Egypt.*
> *Now go and attack Amalek, and utterly destroy all that they have,*
> *and do not spare them. But kill both man and woman, infant and*
> *nursing child, ox and sheep, camel and donkey.'* 1 Samuel 15:1-3

In this passage, we read that the Lord sent a message through the prophet Samuel to Saul: God intended to punish Amalek for attacking Israel. It was God who meant for the Amalekites to receive this judgement. Through Samuel, God was very specific. Saul was to "utterly destroy *all*" of the Amalekites. Men, women, children, and even animals were to be completely and utterly wiped out. No person, no possessions, nothing connected to the people of Amalek was to be spared in this attack. The instructions were harsh, and were meant to be: it was the Lord's intent to destroy not only the living Amalekites, but the possibility that the lineage would continue.

King Saul has an order to follow.

> *"So Saul gathered the people together and numbered them in Telaim,*
> *two hundred thousand foot soldiers and ten thousand men of Judah.*
> *And Saul came to a city of Amalek, and lay in wait in the valley.*
> *Then Saul said to the Kenites, 'Go, depart, get down from among the*
> *Amalekites, lest I destroy you with them. For you showed kindness*
> *to all the children of Israel when they came up out of Egypt.' So the*
> *Kenites departed from among the Amalekites. And Saul attacked*
> *the Amalekites, from Havilah all the way to Shur, which is east of*
> *Egypt."* 1 Samuel 15:4-7

Saul gathers his people together and acts quickly. He leads the attack against Amalek. The Kenites lived near the Amalekites. Before the attack was to begin, Saul gave them an opportunity to escape the coming bloodshed. By this action, it seems Saul's intention was to follow the command of the Lord to the letter. Unfortunately, Saul became so involved in the attack, he neglected to obey an important part of the Lord's command.

> *He also took Agag king of the Amalekites alive, and utterly destroyed*
> *all the people with the edge of the sword. But Saul and the people*
> *spared Agag and the best of the sheep, the oxen, the fatlings, the*
> *lambs, and all that was good, and were unwilling to utterly destroy*
> *them. But everything despised and worthless, that they utterly de-*
> *stroyed.* 1 Samuel 15:8-9

Men, women, children, oxen; the Lord commanded that they be completely erased. However, the custom of the times was that the king be spared (at least for the moment) and brought back as a trophy to show the people. Saul wanted to bask in praise of his people, and share with them this great victory. What better than the head of the defeated king? Saul got caught up in the excitement of the battle, and wanted a token to share with his subjects.

Rather than doing exactly what God had commanded him, Saul destroyed what he deemed worthless and he spared what he deemed best. Saul used his own judgement, rather than trusting the Lord's direction. The passage tells us that Saul, and his people under his authority, were "unwilling" to destroy what they thought represented the best of Amalek. Following Saul's example, his armies took it upon themselves to determine what part of the Lord's command was to be obeyed, and what part could be ignored. Saul spared what was *in his own judgement* the best. He destroyed what was *in his own judgement* the least.

Saul's judgement was sadly and tragically flawed.

By sparing the Amalekites, Saul allowed the tremendous tension between these people and the Jews to continue. While Saul could not have predicted what was to come, God knew the beginning from the end. God desired for the Israelites to live without the animosity of the people of Agag. When God asked Saul to utterly destroy the Amalekites (the people of Agag), He meant for this destruction of the Amalekites to be a means of protection for Saul and the Israelites.

Saul could not see into the future. His own short-sightedness and his unwilling-ness to trust the Lord's judgement in matters which he could not have judged for himself would ultimately lead to his demise. Saul's disobedience would override the Lord's intentions, and this battle with the Amalekites would not be his last.

Though the history lesson for today has already been long, indulge me for a few more minutes. Let's look at one more event: the end of Saul's life.

> *Now it came to pass after the death of Saul, when David had re-*
> *turned from the slaughter of the Amalekites, and David had stayed*
> *two days in Ziklag, on the third day, behold, it happened that a man*
> *came from Saul's camp with his clothes torn and dust on his head.*
> *So it was, when he came to David, that he fell to the ground and*
> *prostrated himself. And David said to him, "Where have you come*

from?" So he said to him, "I have escaped from the camp of Israel."
Then David said to him,"How did the matter go? Please tell me."
And he answered, "The people have fled from the battle, many of the
people are fallen and dead, and Saul and Jonathan his son are dead
also." So David said to the young man who told him, "How do you
know that Saul and Jonathan his son are dead?" Then the young
man who told him said, "As I happened by chance to be on Mount
Gilboa, there was Saul, leaning on his spear; and indeed the chariots
and horsemen followed hard after him. Now when he looked behind
him, he saw me and called to me. And I answered, 'Here I am.'
And he said to me, 'Who are you?' So I answered him, 'I am an
Amalekite.' He said to me again, 'Please stand over me and kill me,
for anguish has come upon me, but my life still remains in me.' So I
stood over him and killed him..." 2 Samuel 1:1-10

To make it as short as possible, David has just returned from battle to find Saul and his best friend Jonathan dead. Saul, already hurt badly from the battle, is found by an Amalekite who "stood over him and killed him". Years before, Saul had an opportunity to destroy the Amalekites, but his pride and own narrow judgement prevented him from following the Lord's command completely. If Saul had obeyed the Lord, this Amalekite would not have been here at the moment of Saul's death.

It is interesting that the Amalekite does not give his name, but his nationality. Upon hearing "I am an Amalekite", I wonder if Saul felt even a twinge of regret at remembering a failure to obey the Lord in battle so many years ago. I wonder if the memory brought to his mind by those four words hurt his spirit as deeply as the sword hurt his body.

This account of Saul's death differs from the account of the same event offered at the end of 1 Samuel. In reading 1 Samuel 31, it appears that Saul died at his own hand, not at the hand of this Amalekite. We are not told whether the battle was going in Saul's favor, but we do know that Saul's three sons had been killed. In an emotional and heartbreaking state, Saul does not want to continue to live. Saul turns to his armorbearer and commands him, "Draw your sword, and thrust me through with it" (1 Samuel 31:4). When the armorbearer refuses, Saul "took a sword and fell on it" (1 Samuel 31:6), killing himself.

David learns of Saul's death in 2 Samuel 1 from the Amalekite. Whether this Amalekite did in fact kill Saul or is merely taking credit for the king's death and claiming to have killed Saul himself is uncertain. The Amalekite states that he found Saul in "anguish" (2 Samuel 1:9). Some Bible scholars believe that the Amalekite was lying to David, hoping for some kind of reward. Some Bible scholars believe that it is possible, though maybe unlikely, that the Amalekite found Saul near death and did in fact finish the job that Saul started. In either case, whether or not you believe that Saul was killed by his own hand due to anguish caused by losing his sons in a battle with the Amalekites or by this Amalekite directly, one fact remains: had Saul completely obeyed the Lord and destroyed the Amalekites when he was given the opportunity, he would not have been in this battle or in this sad position.

While whether the Amalekite actually killed Saul as he claimed may be debatable, a few facts about this situation are not up for debate. This Amalekite offered up Saul's crown and bracelet as proof of his story; Saul spared what he considered best in he Amalekites, and now his best was taken from his by an Amalekite. The Lord meant for all tension between the Israelites and Amalekites to cease; now Saul's sons are killed in a battle between these nations. Whether this Amalekite did kill Saul or simply took credit for Saul's death, Saul did die as a result of events during this battle. An Amalekite was able to triumph over Saul's death. Had Saul obeyed, none of these events could have taken place.

The lesson for us to take from this: obedience is KEY. If the Lord tells you to destroy something in your life, failure to destroy it could mean your own destruction. Do you understand the Lord's direction at all times? No, but you can always understand that the Lord has your best in His heart.

Let's get back to Persia before we close for the day. Haman has just been promoted and exalted, and Mordecai is seemingly forgotten.

Considering the already anti-Semite climate of Persia (remember that the Jews were originally brought here as captives, not welcomed as equals into the community), having an Amalekite in a high office is not a help to the Jews still in this country. If you can, step into Haman's shoes for a moment in order to understand (but certainly not excuse) his actions. He must know the history between his people and the God of Israel. He may even know that the God of the Jews ordered the attack that almost destroyed his own people so many years ago. Haman's attitude is probably hatred toward a God Whom he thinks is "out to get him". However, since he cannot see God, those feelings are translated to the people that he can see: God's people in Persia.

We'll get to that tomorrow!

Truly, Lord, obedience is better than sacrifice... help me to obey Your word regardless of whether I can see Your hand. I trust that Your heart is to protect and bless me.

᪥

DAY TWO: ESTHER 3:2-5

We have seen several situations in which the person at the center is being driven by emotions... Haman is no different. Do not allow your emotions to rule you: ask the Lord to give you peace in all situations, and then accept that peace!

FRIEND TO FRIEND...

I had been running and not paying attention to the oversized hammock strung between the two trees in front of me. How could I miss that? Six years old, I had been more concerned with what was behind me than what was in front of me: it was tag, and my little brother was gaining on me! I ran straight into the hammock, and was flipped over onto my back. When I hit the ground, the wind had been knocked out of me. Little and scared, I looked frantically for my dad. I didn't have to wait long. From my vantage point on the ground, I saw it happen: my dad jumped off the back porch — *jumped off the back porch!* — landed on his feet and ran to my rescue without hesitation. You should have seen our back porch. It was high, I'm telling you. Scary high. Daddy lifted me up, reassured me, and stayed with me until I felt safe again. Already convinced that my dad was Superman, I now had proof: I had seen him fly.

This would not be the only time that my dad came to my rescue. Over and over again in my life, he made it clear through his words and actions that nothing was more important to him than the success and safety of our family. I believe that, in a perfect world, our relationships with our earthly fathers would prepare us for and be a type of the relationship that we would develop with our Heavenly Father. In this way, as in every other possible way, my dad did his job well. He spent time with us, provided for us, protected us, loved us. It was so obvious that the main goal in my dad's life was to care for us and strengthen us. This knowledge made it relatively easy to submit to him. If you were convinced that your authority was dedicated to your success and happiness it would be infinitely easier to obey, wouldn't it? Sure! That was the way it was with my dad.

Of course, I went through my difficult years like most people did. I made my own mistakes and learned my own lessons. Though he always put in his "two cents worth", Dad let me struggle at times. In his wisdom, he knew I would learn even in the struggle. Certainly, there was always a reminder that the situation would have been much easier had I listened, but even when I fell, he was always there to help me up.

Looking back, I honestly cannot remember a time when my dad turned out to be wrong. I didn't always do what he told me, but things always worked to my benefit when I did. From my childhood forward, there were times when I understood his directions, and there were times when I did not understand. In either case, there was one aspect of his instructions that I always understood completely: my dad loved me, and his motive was to see me successful and happy. As I grew, I was able to apply my experience with my earthly father to what would become my experience with my Heavenly Father. Because it had been my experience that fathers were loving and caring and protective, I was able to accept that love more easily from my Father God.

Sadly, everyone does not have the relationship with their fathers as I have had. If your experience was different, you must exchange whatever feelings you have for your earthly father for what you know to be the truth about your Heavenly Father: God loves you! To be successful in obedience, we must become convinced that God loves us and means for us to be fulfilled. As His motives toward us are pure, our motives in obedience must be pure as well. Sometimes it is important for us to know why we do the things we do. When we were children, we did things because we were told. Sometimes we understood why, and sometimes we did not. However, as it is acceptable to use wisdom in helping us to make decisions, it is not acceptable to trust our own wisdom over the wisdom of the Lord. When in doubt of your situation, you must never doubt His heart toward you. Practice being obedient. Make it your aim to please God, whether or not you completely understand His ways.

As we mature and make decisions for ourselves, the reason behind our obedience can help in the process. God searches out our motives as well as our obedience. In Jeremiah 17:10, God speaks to us and tells us, "I, the Lord, search the heart, I test the mind, even to give to every man according to his ways, according to the fruit of his doings." The motives behind your obedience (or disobedience) will produce fruit, and it is according to that fruit that you will be judged. Strive to keep your heart open and pure before Him.

The Word communicates to us over and over again that God is love. Through every act of His providence, we can easily recognize His heart and His intentions toward us: He loves us and He means for us to be fulfilled. As we come to rest in His love, we will be able to minister His love to others. We are taken care of in order that we may pass on the fullness of God's care and comfort to others who need to experience His comfort. In understanding our role in the providential plan of God, we must be aware that all He does for us is not only for us. As we are His agents here on earth, it is up to us to do His work and see His kingdom increased.

Paul communicates this idea perfectly in 2 Corinthians 1:3-4 when he writes, "our Lord Jesus Christ... comforts us in all our tribulation, that we may be able

to comfort those who are in any trouble, with the comfort with which we ourselves are comforted by God." As we understand His motives toward us, and as
we find ourselves cared for and comforted by the Lord, we are to pass that care
and comfort along to the people whom He places in our path. To do less would
be disobedient to His divine plan. As you become more and more accustomed to
obedience and closely following Christ, you will find it easier and easier to serve
others. When your obedience comes full circle in that way, you will be simultaneously fulfilling God's plan for your life and for the furtherance of His kingdom.
In this way, our motives become just as important as our obedience. Many times,
your motives will determine your course: to obey or to disobey.

From my six year old perspective, that porch was high. Scary high. Years later,
after I had left home and married and had children of my own, I stood out in that
same backyard with my dad, my hero. Looking over my shoulder and remembering that day and so many other days when he put me first, I saw that porch from
an adult perspective. Funny: it was only about four feet off the ground. I looked
at my dad again and realized that it didn't change my opinion a bit.

Already convinced that my father was Superman, I had proof: I had seen him fly.

Haman has his motives for rebellion against the God of the Jews, as Mordecai
has his motives to obey that same God. Their motives are the fuel stirring each on
their chosen paths. Let's see where they are led today.

> *And all the king's servants who were within the king's gate bowed*
> *and paid homage to Haman, for so the king had commanded con-*
> *cerning him.* Esther 3:2

According to King Ahasuerus' command, Haman made the people of the kingdom bow and pay homage to him. Surely this served a dual purpose. The first
purpose was to stroke Haman's ego. The second, and not any less important, was
certainly to humiliate the Jews. They were already living in a hostile atmosphere,
and it may have been difficult at times to stay true to their own belief system.
When Haman required them to bow to him, he was requiring them to break one
of the ten commandments. The ten commandments were not just rules, but a
series of commands that were core to their beliefs. The third commandment (Exodus 20:4-5) instructed God's people not to bow before other gods or idols. This
must have included not bowing before a man, for fear of giving man the place of
God in their lives.

> *But Mordecai would not bow or pay homage.* Esther 3:2b

"Mordecai would not bow down or pay homage." It does not get any more
clear than that, does it? Mordecai refuses to give this respect to Haman. There
could be several reasons for Mordecai's refusal. Perhaps Mordecai is simply obey-

ing the commandment of God rather than obeying the commandment of man, and he is refusing to bow as a religious objection to a law that compromises his set of beliefs. On the other hand, Mordecai might have been persuaded to bow to Haman as a matter of respect to the governing authorities. As Mordecai is possibly the only Jew refusing to bow, this act may have been acceptable to the rest of the Jews with whom Haman comes into contact. However, as Mordecai is aware of Haman's background, it is entirely possible that refusing to bow is Mordecai's way of showing Haman where he stands in the old rivalry between the Jews and the Amalekites.

In any case, Mordecai will not bow down. While we cannot understand all of Mordecai's thought processes, we can be certain that he knows where he stands. He means to show his allegiance to God, and only to God.

> Then the king's servants who were within the king's gate said to Mordecai, 'Why do you transgress the king's command?' Now it happened, when they spoke to him daily and he would not listen to them, that they told it to Haman, to see whether Mordecai's words would stand; for Mordecai had told them that he was a Jew."
> Esther 3:3-4

Though the king's servants speak to Mordecai daily for several days, Mordecai cannot be dissuaded from his decision not to bow to Haman. In fact, the Bible does not say that Mordecai participated in a debate with these men. We read simply that Mordecai told them that he was a Jew, and that he would not listen to their arguments. Finally, they decide to talk to Haman about the matter personally.

The king's servants go to Haman "to see whether Mordecai's words would stand" (v.4). Mordecai had already told them that he was a Jew, by way of explaining his refusal to bow to Haman. After speaking to him for several days, they must have understood how passionately he objected to this law. Though they most likely knew that his mind would not be changed, they decide to go straight to Haman anyway.

Does that cause you to wonder about their motives? People sometimes enjoy seeing conflict. Sometimes they even enjoy being right in "the middle of it". Perhaps the king's servants were trying to promote themselves by drawing negative attention to someone else. Take an opportunity now to determine to be better than that. Do not be like these king's servants. Your promotion and your self worth, as we have mentioned before, MUST come from the Lord. You do not need to make yourself feel better by making someone else feel worse. Be who you are, and be true to yourself without unnecessarily causing difficulty to anyone else.

> When Haman saw that Mordecai did not bow or pay him homage, Haman was filled with wrath. Esther 3:5

Mordecai's words did stand! Haman is "filled with wrath" at his refusal, but Mordecai cannot be swayed. Mordecai is a man who is not only obedient to the call of God on his life, but he knows WHY he does what he does. Blind obedience is one thing — and if blind obedience is all you have, then by all means obey. However, when you are able to understand the cause, it makes your obedience that much more effective. At times, understanding will make it much easier to stand. How long would Mordecai have continued in his refusal if he did not truly know why he was refusing? Possibly not too long! It is this strength of character that will serve him well throughout the story, and this strength of character that will inspire Esther later on.

Remember, Haman is a little man trying to fill a big office. He wants to feel important, but he tries to accomplish this by making other people feel less important. Haman goes about in the kingdom and everyone is required to bow down to him. In order for Haman to feel as if he is better than the other subjects of Persia, they must physically lower themselves before him as he passes by. (You know, leadership is often reflected in the people — this could explain the king's servants, couldn't it?) There is an entire kingdom of people — Persia is a big and powerful place — who are more than willing to bow down and pay homage to Haman. The chronicler only tells us about Mordecai refusing to bow, no one else. A lesser ego would have looked at this as a pretty good percentage — Mordecai probably represents less than 1 percent of the population! Not Haman — out of all the people in Persia, only one refuses to bow, and it burns Haman up.

It is important for us to consider not only what people are doing right, but also what people are doing wrong. Some people show us the path to walk on, and others show us the pitfalls to avoid.

A quick prayer before we close the word: Lord, help me be the kind of person that leads by example the right way to walk!

❧

DAY THREE: ESTHER 3:6-9

As women of God, in addition to our obedience, we need to keep our hearts (our motives) pure.... the most important thing to remember is to daily try to please God. Please Him with your actions that are easily seen, and also please Him with the inward things that are not so easily seen!

FRIEND TO FRIEND...

Like free association, words or incomplete phrases seemed to come to my mind when I thought of her. Center of attention, always seems eager to help, confident in her opinions, strong personality, sense of humor... These phrases, when left incomplete, sounded pretty good. However, the closer I became to her, the more I had to fight to keep from completing those phrases.

Center of attention... perhaps it was because she demanded the spotlight in every situation. If it seemed as if the focus might be on someone else, expect that she'll stay home. Always seems eager to help... *seems* is where we lose her, though. Now that I thought about it, I could not come up with a single instance in which what she *said* matched what she *did*. I had been "left in the lurch" on more than one occasion, waiting for her to come through on her eager promises to help. She was confident in her opinions... was it because she refused to listen to any opinion but her own? Strong personality... it always seemed she was in competition with everyone around her, even her own children and husband. Sense of humor... well, she could be funny, but it always seemed to come at the expense of someone else.... Not really funny at all, now that I consider it fully.

Whenever I talked to her, there always seemed to be a "but". After a while, I stopped asking for help. I didn't discourage her help when it was offered, but I always had a back-up plan just in case the inevitable "emergency" arose and prevented her from following through. It became apparent to me that I had grown weary from trying so hard to make excuses for her. I wondered why I had been so intent on forming a friendship with her in the first place. Still, the realization represented a loss, and the loss was a source of sadness to me. She might have been a friend, and I would have liked to have had a friend. She might have been a good friend, but...

Sometimes "but" can be a dangerous word in our vocabularies. Think about it for a moment:

"I would love to help, BUT"....

"We are such good friends, BUT".....

"I should not be doing this, BUT"...

"I wasn't going to say this, BUT"....

Usually, there is a good beginning before the "but". If you truly would love to help, then don't allow the "but" to stand in your way. If you truly are a good friend, then let the thought of friendship be perpetuated before the "but" brings your friendship to an end. If you feel as if you should not do or say something, then stop yourself before the "but" gives you an excuse to continue in that wrong course.

Sometimes the "but" gets in the way of our best intentions, and sometimes the "but" is the beginning of the worst. For Haman, this word opens the door to a much darker plan, and motives are going to be revealed in Persia today. "Haman was filled with wrath. But"..... Esther 3:5b

When we left Haman yesterday, he was filled with wrath over Mordecai's refusal to bow. Today, he is going to take that anger to a much lower level.

> *"But he disdained to lay hands on Mordecai alone, for they had told him of the people of Mordecai. Instead, Haman sought to destroy all the Jews who were throughout the whole kingdom of Ahasuerus — the people of Mordecai."* Esther 3:6

He is angry at Mordecai, but the more he allows his anger to "fill" him, the more that revenge against Mordecai alone seems inadequate. (It's a very simple lesson, but very true: have you ever considered that in order for something to become full, you must continue to pour into it?)

Haman's anger is probably aroused all the more once the king's servants tell him "of the people of Mordecai". He already knows his own history, and now he has been acquainted with Mordecai's history as well. Now his eyes have been opened to the fact that it was Mordecai's God Who ordered the destruction of his ancestors years ago. Haman sees this as an opportunity not only to punish Mordecai, but to take action on the anger he feels against Mordecai's God. His revenge against Mordecai will go far beyond just one refusal to bow.

Haman could have stopped at punishing Mordecai alone, BUT... Haman could have been sufficiently happy that everyone else in the whole kingdom was bowing to him, BUT.... Haman could have directed his anger only at Mordecai, BUT.... (Do you see how that little word is getting us into big trouble here?) Haman decides to devise a plan by which all the Jews living in King Ahasuerus' kingdom will be put to death. Haman "sought to destroy all the Jews..... the people of Mordecai" (Esther 3:6).

A little more research and a little less emotion would have been of benefit to Haman before he went to see King Ahasuerus. Haman did seek advice, but he did not seek it from the right source. We have seen this happen before. Haman made another mistake; he did not ask the right question.

> *In the first month, which is the month of Nisan, in the twelfth year of King Ahasuerus, they cast Pur (that is, the lot), before Haman to determine the day and the month, until it fell on the twelfth month, which is the month of Adar."* Esther 3:7

Casting lots was an ancient practice in the East, and Haman employed it to determine a "lucky day" to attack the Jews. He wanted this information before he went to present his plan to Ahasuerus. While Haman was right to seek advice, seeking that advice from mystics was wrong. While he was right to ask questions, to ask what day to attack the Jews was the wrong question. Perhaps a different source and a different series of questions would have produced different results, (here's that word again) but...

Unfortunately for Haman, after all his seeking and asking he still does not know who "all" the people of Mordecai are. Now he knows when the "lucky day" should be, and he goes to see the king with his plan.

> *Then Haman said to King Ahasuerus,*
> *'There is a certain people scattered and dispersed among the people*
> *in all the provinces of your kingdom;*
> *their laws are different from all other people's,*
> *and they do not keep the king's laws.*
> *Therefore it is not fitting for the king to let them remain.'*
> Esther 3:8

Haman suggests to the king that there is a faction of people in the kingdom who are not abiding by his laws, and therefore should not be allowed to stay. Notice how he phrases the request; he chooses his words carefully and speaks nothing of his own hurt ego and anger. Haman seems to be concerned only for Ahasuerus and his throne. Haman tells Ahasuerus that there are people in the kingdom who are not obeying the king's laws. Not surprisingly, he conveniently leaves out which law the Jews are disobeying.

Notice that Haman calls the Jews "a certain people", as if no one had any idea of who they were or where they came from. He tells Ahasuerus that the laws of these "certain people" are different than the laws obeyed by the rest of the Persians. Haman is trying to convince Ahasuerus that the Jews are a dangerous people, and therefore it is dangerous to allow them to continue to live in Persia.

It is difficult to believe that Ahasuerus would fall into Haman's trap. How could it be dangerous for the Jews to continue living in Persia? The captivity began some 170 years ago. Jews have continued to live and work in Persia since the captivity ended around 150 years ago. The Jews and Persians have been living together for a very long time. Though there may be some degree of tension, Ahasuerus knows that they are not just some strange people as Haman would have him believe. The "different laws" to which Haman is referring (and I doubt that Haman would have been prepared to be more specific about these "different laws") have never before caused a problem. Haman is exaggerating the situation for his own purposes. This "certain people" are not disobeying the "laws" of the king! The truth is Mordecai (one man) is refusing to bow down to Haman (only one law is being broken).

Haman uses a tactic similar to Memucan's in chapter one: to play on Ahasuerus's own self-importance to achieve selfish purposes. Haman tells Ahasuerus it is for the sake of Ahasuerus' own kingdom and greatness that the Jews must be put out of the kingdom entirely. Haman also lies to the king, and tells him that if the Jews are not dealt with swiftly, they could become dangerous to the safety of the kingdom. Haman has grossly exaggerated the fact that one man has broken one law. In response to one man's refusal to bow, he tries to get the king to agree to getting rid of all of the Jewish people. (This sounds like an emotional decision!)

Is that enough for Haman? Apparently not. As he speaks to King Ahasuerus, he continues to pour into his own anger.

> *If it pleases the king, let a decree be written that they be destroyed,*
> *and I will pay ten thousand talents of silver into the hands of those*
> *who do the work, to bring it into the king's treasuries.* Esther 3:9

Haman tells Ahasuerus that he wants the Jews destroyed completely, and he wants the king to order the destruction himself by a royal decree. Now he does not simply want the Jewish people out of Persia; he wants them destroyed completely. An extreme response to such a minor offense, but remember that Haman has kept the offense hidden from Ahasuerus. Furthermore, Haman is so convinced that this should be carried out as quickly as possible that he makes the king's decision easier: Haman offers to pay for the destruction of the Jews from his own pocket. To destroy the Jews will require no effort from the king, and it will require no money from the king. Actually, Haman will pay into the king's treasuries if the plan is carried out.

For Ahasuerus, there may not have been any reason to think twice about Haman's plan. Considering his motives, perhaps Ahasuerus is being driven by a desire to feel important. At this point, we are more than ten years into his reign, and he has not yet done anything truly noteworthy. Perhaps he is also being driven by money — ten thousand talents of silver is a great sum. With no effort whatsoever from him, Haman will put it into his treasuries.

Ahasuerus does not ask many questions. He does not know why Haman desires to punish the Jews; all he knows is that a law (not even which law) is being broken. Because Ahasuerus does not understand the offense, he does not know that destroying them for simply not bowing to one person is a most disproportionate response. In any event, Ahasuerus is not truly considering the consequences of this decision. Remember: just as Haman is ignorant of who "all" Mordecai's people are, Ahasuerus is also ignorant of who is included in this group.

Ahasuerus could have thought this decision through more carefully, but... Without realizing it, Ahasuerus is about to agree to destroy his queen. Let the Lord search your heart before you make any decision this week, and make your decisions out of a pure desire to do what would be pleasing to Him!

DAY FOUR: ESTHER 3:10 - 11

Without truly considering the consequences, Ahasuerus makes a decision. Because we have been focusing on providence, we are beginning to understand that our decisions sometimes reach far beyond us. Ahasuerus does not see beyond himself. Live your life carefully, deliberately serving the Lord!

FRIEND TO FRIEND...

Have you heard the saying, "The only thing needed for evil to triumph is for good men to do nothing"? If that is true, we have a great example of it here in Ahasuerus and in Haman. Haman is angry, but it is not anger that causes one to sin.

In Psalm 4:4, and again in Ephesians 4:26, we are instructed to "be angry" and yet "not sin". God is just. As you can be confident that He would never require something of you which would be impossible to achieve, you can be confident that you can find this balance between feeling anger and having that anger drive you to wrong action.

Proverbs 19:11 offers this wisdom on anger, "The discretion of a man makes him slow to anger, and his glory is to overlook a transgression." To me, this verse goes along with another favorite verse of mine which tells us, "great peace have they who love Your law, and nothing shall offend them" (Psalm 119:165, KJV). Great peace comes from loving the law of the Lord. One tremendous benefit to loving the law of the Lord is that *nothing* will offend you! Another translation says that "nothing will cause them to stumble". This kind of peace is powerful and sustaining. This kind of peace can weather any storm, anger or frustration. This kind of peace can only be achieved through knowing God's love for you and resting in that love. It does not follow that being stirred to a righteous anger has to mean losing your peace.

Jesus Himself experienced anger, and He was stirred to action. In one such instance, He was faced with men who were more concerned with the letter of the law than the spirit of the law, the Pharisees. To the Pharisees, following the law was more important than even seeing people restored and healed by the very God Whom they claim to serve. They did not understand that the Law was meant to point them to the Lord, not keep them in condemnation and bondage. When they confronted Jesus about healing on the Sabbath, Jesus knew what was in their hearts. "He said to them, "Is it lawful on the Sabbath to do good or to do evil, to save life or to kill?' But they kept silent. And when He had looked around at them with anger, being grieved by the hardness of their hearts, He said to the man, 'Stretch out your hand.' And he stretched it out, and his hand was restored as whole as the other" (Mark 3:4-5).

Jesus was angry, but that righteous anger stirred Him to action on behalf of the man who needed healing. Balancing your anger with God's righteousness will bring great and powerful results.

Anger in Persia will not be balanced with righteousness.

> *If it pleases the king, let a decree be written that they [the Jews] be destroyed...* Esther 3:9

Haman presents his plan to Ahasuerus, and makes the terms very easy for him to accept. Ahasuerus does not have to think for long. Without truly considering the consequences of such an evil scheme, Ahasuerus agrees to Haman's plan to destroy the Jews.

> *So the king took his signet ring from his hand and gave it to Haman, the son of Hammedatha the Agagite, the enemy of the Jews.*
> Esther 3:10

Now, in addition to his heritage, our chronicler gives us one more title for Haman, son of Hammedatha the Agagite: "the enemy of the Jews". Most likely not even realizing what he is truly agreeing to, Ahasuerus gives his signet ring to Haman. This was a sign of the king delegating his full royal authority to Haman. Now Haman has the weapon he needs to exact his revenge on Mordecai and all of Mordecai's people.

> *And the king said to Haman,*
> *'The money and the people are given to you,*
> *to do with them as seems good to you.'* Esther 3:11

Ahasuerus decides to give his permission to Haman, but notice that he does not say, "Haman, I give you full authority to utterly destroy all the Jews." Ahasuerus says to "do with them [the Jews] as seems good to you." I wonder if the king was, inside himself, thinking that Haman would "cool off" as the season went on, and that the end of this angry tirade of Haman's would certainly not be killing the Jews. Another possibility is that Ahasuerus wishes to be separated from this decision. In his own mind, Ahasuerus was seemingly able to separate himself from what had happened to Queen Vashti. Remember in chapter two? Ahasuerus remembered what "Vashti had done and what had been decreed against her" (Esther 2:1), as if he shared no responsibility in the situation. This could be considered a sign of his weakness.

Consider Ahasuerus' situation at this moment. If this remnant of Jews stayed in Persia for this many years after the captivity ended without incident, certainly they could not have been the danger that Haman presents them to be. Ahasuerus knew the Jews were not dangerous people, but we have seen this king easily swayed by the opinions of the people closest to him. This circumstance may be different only in the king's attitude. Ahasuerus is swayed by Haman's argument, but he has no personal interest in this matter as he did in the situation with Vashti. Of course, like Haman, Ahasuerus still is ignorant of who is included in "all the Jews".

Haman is acting out of anger, and Ahasuerus is acting out of complacency. We mentioned it earlier, but it seems worth repeating: "the only thing needed for evil to triumph is for good men to do nothing". If that is true, we have a great example in Ahasuerus.

Pray today that God will show you if there is an area in your life where you have a tendency to let your emotions take control — possibly even get OUT of control. Ask Him to help you recognize these tendencies, and lean heavily on His spirit to keep you in check. Praise God for placing in you all the wonderful emotions and passions that make you who you are, and praise Him for giving you balance in the roller coaster that your emotions can cause!

☙

DAY FIVE: ESTHER 3:12-15

A terrifying development in Persia today... but a great opportunity for us to see God at work! As we see God working behind the scenes in Persia, try to see Him working behind the scenes in your own life today. If you seek Him, He will reveal Himself to you!

FRIEND TO FRIEND...

We discussed how the little conjunction "but' can get us into big trouble sometimes. However, everything has two sides, and "but" is no different. As easily as it gets us into trouble, "but" can help us do and receive good.

Genesis chapter 30 records the birth of an important man named Joseph. The extraordinary events of his life are recorded in the following chapters. God saw Joseph faithfully through many twists and turns. Separation from his family, unjust accusation and wrongful incarceration were just a few of his trials. However, as he was steadfast in his devotion to the Lord, the Lord saw him through it all. As his life was completely in God's hands, Joseph began to experience restoration, promotion, favor, and reunion.

When his brothers, who had originally betrayed Joseph at the deepest and lowest level, were ultimately brought full circle to Joseph's door, we see the flip side of this powerful little conjunction "but". Joseph forgives his brothers their horrible trespasses against him. With kindness that could only come from a heart dedicated to the Lord, he tells his brothers, "you meant evil against me; but God meant it for good" (Genesis 50:20).

But God meant it for good. Where this little conjunction has caused trouble before, it brings joy now. God is the same today, and has the same desire and ability to turn your difficult situations into triumphs, just like He did for Joseph. Place your trust in Him, place your life in Him, and you will find there is no safer situation. Storms may come, *but God* will save. Hearts may break, *but God* will heal. Lack may threaten, *but God* will provide.

Let's return to Persia. If Ahasuerus had actually thought that Haman might reconsider his anger against the Jews over a period of time, he was horribly mistaken. Haman is still "filled with wrath", and he is continuing to pour into that anger.

But God...

> *...they cast Pur (that is, the lot), before Haman to determine the day and the month...* Esther 3:7

Earlier in the week, we read that Haman casts lots to determine when to attack the Jews. He consults with what he considers a "higher power", certainly not the God of the Jews. Haman does not realize that the God of the Jews is actually using Haman's own superstitions to continue His providential work on behalf of the Jews.

Matthew Henry writes,

> He [Haman] then consults with his soothsayers to find out a lucky day for the designed massacre, v. 7. The resolve was taken up in the first month, in the twelfth year of the king, when Esther had been his wife about five years. Some day or other in that year must be pitched upon; and, as if he doubted not but that Heaven would favour his design and further it, he refers it to the lot, that is, to the divine Providence, to choose the day for him; but that, in the decision, proved a better friend to the Jews than to him, for the lot fell upon the twelfth month, so that Mordecai and Esther had eleven months to turn themselves in for the defeating of the design, or, if they could not defeat it, space would be left for the Jews to make their escape and shift for their safety. Haman, though eager to have the Jews cut off, yet will submit to the laws of his superstition, and not anticipate the supposed fortunate day, no, not to gratify his impatient revenge.[1]

It bears repeating here: **providence** is *"that continuous agency of God by which He makes all the events of the physical and moral universe fulfill the original design with which they were created"*.[2]

Haman is consulting his own gods and soothsayers to determine the best course of action, but God is using Haman's tactics against him..... God is making all the events fulfill the original design! We were meant to search out a higher power, and we were meant to desire confirmation and approval from our God. Haman desires approval and confirmation, but he does not know where to look. Haman does not know that he is under the providential power of God!

> *Then the king's scribes were called on the thirteenth day of the first month, and a decree was written according to all that Haman commanded — to the king's satraps, to the governors who were over each province, to the officials of all people, to every province according to its script, and to every people in their language. In the name of King Ahasuerus it was written, and sealed with the king's signet ring.* Esther 3:12

The letter from Ahasuerus went out on the thirteenth day of the *first* month. The command was to be carried out on the thirteenth day of the *twelfth* month. This must have taken a tremendous amount of patience on Haman's part. Considering his anger, it had to have been difficult to wait eleven months. In addition to this patience, Haman must also have a tremendous amount of faith in his soothsayers and lot casting. He must have been determined that this was the proper way to carry out his plan against the Jews. Though it must have been difficult for him to wait, Haman decides to plan according to the lots he cast. Haman determines to wait eleven months to carry out his evil plot against the Jews.

> *And the letters were sent by couriers into all the king's provinces, to destroy, to kill, and to annihilate all the Jews, both young and old, little children and women, in one day, on the thirteenth day of the twelfth month, which is the month of Adar, and to plunder their possessions.* Esther 3:13

The command was "to destroy, to kill, to annihilate all the Jews, both young and old, little children and women, in one day". This must have been much more severe than Ahasuerus had expected. Even if the severity was a surprise to him, Ahasuerus most likely would not have changed his mind about allowing Haman to continue with the plan.

> *A copy of the document was to be issued as law in every province, being published for all people, that they should be ready for that day. The couriers went out, hastened by the king's command; and the decree was proclaimed in Shushan the citadel. So the king and Haman sat down to drink, but the city of Shushan was perplexed.* Esther 3:14-15

As a command is being decreed throughout the kingdom that will cause the destruction of an innocent people, King Ahasuerus and Haman sit down to a drink. What a time to celebrate or even relax! The blood of these people — the children and women, the young and the old — will be on their hands. At this point, Ahasuerus and Haman have no reason to believe that the command would not be followed in every aspect. Apparently Ahasuerus was not disappointed in Haman's decision. Besides, he has no connection to the Jews, right? How could this decree affect his life?

It won't be long before Ahasuerus' blissful ignorance will come to an abrupt end. Before long, he will find out exactly how this decree affects him.

As Ahasuerus and Haman join each other in the palace for a drink, the king's couriers go out to proclaim the decree in the city of Shushan. The people of Shushan get the word first, and they are perplexed. They are confused, they are upset…. Considering the reaction of the people of Shushan, the Jews could not have been the dangerous people that Haman was trying to have Ahasuerus believe that they were.

One more thing to notice here: Mordecai had been able to keep his Jewish heritage a secret until the issue of bowing to Haman arose. Esther has been living in the palace with Ahasuerus for five years now, and she is still successfully keeping her heritage a secret also. It is a great possibility that other Jews in Persia have been living there not only quietly, but anonymously. If the people in Shushan (the non-Jews) were perplexed and confused by the order to kill the Jews, imagine how the Jews must have felt. For generations, the Jews have been living quiet and productive lives in Persia, and now comes this decree.

Imagine the confusion: the decree is to "annihilate all the Jews", but the Jews do not know the cause. Since Haman did not even tell Ahasuerus the reason behind his anger against the Jews (Mordecai's refusal to bow to him), it is entirely possible that no one else knows either. They only know that a terrible day is coming. They are to be killed, and they have no idea why.

Satan is busy, *but God* is real, and He is faithful. Even in the midst of this traumatic time, the Jews will find peace in their faith and in the confidence that God's love provides for them.

The Jews may be in danger now, *but God* has a great plan!

As we close out week three, pray that God would open your eyes to His power. Trials may come "out of the blue", but in every situation, make an honest effort to see God's hand. Even if you are not able to see his hand, trust His faithfulness to you. God is good!

❧

the peace of God, which surpasses all understanding, will guard your hearts and minds through Christ Jesus. Philippians 4:7

Father, Your love gives me peace.
If I allow it to, Your love will free me.
Your love will free me from being driven by emotions —
emotions that threaten to take away
my peace, my quiet, my rest, my oneness with You.
I thank You that Your peace will
guard my heart (my feelings)
and I thank You that Your peace will
guard my mind (my perceptions).
I know that if I can get these two areas of my life
in balance with You,
I will be able to fully experience Your peace.
I love You, Father,
and I desire to operate daily in the quiet of Your peace!

❧

---

1.   Dr. Augustus Hopkins Strong, Systematic Theology, p. 420.

2.   Matthew Henry, Matthew Henry's Commentary on the Whole Bible, (USA: Hendrickson Publishers, 1996), p.873

ESTHER: CHAPTER 4
Esther Agrees to Help the Jews

At the end of last week, we left Haman "filled with wrath" as Mordecai refused to bow to him. Haman's anger leads him to plot revenge against not only Mordecai, but against all of the Jews. He presents his plan to Ahasuerus. The king, as seems to be his pattern, is easily swayed to Haman's plan to destroy the Jews. In eleven months from the time of the decree, all the Jews are to be annihilated in one horrible day. Upon hearing this terrible news, all the people in the city of Shushan (all the people — Jewish or not) are blindsided by the king's sudden and devastating decree. In Esther 3:15, our historian records that Ahasuerus and Haman sat down for a drink, but that the "city of Shushan was perplexed."

An important member of the Shushan community is experiencing these feelings of confusion and fear over this situation as well: Queen Esther.

Confusion and fear. You have most likely had those feelings and experienced those moments as well; the ones that require so much more than you thought that you had inside you. Were you prepared? Whether or not you were, the possibility to be prepared was always in you! Like an acorn has all the potential of a great oak tree inside it, like Esther was born with all the potential to become queen and eventually rescuer of an entire race, you have inside you all the potential to become what God intends for you to become. Placed in a specific location, surrounded by specific people, your heart inclined toward specific passions, a providential God has placed everything that you need to be successful within you.

As you follow the Lord, you will find within yourself the ability to fulfill His plan for you. In each day, you will find that God provides you with opportunities to grow in grace and demonstrate His love. In practicing faithfulness to the Lord, you will find that He is always faithful to you. As a result of this faithfulness, you will become confident in His love. You will become full of praise in the good days and full of faith in the not so good days. Tests will come, trials will come, storms will come, but as you are true to the Lord, He will show Himself strong on your behalf. This week, begin to exercise your faith to that end.

Esther comes to a defining moment in her life this week. She had prepared to be queen for a full year before ascending to the throne, and this is the moment that will require all of her preparation, all of her wisdom, all of her strength... However, the preparation required for this situation is more than Hegai, Ahasuerus' custodian of the women, ever had to offer.

Actually, this test will require more than just the preparations of the past year. To consider the situation rightly, we must see that Esther has been preparing her entire life for this time. Though she herself could never have predicted this situation, she has been serving the God who knows the beginning from the end, and He knew what was coming for Esther. God Himself had been preparing her from birth. From her home and family to her faith, God had considered every detail and provided opportunities that would challenge and grow Esther as she submitted herself to Him. Esther had submitted herself fully to the preparations. Confident in her call and in God's love for her, Esther is well able to extend herself further than she might have thought she could for the sake of her people.

Esther's trial has come. How will she respond? How will the Lord meet her faith? Let's find out together as we begin Esther chapter 4.

🙚

DAY ONE: ESTHER 4:1-3

We have talked often over the past few weeks about being prepared for what the Lord is calling us to, and obedient to that call at any price... even through tragedy, our faith must remain steadfast.

FRIEND TO FRIEND...

Some days it seems that the sun shines brighter than others. Some days, we seem to be in the shadows. We already know and understand that God is good in both days, however, the challenge is in letting our actions reflect our knowledge of the Lord... to make it plain: act like the children of God that we are — *even when it's tough!*

Some days, my children are happy and my house is clean. Some days, I have cookies in the oven for an after school snack and chicken marinating in the refrigerator for dinner. Some days, my husband's work brings him joy, and the sanctuary of our home brings him peace and comfort. Some days, all the bills are paid and all the worries of life seem far away from us. Some days our church is exciting and our congregation is blessed. Of course, in every day there is reason to be thankful. On any given day, any number of these happy situations occur one at a time or all at once. On the rarer day, all these reasons for thanksgiving happen on the same day, and we float through the day and try to remember in our joy to "praise God from Whom all blessings flow."

Of course, there are days when none of these things seem to happen. To make it worse, we experience the opposite. The pantry is empty (because I didn't make time to go grocery shopping yesterday). The rain is keeping us inside and out of the pool. The children are irritable, not to mention irritating. We get a letter from the orthodontist explaining the fees for braces; expenses for all three children will be due next month. My husband had a hard day and comes home tired. Someone has left the church. On any given day, any number of these unhappy situations occur one at a time or all at once. On the rarer day, all these reasons for discouragement happen on the same day, and we struggle through the day and.... well, try to remember in our weariness to "praise God from Whom all blessings flow."

Sometimes people use times of heartache (big and small) as an excuse for behavior that is less than desirable. We are guaranteed in this life that there will be trials, but we are also guaranteed that there will be hope and help through the trials. Tragedy can make us stronger as we put ourselves completely in the hands of the Lord, or it can make us bitter and resentful. It is up to us!

Even in the best of us, there is the possibility of becoming tired through trials. Paul writes to the Hebrews, "For consider Him who endured such hostility from sinners against Himself, lest you become weary and discouraged in your souls" (Hebrews 12:3). Are you tired, friend? If you are, remember that you are in good company. Jesus had to endure suffering beyond what we can imagine, *and yet* He continued in His purpose. Jesus, "being found in appearance as a man, He humbled Himself and became obedient to the point of death, even the death of the cross" (Philippians 2:8). What a powerful picture, and what a precious Savior.

As time of joy call us to praise, times of heartache should call us to prayer. Our friend Paul encourages us in this way: "Rejoice always, pray without ceasing, in everything give thanks; for this is the will of God in Christ Jesus for you (1 Thessalonians 5:16-18). Always has to mean *always* — good and bad days alike. Without ceasing has to mean *without ceasing* — never allowing your praise to stop, never allowing your prayer to stop.

How can this be accomplished? Is it possible? It is, and you will do it! Jesus said to him, "If you can believe, all things are possible to him who believes" (Mark 9:23). All things possible to you as you believe... no need to expand on words so powerful as those! It is our response to these days, good and bad, that define us. Faithful to the Lord on the good days, we must be faithful to the Lord on the not-so-good days. In times of personal tragedy, what has been your response? Reflect for a moment within yourself. Consider a time of tragedy in your life. How was the Lord faithful to you? Better yet, how were *you* faithful to the *Lord*?

How will Esther and Mordecai respond to hard times?

> *When Mordecai learned all that had happened,*
> *he tore his clothes and put on sackcloth and ashes, and went out*
> *into the midst of the city. He cried out with a loud and bitter cry.*
> Esther 4:1

In Persia, "wrongfulness of character" is behind the tragedy about to befall the Jews. In the face of this crisis, Mordecai has important decisions to make. His response to Ahasuerus' decree is more important than even he may realize himself. When the news of Haman's plan reaches him, Mordecai goes into mourning. Tearing his clothes and putting on sackcloth and ashes, Mordecai is in utter despair over the decree that has gone out from King Ahasuerus. Mordecai is not only mourning for the seemingly inescapable death that Ahasuerus has just ordered, but he is also mourning for the king. Mordecai knows it is dangerous to come against God's people.

Even though Mordecai has refused to bow to Haman, he still is loyal to the king and to the government. Remember — just a few verses ago, this very same man had rescued the king from an assassination attempt. This is not a man who is dangerous or rebellious to authority as Haman had described to Ahasuerus in chapter 3. Mordecai, within the parameters of his faith, is not only dedicated to his people. He is dedicated to his country as well. In a situation where Mordecai felt pressed to be of service to the king, he did not hesitate to bring the assassination plan to Esther's attention so that the murder could be averted and the king's life saved. However, this time is different. It is not a matter of Mordecai saving the king from the evil outside of the palace; it is a matter of Mordecai saving the king from the evil in his own heart. This decree and the direct consequences of it is something from which Mordecai feels helpless to rescue his people or to rescue the king.

During chapter 3, we explored the tension between Mordecai and Haman. We read in 1 Samuel how this tension had possibly stemmed from the Lord's order to destroy the Amalekites, and how it had been going on for several generations. When the order had been given to destroy the Amalekites, Saul chose to disobey the Lord. Rather than utterly destroying the Amalekites, Saul spared the king and all that was best in his own judgement. We learned the end result of Saul's disobedience in 2 Samuel 1:6-10. Saul was killed by an Amalekite; a member of the same group of people that the Lord had commanded him to destroy.

Let's look quickly at David's response to Saul's death.

> *Therefore David took hold of his own clothes and tore them, and so did all the men who were with him. And they mourned and wept and fasted until evening for Saul and for Jonathan his son, for the people of the LORD and for the house of Israel, because they had fallen by the sword. Then David said to the young man who told him, "Where are you from?" And he answered, "I am the son of an alien, an Amalekite." So David said to him, "How was it you were*

not afraid to put forth your hand to destroy the LORD's anointed?"
2 Samuel 1:11-14

David asked the Amalekite, "How was it that you were not afraid to put forth your hand to destroy the Lord's anointed?" As Saul was his enemy, the Amalekite might have expected David to rejoice at Saul's death. David did not rejoice. He mourned, and he had his men mourn as well. To David, it did not matter that Saul was his enemy. David recognized Saul as one anointed by the Lord. Saul was in a position of authority, and that in and of itself was worthy of a degree of respect from David.

At this moment in Persia, Ahasuerus has seemingly become Mordecai's enemy, having just decreed death to all Jews.

Mordecai's response to the situation in Persia is respectful and appropriate. Haman's action has made it clear that he is an enemy of the Jews, but Mordecai is not full of hate for Haman. Ahasuerus is allowing this terrible thing to be done, but Mordecai is not filled with hate for Ahasuerus. Hatred toward these men would have blinded Mordecai and made it impossible for him to see the right course of action. Mordecai knows Ahasuerus has done a fearful thing. He mourns for the Jews who are now in grave danger, as well as for the king who was not afraid to "raise his hand" against them. What does Mordecai decide to do?

*He went as far as the front of the king's gate, for no one might enter
the king's gate clothed with sackcloth.* Esther 4:2

Even though Mordecai is in mourning, he still goes to the king's gates as he has done every day since Esther was carried away to the palace. Once again, Mordecai demonstrates his faithfulness and constancy. Mordecai is still concerned for Esther, and has maintained his commitment to her. Even through a time of personal tragedy, he does not use his pain as an excuse to shirk his responsibility. (There's a great lesson in that!) The verse also records that Mordecai stopped at the gate because no one was allowed to enter the king's gate while clothed in sackcloth. In this, Mordecai demonstrates his submission to authority. He is respectful of the law in Persia, and abides by it.

Now that the decree has gone out, Mordecai is not the only one who has a strong reaction.

*And in every province where the king's command and decree ar-
rived, there was great mourning among the Jews, with fasting, weep-
ing, and wailing; and many lay in sackcloth and ashes.* Esther 4:3

As Jews throughout the provinces hear the decree proclaimed, there is great mourning. Please keep in mind these people have been raised here in Persia, have made lives here in Persia... In spite of that, most of them have never seen the king, and he has not seen them. There is confusion as well — why does Ahasuerus want them destroyed? They do not know. They are possibly feeling helplessness. They know the law, and know that this decree, written into Persian and Median law, can never be reversed. In this situation, who is more helpless than a Jew?

As the Jews immediately experience confusion and fear in hearing this decree, they are moved toward their faith, not drawn from it. The Jews mourn *with fasting*. At this moment, they do their best to turn their eyes upward and demonstrate their faith in God. God is a refuge and strength — a very present help in time of trouble... The Jews turn first to God, and in doing so they set a great example for us.

Of course, the Jews do not know about the "secret weapon" that God has in the palace! God, in His *providence* (you knew that was coming, didn't you?) had prepared for this moment long ago!

Lord, help me to respond in a godly way to the trials that I must sometimes face on this earth. It is not Your will that I deny my emotions; however, it is not Your will that I give in completely to them. Help me to find that balance and find that my hope is always in You.

☙

DAY TWO: ESTHER 4:4-5

Though the situation may seem hopeless, with God we are never helpless. Remember to always consider God's power before you allow yourself to despair over your circumstances. In comparison with His power, your problems will surely pale!

FRIEND TO FRIEND...

When Michael and I first moved to Miami, I was beyond homesick. I cried every day for six months straight. Not just regular tears here and there, either. I'm talking about sobbing-can't talk-can't breathe-crying so hard. It wasn't the church; they were wonderful to us. I just missed being *home*, and it took a while for Miami to become home.

I remember calling my college roommate, Andrea. I tried not to sound too pathetic, but a girl can't fool her best friend, especially if that friend is a woman of prayer! After a few minutes on the phone, she said, "I'll call you back in thirty minutes, okay?" Okay, but I wondered what was going on. When Andrea called back, she asked, "Can you pick me up next Friday? I thought I'd fly in for the weekend." When I saw her at the airport the next weekend, I cried again. This time, it was tears of joy. Andrea just smiled, "Sounded like you needed your best friend!" I knew what a sacrifice that trip was for her — plane tickets are expensive, and we were young. We had a wonderful weekend, and the memory of that time would sustain me through other sad days. What I remember most, and what I remember still, is as simple as this: she recognized that I needed her; and without hesitation, she came.

John records the words of Jesus in John 15:13: "Greater love has no one than this, than to lay down one's life for his friends." Consider quietly: how much of your life do you actually have to give? The past is over, the future is not yet here. The only part of your life you have to give is this moment. If it's all you have, give it willingly! Put someone else's needs above your own — you will be surprised to find that you are the one who is blessed! I'll have to remember to ask Andrea if that weekend blessed her as much as it did me. That weekend she demonstrated the "greater love"; that sacrifice, that expense, those days. She "laid down her life" (put aside what other things she had planned for that weekend) for my benefit.

As we discussed yesterday, hard times come to us all. It is our response to difficult times that demonstrate our character. Through the hard times of the people around us, we are given opportunities to demonstrate our compassion. Paul writes in Philippians 2:3-4, "Let nothing be done through selfish ambition or conceit, but in lowliness of mind let each esteem others better than himself. Let each of you look out not only for his own interests, but also for the interests of others." Paul admonishes us to be guided not by selfish ambition, but by the needs of the people around us. In a time of need, we should be moved to prayer and action out of a desire to be a help to others. (Interesting — most scholars agree that Paul was in prison while he wrote this letter to the Philippians — at that moment, he is not only *writing* about esteeming other people, he is *doing* it! His concern was for these Christians, when he had "every right" to feel sorry for himself!) Extraordinary that at this moment, Paul is not concerned with his own comfort; he is consumed with the well-being of the church in Philippi.

I know that being homesick hardly qualifies as a great tragedy in life. I realize that it seems ridiculous to even bring it up. At the time, though, it sure seemed hard. Looking back now, it seems silly. I was so young, and so many other trials have come that make missing home seem like nothing. What I really remember is this: Andrea was not looking out for her own needs that weekend a million hours ago; she was looking out for me. It feels good to have someone like that on my side, and since then I have been inspired to be that person for others.

Something else about that weekend stands out: as we are encouraged to take the struggles of others seriously and offer help, God takes our struggles seriously. When my heart was broken miles away from my comfort zone, God did not criticize me for being young and short sighted. He sent a friend to minister His love to me and remind me that I was not alone. Andrea was not the only one who came to me that weekend: Jesus came, too, and He made all the difference.

The way we respond to our own struggles defines us. If we are faithful to the Lord during those times, those trials will strengthen us. The way we respond to the struggles of other people inspire us. If we continue walking in the love of the Lord, those trials will make us compassionate. Strength and compassion are precious qualities — gifts that must be practiced, and then continually given away.

Esther and Mordecai are going to demonstrate these two gifts, strength and compassion, in Persia.

> *And in every province where the king's command and decree arrived, there was great mourning among the Jews, with fasting, weeping, and wailing; and many lay in sackcloth and ashes.* Esther 4:3

Mordecai stops at the king's gate, and possibly realizes that he is the only Jew in Persia that may be in a position to do some good. All the Jews in Persia are mourning and fasting — feeling as if their only choice is to pray and wait for the Lord to deliver them (not a bad choice!). Even leaving Persia does not seem a likely option, since Ahasuerus rules all lands from India to Ethiopia (Esther 1:1). Where would they go?

Queen Esther is in the palace, but clearly does not know anything about what is happening in the kingdom. Esther is in her own quarters, away from the king, and does not see him unless he calls for her. Even if he requested her presence often, there was no reason for Ahasuerus to talk to Esther about political matters; he was surrounded by advisors. Why would he burden his queen with such news? Esther will not remain unaware of her husband's decision for long.

> *So Esther's maids and eunuchs came and told her, and the queen was deeply distressed. Then she sent garments to clothe Mordecai and take his sackcloth away from him, but he would not accept them.*
> Esther 4:3-4

Esther finds out that Mordecai is in mourning through her maids and eunuchs. She is "deeply distressed", the Bible tells us. Though she is in the dark as to the reason for his depression, she takes action immediately. Esther sends Mordecai some new clothes, and intends for her servants to take the sackcloth away from Mordecai. Esther is hoping to end his mourning. However, Mordecai does not accept the garments that she has sent.

Initially, Esther does not ask her servants to find out *why* Mordecai was in mourning. Esther is moved to action at the mere suggestion that Mordecai is experiencing discomfort. She does not ask "why" or "what". Details such as these were not as important as the one fact she already knew: her cousin was deeply upset. Finding out the reason why was much less important at this moment than making an attempt to comfort Mordecai, and making sure that he knew he was not alone.

Esther's example presents a great lesson for us: while there are times when it is helpful to know "the whole story", there are many times when it is completely unnecessary. Our concern for other people ought to be *honest* — not motivated by curiosity. Pray that God will help you discern these times, and pray that He will help you to be motivated by concern for others and not out of curiosity for details.

Once Esther's servants return with the news that Mordecai will not change, she sends out another servant.

> *Then Esther called Hathach, one of the king's eunuchs whom he had*
> *appointed to attend her, and she gave him a command concerning*
> *Mordecai, to learn what and why this was.* Esther 4:5

Esther commands Hathach, one of the king's eunuchs, to find out what is going on with Mordecai, and to find out for her exactly why he is in mourning. Esther was "deeply distressed" before she found out *why* Mordecai was in mourning. Imagine how she will feel once she knows the reason.

It is important to notice that Mordecai and Esther both put other people's needs before their own. Esther is deeply distressed simply at the idea of Mordecai in mourning — before she even knows what has made him so upset, she takes steps to care for him. Mordecai is mourning not for himself, but for the danger of his people. He is also mourning for the king who has sentenced them to death.

Willingness to put aside everything that is going on in his world at the moment to mourn for the Jewish people, for Persia, and for his king, Mordecai gives his full attention to the most important issue. When Esther learns of Mordecai's distress, she puts aside everything else in order to give him comfort. Just as we read earlier Paul's admonishment that everyone should "esteem others more highly than ourselves", Esther has placed Mordecai's feelings above her own. She displays this principal in a time of great turmoil beautifully.

Esther and Mordecai are about to find out exactly how much they have to give.

Father, help me to put others before myself — even in times of tragedy. Help me to remember that I don't have time for self-pity... Stir me to action in the good times and the not-so-good times! I praise You, Lord — Your providence is always at work!

DAY THREE: ESTHER 4:6-9

Your actions during a trial are important — and so is your attitude! Keep an attitude of victory — and be assured that you will be victorious, woman of God!

FRIEND TO FRIEND...

Have you ever noticed that sometimes people in trouble exaggerate the situation they are in? Sometimes for attention, sometimes for sympathy...(None of us have to admit it, but women can be especially given to exaggeration!) Whatever the motive to exaggerate is, exaggeration is really magnifying the PROBLEM rather than the SOLUTION. Even during difficult times, **praise** your way to the victory!

Paul writes of a treasure that we hold on the inside in 2 Corinthians. Through difficult times, he reminds us, "But we have this treasure in earthen vessels, that the excellence of the power may be of God and not of us. We are hard-pressed on every side, *yet not crushed*; we are perplexed, *but not in despair*; persecuted, *but not forsaken*; struck down, *but not destroyed* – always carrying about in the body the dying of the Lord Jesus, that the life of Jesus also may be manifested in our body" (2 Corinthians 4:7-10).

Paul tells the Corinthians that they have a "treasure" on the inside: that the excellence of God may be demonstrated through them. We have this same treasure inside us! When trials come, we are presented with a great opportunity to demonstrate the power of God working in our lives. We are hard-pressed, *yet not crushed*, we are perplexed *but not in despair*, persecuted *but not forsaken*, struck down *but not destroyed*.....God has a plan that is being worked out in your life through times of both triumph and tragedy. Faithfulness through both times is part of the process of growth that we discussed yesterday.

James 5:11 also holds an encouraging promise: "You have heard of the perseverance of Job and seen the end intended by the Lord --that the Lord is very compassionate and merciful". Some days, I am especially encouraged by the assurance that the Lord is "very compassionate and merciful". Other days, I am especially encouraged that there is an "end intended by the Lord". Though you may be in the middle of a trial now, you can be assured of one thing: *it will end*! The Lord has an intended end, and He is so merciful and compassionate. Trust in Him. There is no need to exaggerate your problem. The need is only to magnify your God.

When our church was young, Michael found an "opportunity to grow" in our post office box. This letter forced him to prayer, and would force him to a decision: our landlord had written to let us know that he would not be renewing the church's lease. Though the relationship had been good and the landlord had been generous, he had found a business able to pay a higher amount each month in rent. In a few months, our church would have to find a new home. I panicked a little: how would we afford something else? Where would we find available property in our rapidly growing county? Problems were magnified and exaggerated in my mind as I considered the list of "cons".

In contrast to my "half empty" attitude, and in keeping with his cheerful "half full" personality, Michael explained this new challenge to our congregation the very next Sunday morning. So relational and genuine, being transparent and sharing his heart with his flock comes naturally to Michael. Joys and concerns alike are communicated regularly from his pulpit. Michael held up the envelope and told the church, "This week the Lord presented us with a divine opportunity to grow! Of course, it came cleverly disguised as an eviction notice!" The church laughed with him, and what might have been cause for worry became the next step in the church's vision. As Michael honestly presented the next step to the church and trusted the Lord, the congregation stood with him and trusted the Lord with him. No need to panic, and no need to exaggerate: it was what it was, and the Lord would continue to be faithful.

Mordecai does not need to exaggerate the situation in Persia. It would be difficult to imagine it being any worse. Esther, determined to learn the cause of Mordecai's mourning, sends her servant Hathach out to him.

> *So Hathach went...* Esther 4:6.

"So Hathach went". The first step is always obedience, isn't it? The queen sends this servant out to Mordecai to find out why he is in mourning.

> *So Hathach went out to Mordecai in the city square that was in front of the king's gate. And Mordecai told him all that had happened to him, and the sum of money that Haman had promised to pay into the king's treasuries to destroy the Jews.* Esther 4:6-7

Mordecai tells Hathach "all that had happened to him". He acquaints Hathach with the entire story, and also tells him about the sum of money that will be placed in the king's treasuries. However, Mordecai wants to make sure that the account is given to Esther in its entirety, with no exaggerations. He tells Hathach what has happened, but goes one step further.

> *He also gave him a copy of the written decree for their destruction, which was given at Shushan, that he might show it to Esther and explain it to her, and that he might command her to go in to the king to make supplication to him and plead before him for her people.* Esther 4:8

Rather than just telling Hathach what is going on, Mordecai gives a copy of the decree signed by Ahasuerus to Esther's servant. There is no room for exaggeration here — Mordecai is very careful not to present the situation to Esther as anything but exactly what it is. Once Esther understands what is happening outside the palace gates, Mordecai is hoping against hope that his adopted daughter will step out in faith and intervene on behalf of the Jewish people. Mordecai asks Hathach to tell Esther to go to Ahasuerus and plead for the lives of her people. Mordecai hopes that Esther will be moved to action by the decree, and use her influence in the palace to help. Esther's heritage will not be a secret for too much longer!

Meanwhile, in Persia, Mordecai is still being true to his character. During this tumultuous time, he is operating in quiet faith to his God. Mordecai is praying, he is continuing to be faithful, he is doing what he knows to do.... Like Paul described to the Corinthians, he is hard-pressed, he is perplexed, he is struck down... but he knows he is not forgotten by his Heavenly Father. Neither are you forgotten by your Heavenly Father, woman of God! Keep your eyes on the Lord. Be assured that He is keeping His eyes on you!

When Esther learned of Mordecai's distress, she sent him clothes. Once she hears the entire story, she'll realize just how insufficient that gesture was. Esther is about to be presented with an important opportunity: to allow the power of God to be demonstrated through her.

So Hathach returned and told Esther the words of Mordecai.
Esther 4:9

Esther sent a little help to Mordecai without knowing the details — once presented with the full details of the situation, how will she respond?

A quick prayer before we close for today: Father, help me to magnify one thing and one thing only during the hard times: YOU! Your greatness is something that I could never exaggerate!

※

DAY FOUR: ESTHER 4:10-14
Regardless of the consequences, we must obey. Whether or not we understand, we must obey. If we really trust, we will trust even when we can't see!

FRIEND TO FRIEND...

As every mother is by her own child, I am captivated by my daughter Lindsay. She has always demonstrated confidence and independence, passion and creativity. I am continually amazed with how well she knows herself. Lindsay does not always fit into my "routines", but she is always full of surprises. God knew I needed her! While Lindsay's free-spiritedness is very charming and can be lots of fun, I have to admit it is an occasional (but very small source) of frustration to my "type A" personality.

One morning, I was especially interested in maintaining my schedule. Even though three-year-old Lindsay had not yet started school, I had decided to get her up and dressed with the twins each day. This way we could all have breakfast together. Also, once Jacob and Tyler were dropped off at kindergarten, Lindsay and I would be ready to go if there were any errands to run or appointments to make. The theory was great, but the execution was difficult with my free-spirited, independent, creative butterfly girl. Jacob and Tyler usually fit easily into my routine, but Lindsay came with routines of her own.

On this particular morning, I had planned to go grocery shopping. Michael took the twins to school, and according to plan, Lindsay was already dressed and ready to go. I placed her little sneakers by the front door and went to have a mother/daughter talk with my Linds. She was in the family room with her favorite stuffed animal, a large pink rabbit she lovingly referred to as her "sister bunny". I began gently: "Lindsay, baby, Mommy needs to run a few errands after I do a few things around the house. Your sneakers are by the door, and I need your socks to stay on your feet so that we will be ready to go when its time, okay?" Lindsay smiled sweetly. "Okay, Mommy."

A simple "okay" might have been satisfactory from the twins, but from Lindsay, I wasn't sure. We had had this conversation before, so I decided to continue explaining. Lindsay was a "crammer", and many a morning had been spent searching for shoes, socks and hairbows in between sofa cushions, under beds or behind chairs. I wanted to maintain a schedule today, and had not included time in that schedule to search for these missing items. "Honey, listen. Mommy will be in a hurry and I do not want to look for missing socks. You have to keep them on your feet this morning, or there will be consequences. Do you understand?" She assured me that she did understand, so I left her and the "sister bunny" to play.

After a few minutes, I was ready to go. When I came down the stairs into the family room, Lindsay's eyes met mine and she gave me a knowing little smile. Even at three years old, she always seemed to know more than I did. Sitting on the couch with her sister bunny in her arms and her little ankles crossed, Lindsay might have looked sweet. Today, however, the sight of those ten precious toes exposed made me feel as if my head might explode: toes without socks. I took a deep breath, and in my own sweet-but-firm voice, I spoke first.

"Lindsay, baby, Mommy is disappointed. Don't you remember what Mommy told you a few minutes ago?" Before I waited for her answer, I proceeded to gently remind her of our earlier conversation. Now it was time to follow through. After all, I had said that there would be consequences.

As usual, Lindsay was a step ahead of me — I told you about that knowing smile of hers. She smiled, pulled up her pant legs and excitedly told me, "Look, Mommy! I didn't take my socks off!"

Her socks were tied around her ankles.

Outsmarted again (well — the socks were ON and that was what I had instructed her), I smiled, stifled a laugh and helped her put her socks and sneakers on. She had figured out a way to satisfy both of us: she had been barefooted like she enjoyed, and I was still on schedule like I enjoyed. After buckling Lindsay and the sister bunny into her car seat, we were ready to go.

Lindsay's "choices" do not always work out so well as they did that day. Sometimes there is simply no way around doing what Mom says exactly how Mom says it. Part of my job is to teach her that just as there is freedom in the ability to make her own choices, there can be freedom in the ability to obey as well. With Lindsay, I use train tracks as an analogy: while there are different directions that a train could go, it cannot go anywhere if it is not on the track. The only way for us to experience freedom and success is to be on track with the Lord. It's simple, but I pray that it works for her until she can understand more.

It is the same with us and our Heavenly Father. Sometimes there are choices. There are times when the Lord might say to us like he said to Jeremiah, "See, all the land is before you; wherever it seems good and convenient for you to go, go there" (Jeremiah 40:4). Jeremiah was "on track", and he was free in the Lord. As Jeremiah was free to seek the Lord and determine the right course, God encouraged him by letting Jeremiah know that wherever he went, God would be with him. Jeremiah's obedience in former situations opened the door for this choice, because God knew that Jeremiah could be trusted to obey Him wherever he went.

Other times, there are not choices. Earlier, we discussed the rich young ruler in Matthew 19. He wanted choices, and he asked questions. Asking a question was not wrong; this young man's response to the answer that Jesus gave him was wrong. Jesus is not frustrated with the questions. Patiently, lovingly, Jesus answers. After hearing Jesus' final answer and instruction, the young man, unwilling to obey fully, went away in sorrow. I believe that this young man was looking for a "shortcut" or an easier choice. Sometimes, many times, there is no "easy way out". We must trust and obey the Lord, follow Him as closely as we can, and live joyfully in the freedom that this obedience provides for us.

Today Esther comes to her crossroads. She has found out the cause of Mordecai's mourning, and learned what he is expecting her to do. She may look for an easy way out, but will she try to take it? A turning point for her, and by extension for the Jews. Esther could not have measured the repercussions of her boldness in this matter.

Esther has an important decision to make.

> *Then Esther spoke to Hathach, and gave him a command for Mordecai: "All the king's servants and the people of the king's provinces know that any man or woman who goes into the inner court to the king, who has not been called, he has but one law: put all to death, except the one to whom the king holds out the golden scepter, that he may live. Yet I myself have not been called to go in to the king these thirty days."* Esther 4:10-11

Esther reminds Mordecai of the Persian law: no one can go into the king's chambers unless the king calls for him or her. Different Bible scholars have interpreted Esther's answer to Mordecai in different ways. Some are sure this was an excuse on Esther's part, asking Mordecai to find another way of rescue for the Jews. Some scholars say that, at least for this moment, Esther is glad that her heritage has remained a secret; that perhaps she is thinking that this decree will not apply to her, since Ahasuerus is unaware that she is a Jew.

One study suggests that this was not

> "an excuse on Esther's part, but rather a plea that Mordecai give her some guidance. He knew palace protocol, he was a man, and he was in touch with what was going on. She was isolated in the harem and incapable of devising the kind of strategy needed to solve the problem. Besides all this, she hadn't seen the king for a month; and it was possible that she had somehow fallen out of favor. Ahasuerus was unpredictable, and she didn't want to make matters worse."[2]

Maybe we can give Esther the benefit of the doubt here. As we have seen, she is selfless and honest, and surely her intention was to help in spite of the fear that she must have felt. Remember, it is not wrong for us to admit our emotions, and it is not wrong to ask questions. Our responses can be wrong, but the questions are not wrong. Esther feeling fear and admitting to Mordecai that fear was not wrong. However, in certain situations, it can be wrong to act upon emotions. Esther was not wrong to be afraid, but it would have been a grave mistake to allow that fear to cause her to hide behind her position. However, it seems from Mordecai's response that he thought Esther was trying to make an excuse to stay away from this situation. Let's read what Mordecai says to Esther after hearing her reply to his message.

> *So they told Mordecai Esther's words. And Mordecai told them to answer Esther: "Do not think in your heart that you will escape in the king's palace any more than all the other Jews."* Esther 4:12-13

Mordecai replies to Esther that she is mistaken if she feels as if her position will save her. He thinks that her reply was an excuse to stay out of the situation and hide in the palace. To paraphrase the conversation between Mordecai and Esther, she tells him that if she goes to the king without being summoned, she could die. Mordecai tells her that the possibility of death is real, *even for the queen*, whether or not she goes to the king on behalf of the Jews.

Mordecai does not stop there. He says one more thing to further convince Esther that her involvement is vital.

> *For if you remain completely silent at this time, relief and deliverance will arise for the Jews from another place, but you and your father's house will perish. Yet who knows whether you have come to the kingdom for such a time as this?"* Esther 4:14

Mordecai tells her that relief for the Jews is coming regardless of her action at this moment. God will not allow His people to be destroyed. Mordecai must be convinced within himself of this — all of his faith depends on it.

This moment is easily recognized as important for Esther, but it is an important moment for Mordecai as well. This is possibly the first moment that he realizes his purpose and Esther's purpose in Persia. Imagine how Mordecai may be feeling. All these years of being out of place, exiled in the anti-Semitic climate of Persia. Even though the Jews were released by Cyrus so many years ago, Mordecai never felt a release from the Lord to leave.

For Mordecai, it must have been so confusing to see Esther taken to the palace to prepare to be queen, knowing she was a Jew. It must have been heartbreaking as well, losing her and considering the probable outcome in the event that she was not chosen by the king. Imagine how he must have felt when Esther was actually chosen. It was an honor, yes, but why would God put a Jewish girl on the throne in this country? Now all of these details of his life that Mordecai had simply been trusting to the Lord, operating in faith and obedience even though he may not have understood... now all of these details are starting to fall into place in his mind.

Mordecai sees the *providence* of God in action now. What had previously been hidden from him is now revealed. Mordecai must have felt humbled to realize he had been preparing a queen for this moment. He must have felt humbled to realize that the Lord trusted him to raise Esther, the hope for the Jews. Now his job is to make Esther see the hand of God here as well.

So *this* is why he stayed in Persia...

So *this* is why he raised Esther as his own...

So *this* is why Esther was chosen as queen...

Mordecai responds to Esther, "Who knows whether you have come to the kingdom for such a time as *this*?"

Who knows?

Father, help me to trust You even when I don't understand. Help me to praise You and act quickly when Your purposes are revealed to me. If you can use me to demonstrate Your power, Lord, I am available to You!

❦

DAY FIVE: ESTHER 4:15-17

Father, help me to understand today importance of obeying You quickly. Help me to feel the urgency in my spirit. Give me Your view and let me experience Your passion. Let me follow You without fear, and let me more than a blessing to the people You place in my path: let me be Your instrument of rescue.

FRIEND TO FRIEND...

I argued with the Lord for several days. Truth be told, the argument (one sided, I should point out — my gentle and loving Father never argued back) lasted for several weeks before I got in line and obeyed what the Lord had put in my spirit to do: He was calling me to a fast. This feeling, this sensing, this urging in my spirit to draw closer to the Lord in prayer, was oftentimes indicative of an upcoming battle. Many times, fasting would provide me with the tools that I would need to fight. At the same time, fasting would provide me with the humility before the Lord that was needed to handle the victory He would surely give.

I knew when I fasted, I was more sensitive to the Spirit of God. I knew when I took advantage of these times to draw closer to Him, He would draw closer to me. I knew in these times when I denied my flesh (whatever specific desire it may be at the time, whether it was turning off the television or pushing away my plate), I found it easier to hear His voice. Even knowing these things did not make it any easier to "bite the bullet" and begin.

However, obedience is vital, not only to me, but to those around me. Thinking about my husband, my children, my ministry, and those people within my sphere of influence changes me. I realize it was the Lord Who reminded me that it's not all about me, and I decide: my fast will begin tomorrow.

Take a few minutes to read Numbers 16:46-50. In this passage, Moses, when faced with a plague that was killing people by the literal thousands, commanded his brother Aaron to fill a censer with incense and run to the congregation. When Aaron got to the center of the group to make atonement for them, the plague had already begun. In Numbers 16:48, the Word says, "he stood in between the dead and the living, so the plague was stopped."

Can you imagine that picture in your head? Close your eyes for a moment and try to visualize Aaron standing in the midst of these people. All the people to his left are dead, all the people to his right are alive. It's a pretty powerful picture, isn't it? Imagine how many people were saved because Aaron obeyed and acted quickly. Notice that Aaron did not stop and ask what would happen to him; his was concern for the dying people. Aaron knew God would take care of him. Numbers 16:50 says, "the plague had stopped." Praise God; all because one person was willing to stand in the gap.

Proverbs 24:11 instructs us to "deliver those who are drawn toward death, and hold back those stumbling to the slaughter." Every day, we are faced with people who are literally dying and going to hell. We may even feel somewhat cavalier about it; it's not as if they are dying in front of our eyes, is it? Are you willing to stand in the gap for the lost in your community? They are ignorant of the things of God and they are headed for certain destruction. As they totter to the slaughter, are you doing anything to hold them back?

The ability to stand between the living and the dead does not come altogether naturally to us. Sometimes, acquiring the kind of strength that it takes requires something extra. In Mark chapter 9,when Jesus' disciples became frustrated at their inability to prevail over the devil, they asked Him a simple question: "Why couldn't we cast it out?" Why were they unable to stand between the living and the dead at the moment when it was most needed? Jesus answer was simple to hear, but sometimes more difficult to perform: "This kind can come out by nothing but prayer and fasting" (Mark 9:29).

Isaiah 58:6-12 is a wonderful passage concerning fasting. In verse 6, it says the fast chosen by the Lord will "loose the bonds of wickedness...undo the heavy burdens...let the oppressed go free, and... break every yoke". Powerful words: loosening the bonds of wickedness, undoing heavy burdens, freeing the oppressed, breaking every yoke... and there is even more. In verse 9, Isaiah writes, "you shall call, and the Lord will answer". This is what the Jews in Persia needed during Ahasuerus' reign. It's also what we need today, isn't it? You can be assured that when you call upon the Lord that He will answer you. What a great assurance!

Another passage on fasting can be found in Ezra 8:21. Ezra calls for a fast for a specific reason. He fasted that he and his people might "might humble ourselves before our God, to seek from Him the right way for us and our little ones and all our possessions". Later, Ezra writes that God heard and answered their prayer after their fast (Ezra 9:23). The fast was for specific purposes: for direction, for protection and for provision. More examples of what the Jews in Persia needed, and more examples of what you and I need today!

Esther needs this direction from the Lord and this assurance of the Lord's answer now. This is Esther's opportunity to stand in the gap for her people; her opportunity to stand between the living and the dead. Her opportunity to be the instrument of God in rescuing the Jewish race, as God in His providence has positioned her to be. Outside the palace gates, we have a group of people who have been condemned to death. Inside the palace gates, we have a woman who has been commissioned by God Himself to stop the destruction. God always has a remnant, and He always has a plan.

Will Esther take advantage of this divine opportunity?

> *Then Esther told them to reply to Mordecai: "Go, gather all the Jews who are present in Shushan, and fast for me; neither eat nor drink for three days, night or day. My maids and I will fast likewise. And so I will go to the king, which is against the law; and if I perish, I perish!"* Esther 4:15-16

Esther sends her message back to Mordecai. It is apparent that she understands, as Mordecai understands, the purpose God has for her in the palace. Just as the Jews throughout Persia were stirred to action upon hearing the decree, Esther is stirred to action. She tells Mordecai to ask the Jews to fast on her behalf, and tells him that she and her maids will be fasting as well. She demonstrates her faith in God, lifting her eyes to the hills just as the rest of her people did.

Fasting and prayer are a powerful combination, and Esther shows her determination here. Esther knows there is power in fasting. She begins a fast immediately upon hearing Mordecai's terrible news. She is preparing for a battle, and hopeful for a victory.

Esther tells Mordecai, "I will go to the king, which is against the law; and if I perish, I perish!" Esther understood her purpose. Beyond understanding, she is going to follow through. She has prepared for this moment, and she is going to be obedient regardless of the consequences.

Let's read the last verse of chapter 4 together:

> *So Mordecai went his way and did according to all that Esther commanded him.* Esther 4:17

After all these years of obeying the Lord and preparing Esther, the roles are reversed now. Esther is the queen and she is a godly woman. She has come to the kingdom for such a time as this, and she is walking in her purpose. Esther rises to the challenge, and "takes charge"! Now Mordecai is obeying her and doing "all that Esther had commanded him". Esther is going to the king, and in order to be prepared she has called a three day fast. Mordecai gathers the Jews who are in Shushan to fast and pray as well. Esther, Mordecai, her servants, and the Jews who live in Shushan agree together for Esther to have favor when she goes into the king's chambers.

Like Aaron stopping the plague, like Esther going to the king.... become determined in your heart today to be passionate about the lost. Esther was faced with a literal trauma that would be played out before her very eyes. Every day, you come into contact with people who are lost and dying. Ask yourself: what is the difference? Take a cue from Esther and pray for opportunities to stand in the gap for the people around you. Be a road block for the people stumbling to the slaughter, not merely a speed bump.

Lord, help us. Help us to be bold in our witness — bold in our RESCUE of the people that You place in our path. Open our eyes to the people around us... help us to see beyond ourselves.

❧

For I say, through the grace given unto me, to every man that is among you, not to think of himself more highly than he ought to think but to think soberly... For as we have many members in one body, and all members have not the same office: So we, being many, are one body in Christ, and every one members one of another."
Romans 12:3-5

❧

Father, Your love is more than enough for me.
If I allow it to, Your love will free me.
Your love will free me to love other people the way that You desire me to love them.
Because Your love for me is so great,
I can be confident daily that You are taking care of me.
As a result of that confidence,
I will be able to take care of others without worry:
no worry that if I put the needs of others first, that my own needs will be put last;
No worry that my own needs will go unmet... No worry that I will be unequal

to the task
if I should be called upon to stand "between the living and the dead".
Your love will free me to walk in a manner truly fitting a child of God -
I know that You love me, and I know that You desire that
I share Your love with anyone within my reach!

🙞

---

1.   (Biblesoft's New Exhaustive Strong's Numbers and Concordance with Expanded Greek-Hebrew Dictionary. Copyright (c) 1994, Biblesoft and International Bible Translators, Inc.)

2.   Warren Wiersbe, Be Committed: Doing God's Will Whatever the Cost, (Colorado Springs, Colorado: Chariot Victor Publishing, 1993), p.111.

ESTHER: CHAPTER 5 - "PROVIDENCE"
Esther's Banquet

In Esther 4, we read about turning points in the lives of Esther and Mordecai. For Mordecai, he had been the one in authority until this most crucial moment. Now he is submissive to Esther's wishes (remember Esther 4:17). In a time of great tragedy, Mordecai is able to focus on the Lord and realize his purpose in Persia all these years. For Esther, she is no longer simply under authority; she recognizes that God has given her authority as well. Though we saw change in both Mordecai and Esther, the change does not come as a surprise: they are moved to action, yet maintain their integrity and character throughout the turmoil wrought in Persia by Haman and Ahasuerus.

The apostle Paul said it best in Ephesians 4:26, "Be angry, and do not sin". Even Jesus felt anger at times — remember the fury in the temple (Mark 11:15-18)? Sometimes the very thing that brings about the most emotion in you can be a key to your anointing. As we discussed before, our emotions are God-given. If we maintain control, our emotions can be a force to bring about change; not destruction.

However, chapter 4 did not bring a turning point for Ahasuerus and Haman. They must be the same as always, as our chronicler does not tell us anything new about either of them. No change in their actions or their characters: Haman has planned for revenge against Mordecai and the Jews for his own selfish pride; while Ahasuerus stands by and allows this evil to happen. The only time their names are mentioned during chapter 4 was when Esther or Mordecai talked about what had happened previously.

During her very first encounter with him, Esther found great favor in the eyes of the king. Ahasuerus "loved Esther more than all the other women" (Esther 2:17). Even with this extremely positive beginning, Ahasuerus has proved to be moody and unpredictable. Though Esther has been his wife and queen for nearly five years, she is not given an exception to this law: no one may come into the king's chambers without an invitation. As Esther is preparing for this most important meeting with Ahasuerus, she is most likely painfully aware of one fact: she has not been invited into the king's inner court for thirty days. Whether or not it was unusual for Esther to go thirty days without an invitation from the king, the wait for an invitation must have been caused some measure of anxiety. Every time she left his chambers there may have been some feeling of uncertainty. Did she please him or displease him? Is she in favor or out of favor with the king? Esther could never be sure.

While Esther may feel uncertain at times of her personal standing with Ahasuerus, she is not uncertain concerning the law. When Mordecai suggests to Esther that she make a visit to the king in an attempt to block the impending sentence against the Jews, Esther reminds Mordecai of the single most important order pertaining to guests in the royal chamber. "All the king's servants and the people of the king's provinces know that any man or woman who goes into the inner court to the king, who has not been called, he has but one law: put all to death" (Esther 4:11).

As with many rules, there is an exception. If, at the beginning of the unsolicited visit, Ahasuerus extends the golden scepter, his visitor is granted access without fear. With the lives of the Jewish people on the line, the stakes of this visit are high. Esther may be risking her life by entering the king's chambers unannounced, but in failing to speak to the king about this matter she would be risking the lives of all the Jews. For this visit, it is most crucial that Esther is prepared. Esther is going to Ahasuerus without a summons, and she needs to see Ahasuerus extend his golden scepter to her.

To relieve her initial feelings of insecurity, Esther turns to her faith. Though there may be uncertainty with the king of Persia, there is no uncertainty with the King of Kings. Esther has been praying and fasting for three days. She has not been alone. As recorded in Esther 4:15-16, Esther asks that Mordecai and the Jews fast for three days, and gives them her assurance that she will be fasting and praying as well. The Jews stand with her in agreement.

Now at a crossroads, we see submissive Esther stepping into her own authority. She is demonstrating an important leadership principle: she knows that she must lead *by example*. In His wisdom, God has entrusted her with an important job and given her a great responsibility. Esther does not disappoint. As she asks the Jews to fast and pray for three days, Esther does the same.

At the close of chapter 4, Esther seems determined: now we find out if she follows through!

DAY ONE: ESTHER 5:1-2

This week, we begin to see Esther step out in her God-given authority. God has also trusted you with some amount of authority in your life. Woman of God, in areas where you are in authority, take your cue from Esther: pray that you will recognize the opportunity as from God, and be trustworthy!

FRIEND TO FRIEND...

Though I cannot be sure that any of them will prove effective, I have all of these little theories about raising children. I share my ideas with a good friend of our family sometimes. When I do, one of two things usually happens: either a discussion between us begins, or he enjoys a good belly laugh at my expense. (My friend's children are grown, and he knows many things that I do not yet know. Also, we have been close friends for so long that he can laugh with me at my inexperience and know that my feelings will not be hurt at all!) He will tell me, "Jennifer, when the twins turn eighteen, you and I will write a book. We'll either call it *Parenting: Here's How You Do It* or *Parenting: Please Don't Do it This Way!*" Sometimes I wonder if he is teasing me, and sometimes I know.

One of my theories is that my children respond better to my guidance if I also "practice what I preach". For example, I have never presented household chores as drudgery; in our house, chores are just one way we come together as a family and help each other. Everyone has their own job, and when each of us does his or her job well, our household runs smoothly and happily. On Saturday morning, when I ask my children to do a few things around the house, I make sure I am working along with them. In this way, I am demonstrating to them that I am caring for them and for our house and leading them by example. My theory is this: if I continue to present chores in this way, then we won't have arguments or fusses in this area, but that my children will grow into responsible young people and eventually into adults who know how to take care of the things that God has provided. I'm sorry to admit that I know children who won't clean their rooms or sort laundry without a "war" with their mother. So far, so good in my house, though I don't have teenagers yet. I'll let you know how it goes asking my fifteen year olds to scrub their tub when we get there! For today, leading by *example* seems to be very effective.

Jesus led by example as well. He is our greatest example of leadership. Though His examples are innumerable, one area in which Jesus led us by example is baptism. As recorded in Matthew 3:13-15, Jesus came to John and asked John to baptize Him. John is surprised, and even suggests to Jesus that this was not necessary for the Son of God to be baptized. John tells Jesus that he is the one who needs baptism, not Jesus. In spite of John's initial attempt at preventing Him, Jesus insists upon being baptized by John. Jesus tells John, "*Permit it to be so now, for thus it is fitting for us to fulfill all righteousness*". Jesus is explaining to John that even He is not exempt from doing right.

When Jesus was baptized, the heavens were opened. For the only time in the Scriptures, all three Persons of the Godhead show up in one place. The Son being baptized. The Holy Spirit descending in the form of a dove. The Father's voice: "This is My Son, in Whom I am well pleased." What an awe inspiring picture! Though He did not need to be baptized for any reason other than demonstrating to us that it was important, His following through should make an impression on us.

As Jesus recognized the importance of leading by example, we must appreciate the value of this principle as well. In your life, there are areas in which you have been entrusted with a certain amount of authority. If you are a mother, you have been given authority over your children. As a wife, you have been given authority over your household (not over your husband). As a career woman, you may have authority over people working under you. Part of acting responsibly in your level of authority is leading by example. In many situations, your actions speak so much louder than words.

You cannot measure the value of your children *seeing* you reading the Bible on a daily basis. You cannot measure the value of your husband *being blessed* by your prayers. You cannot measure the value of your co-workers *witnessing* you turning every new project over to the Lord before you begin your work. Leading by example is not about making a "show" to make people notice something good in you for your own benefit. It is about you being honest and unashamed in your faith. It is about understanding that your example may cause someone around you to believe on Christ. Leading by example is about you doing and becoming your utmost best in order that the people around you will be inspired to do and become their utmost best as well. It is about living your life in excellence. As you live your life well in front of others, following through with the instructions that the Lord gives to you and setting an example, you will be astonished by the results.

Esther understands the importance of leading by example, and does not ask anything of the people around her that she is unwilling to do herself. At Esther's request, and following her example, the Jews have been fasting and praying for three days. Now the fast has come to a close, and it is time to find out if the Lord honored their prayers.

> *Now it happened on the third day that Esther put on her royal robes and stood in the inner court of the king's palace, across from the king's house, while the king sat on his royal throne in the royal house, facing the entrance of the house.* Esther 5:1

Imagine the uncertainty of this moment for her, as she stands and waits for the king's response to her boldness in coming to his courts without an invitation. She dresses and prepares herself, as she has done every time she goes in to his court. She leaves her chambers, walks deliberately to the inner court, and stands facing the entrance of the king's house. Considering the weight of this moment, however, she is facing much more.

Waiting on the other side of that door is life (if the golden scepter is extended to her in welcome), or death (the sentence that she will receive if she is unwelcome in the court). Esther faces the prospect that her words to Mordecai may prove prophetic: the possibility of death on the other side of that door is real. Her determination showing strong before her fast even began, Esther is now willing to risk death rather than do nothing on behalf of the Jews. Hearing her own words echoing through her mind to Mordecai, perhaps she wonders at this moment if they will become prophetic: "I will go to the king... and if I perish, I perish!" Confident now that she is acting inside of God's will for her, Esther knows that she is pleasing to the Lord whether or not she pleases Ahasuerus. Without regard for the result, without regard for her personal safety, Esther places herself completely in the hands of God. Esther's sole responsibility is to obey. Life or death, the outcome must be left up to the Lord.

Esther has not seen her husband in over a month. Ahasuerus has not invited her, or shown an interest in her presence. Who knows what was going on in his mind? As Esther stands in the inner court, she can only be sure that she is acting in obedience to the Lord. Whatever transpires from this point on must be in the Lord's hands. As Esther waits for Ahasuerus to see her, she must be confident that the Lord sees her as well.

> *So it was, when the king saw Queen Esther standing in the court,*
> *that she found favor in his sight, and the king held out to Esther*
> *the golden scepter that was in his hand. Then Esther went near and*
> *touched the top of the scepter.* Esther 5:2

Ahasuerus is looking out facing the entrance of the house, and sees Esther standing in the court. On this particular day, Ahasuerus is glad to see his queen. Once again, Esther experiences favor with the king, and to demonstrate his pleasure in seeing her, he extends his golden scepter.

No chance or casting of lots involved here: this day was ordained by the Lord. Ahasuerus does not realize that Esther did not come alone into his chambers today; she was accompanied by the Most High. She is surrounded by His anointing, and covered by the prayers of all the Jews. Esther has God's favor on her life, and that is all she needs.

Like Esther, God's favor on your life is all you need — seek God and His favor before every step you take! It is His desire to bless you as you obey Him!

DAY TWO: ESTHER 5:3–5

If God has given you authority in any area, trust Him to work through you in that authority. Do your utmost to reflect His love and care with everyone He puts in your path — and be prepared for Him to do the extraordinary through you!

FRIEND TO FRIEND...

"New backpack and shoes day" is a special tradition we have at our house. Two weeks before school starts, we make a family day of it. Starting with breakfast at our favorite bakery, everyone always orders the same thing: bagels and peanut butter for the kiddos, and croissant sandwiches for Michael and me. After breakfast, we're off to get haircuts for the boys, and then to the store to choose our new backpacks and school supplies. Once our backpacks are full, we head to the shoe store and everyone gets new sneakers. When the children's feet are measured, they are beside themselves with excitement over how much they have grown, and they are off in search of every box they can find with their "new number" on the side. Of course, their most important criteria is not whether the shoes fit: the children want to make sure that, in these new shoes, they will be able to run faster and jump higher!

As we finish our errands, I realize that my favorite part of the day is seeing the children excited about being prepared. I hope they will continue to learn the value of preparing beforehand. Beyond simply being prepared, I hope they will learn that they are preparing for success: a pencil with which to do their best work, a sneaker with which to put their best foot forward... I want them to realize single every day that they will have an opportunity to "work heartily as unto the Lord" (Colossians 3:23). I want them to prepare to accomplish great things for the Lord, and to be confident that He will bless their efforts for Him. This powerful life lesson would serve all of us well.

Back in Persia, Ahasuerus has accepted Esther into his chambers, and she has a request to make of him. As she prepares her request, she is also preparing for victory over this sentence against the Jews. After she touches the end of his golden scepter, Ahasuerus speaks.

> *And the king said to her, "What do you wish, Queen Esther? What is your request? It shall be given to you -- up to half the kingdom!"*
> Esther 5:3

As Esther has fasted and prayed for three days, God was moving in Ahasuerus' heart and preparing a way for her to fulfill her purpose. Esther has made wise decisions, but it is God Who led her to those decisions, and God Who is blessing her obedience to Him. As Esther stands before the entrance to Ahasuerus' chambers, he see her. Esther finds favor with him once again, and he invites her to come to him. When he extends the scepter, he is assuring her of his good will toward her. When Esther comes forward and touches the scepter, she is showing her respect and gratitude. She must have felt relief — though the one she is truly thankful to is God! Ahasuerus has no thought of any power other than himself, and he has no idea that his wife does either.

Ahasuerus is pleased to see Esther, and tells her that whatever her request is, she may have it from him — even up to half his kingdom! Perhaps the king was being sincere in his response. It is equally as likely that Ahasuerus may have been saying this in the presence of the officials who are in his chambers to show them that she is in his favor. We know how Ahasuerus loves to display his power. In this positive atmosphere, Esther makes her request.

> So Esther answered, "If it pleases the king, let the king and Haman
> come today to the banquet that I have prepared for him."
> Esther 5:4.

In light of the desperate situation outside of the palace gates, does this request surprise you? Haman has determined the date and set the plans in motion for the genocide of the Jews. Ahasuerus agreed and gave his full approval for this wicked plan. Every day brings the Jews one step closer to death. In the midst of this incredibly tense time, Esther finally is welcomed into Ahasuerus' presence. He makes his intentions toward her very clear: whatever Esther desires will be done for her. Anything.

"So, Ahasuerus, would you like to come for dinner? Bring your friend, too."

Considering that she has had the Jews as well as her own (non-Jewish) servants fasting for three days, do you think anyone was confused when Esther goes into the court to invite Ahasuerus and Haman to dinner? "We fasted for three days and prayed for three days for a dinner?" Don't worry — our heroine is working on a plan!

Esther has prepared a banquet for the king and for Haman. When the king tells her that she can have anything she wants up to half his kingdom, Esther asks for an opportunity to bless him and his closest advisor. She invites him to dinner, and does not give him time to change his mind if he does accept: she knows how erratic her husband's behavior and moods are. The banquet is already prepared, and it is set for *today*. Esther knew that if Ahasuerus was in a favorable mood, she could not count on it to last long. She knows very well the erratic and emotional behavior of her husband. Esther prepared beforehand for a positive outcome to her request to Ahasuerus: the banquet was prepared before she went into his courts. Esther prepared for victory!

Esther does not have to wait long for a response from her husband.

Then the king said, "Bring Haman quickly, that he may do as Esther has said." So the king and Haman went to the banquet that Esther had prepared. Esther 5:5

If there is a party or a banquet going on, the king's response to Esther's invitation is no surprise: count Ahasuerus in! He rounds up Haman "quickly", so he can go to Esther's banquet as she requested. After years of being submissive to Mordecai, Hegai, and Ahasuerus, Esther has stepped up now into her own authority. Let's read the king's exact words to his servant; he tells him to bring Haman quickly so "that he may do as *Esther has said.*" Now it is Ahasuerus *rushing* to submit to Esther!

Esther is laying a foundation right now, and she is not acting out of emotion. Esther is carefully choosing her words, and carefully choosing the timing. It is true that she is up against an issue of time, but it does not follow that she has to rush. Esther is operating in faith, and she must operate in God's timing as well.

Pray that the Lord would help you to be patient as you trust Him to work out the best in your life... trust His providence!

⁂

DAY THREE: ESTHER 5:6

Like Esther, we need to recognize the importance of timing and faith working together... but also we also need to recognize when it is time for action! The right action at the right time... does this seem like a lot to put together? Be thankful today that you do not have to work things out on your own — you just have to obey your Heavenly Father! He takes such good care of you!

FRIEND TO FRIEND...

It was an awful lie. Not just wrong, but also ill-intentioned, deliberate, even mean-spirited. I wanted to correct it, but... well, I couldn't figure how to do it. Well, I couldn't figure out how to do it *kindly*. By the time I understood what had happened, the lie was told and accepted, and the situation had been resolved to everyone's satisfaction. Everyone's satisfaction but mine, of course. The lie was about me.

I had been guilty of many things, but in this instance my mistake was simply my naivete. I hadn't considered people capable of protecting themselves at my expense. I wanted the truth to be heard, but I didn't want to defend myself. I had

determined long ago that I would let the Lord be my defense, but I hadn't anticipated a situation such as this. As my heart was breaking, I took my pain to my
gentle husband. His advice would change my life and my outlook. Michael told
me, "Sometimes you can be right, and sometimes you can have a relationship.
Sometimes you cannot have both. You have to decide which is more important:
being right or being in relationship."

At first, I wanted to be right. In the natural, I wanted to "get even". However,
as I thought about it more, I realized that Michael was right. These people had
wronged me, but I had to leave it where it would be best handled: in the hands
of the Lord. I had to be content in the knowledge that He would heal my heart. I
also had to be satisfied that if there were to be consequences for anyone else, that
was for the Lord to determine. I had to let it go. Someone else's attitude was not
my business; my responsibility was to keep my heart pure. I would forgive, and I
would forget. I would serve these same people tomorrow, and I would not allow
fear to control my relationship with them. God would protect me.

Weeks later, I got a phone call from the person responsible for my heartache.
The very one who had sold me out so that her own shortcomings would not be
exposed needed me. Her daughter was struggling, the family was hurting. She
was in need of a friend, a confidante, a prayer partner to hold her arms up during
this battle. "Jennifer, will you come?" For a moment, my flesh reared up inside
me: this was my opportunity to leave her "out in the cold" as she had done to me.
Thank God, my spirit was stronger that day. My flesh was crucified anew as I told
her, "I'm on my way, don't worry... You won't go through this alone..."

Had I wanted to be right? Sure, but I wanted that relationship even more. Without it, I would never have been able to maintain that open door. Without it, I would
not have been given this opportunity to serve. After the wounding came the healing,
and I was able to serve the Lord and His people (all of His people) again.

Esther has a similar choice to make: to only expose the wrong or to operate in
patience and keep an open door for service between herself and the king.

> *"If it pleases the king, let the king and Haman come today to the
> banquet that I have prepared for him."* Esther 5:4

In the center of a storm that would throw anyone into a panic, Esther is patient and deliberate. She decides to serve a meal to the king and his highest official. Though an invitation to dinner may not have been what the Jews in Persia
expected after their time of prayer and fasting, Esther is acting in wisdom and
humility. Though time is of the essence here, she is not in a rush. Long before
Jesus spoke a word, Esther practiced a principle He would teach during His time
on earth: "I say to you, love your enemies, bless those who curse you, do good to

those who hate you, and pray for those who spitefully use you and persecute you" (Matthew 5:44).

If there were any Jews in Persia who misunderstood Esther's intentions, let us not make the same mistake. In choosing to serve Ahasuerus, Esther is not lowering herself. In showing respect *to* him, she is more likely to receive respect *from* him. It is never a mistake to be kind. It is never a mistake to show respect when you can. The true mistake is allowing your own pride to stop you from adopting a right attitude toward other people.

It isn't easy, of course, but God sees your heart. As you trust Him to guide you, trust Him also with the results of your obedience. Refuse to allow pride to keep you from maintaining a servant's heart. What if you are misunderstood, as Esther may have been misunderstood? What if the person whom you are serving misunderstands your kindness? No matter. Convince yourself that it doesn't matter. The primary thought must be to serve God and His people. God sees you!

Esther is not the first person to use kindness to soften a hardened heart, or to stand in the gap on behalf of someone else. 1 Samuel 25 details the story of a wise woman named Abigail. In verses 2-3, Abigail is described as having good understanding and a beautiful appearance. However, her husband, Nabal, is described as evil and harsh in his doings. (Does this bring to mind another couple? Possibly a woman who has lived a quiet and submissive life, and a man who has just consented to allow the destruction of an entire race of people?)

In the following verses of this same chapter, Nabal and Abigail cross paths with David. At this time David is not yet king of Israel, though many years have passed since Samuel the prophet anointed David to be king. As the years wore on, Samuel passed away. With his passing may have also passed David's hope of actually ascending to the throne. In David's eyes, Samuel might have been the only person on earth who actually believed he would become king. After so many years of waiting for this prophecy to come to pass and losing possibly the most significant person in his life, David may be discouraged. Though he has received a promise that he would ascend to the throne of Israel, that promise may become harder and harder to believe with each passing day, month, and year.

At this time, David is in the wilderness with his men, and he has been protecting Nabal's property and his servants. David sends ten of his men to Nabal, and makes a request: David would like a dinner prepared for him and his men. This request is very minimal, considering that David and his men have been protecting Nabal's interests. Small also considering that David is probably in a position to take by force everything Nabal owns.

When David's request meets his ears (1 Samuel 25:10-11), Nabal refuses. In refusing, he also insults David. Nabal replies, "Who is this David, son of Jesse?

There are many servants nowadays who break away each one from their master....." Nabal calls David a lowly servant, not worthy of his attention. He treats this request as if it came from a criminal of sorts: a servant who did not have the integrity to serve; a servant who had escaped from his master. Nabal does not seem to care that David has been protecting his property. Nabal obviously does not consider that one meal is a small price to pay in light of what he might have lost if David had decided to attack rather than to defend.

In Samuel 25:12, David hears Nabal's response, and has a response of his own: he decides that he is going to kill Nabal. He plans and takes four hundred men along with him for the attack. In a time when David is already struggling with his identity (who he is versus who he will be), Nabal attacks David at the core of his personal crisis: "Who is this David? Some criminal? Some escaped servant?" When Nabal's servants hear what David's intentions are, they do not go to Nabal. Nabal's servants go to his wife, Abigail, instead. Apparently, they know their master well. Remember, he is "evil and harsh in his doings" (1 Samuel 25:3). The servants tell Abigail what has happened, and describes how David and his men have been protecting Nabal's property. They explain to her what was asked and how Nabal refused. Abigail quickly goes into action.

As recorded in Samuel 28:18-28, Abigail intercepts David with a meal for him and his men. Abigail begs for forgiveness and mercy for her husband. As soon as she sees him, she falls on her face and bowed at his feet... what man wouldn't respond favorably to that kind of treatment? For that matter, what person, male or female, wouldn't respond to such a gracious gesture? David responded favorably. Admitting that his original intention was attack and ensure that "by morning light no males would have been left" (1 Samuel 25:34), David's anger is appeased. Abigail's foolish and hard-hearted husband is rescued. Abigail is protecting her husband, even though she knows he is acting foolishly.

Much like Abigail's love for Nabal caused her to cover his stupidity with her generosity, Esther's love for her people caused her to stand in the gap for them and go to Ahasuerus. Also, remember that Esther has been his wife for a little over five years; she may also love Ahasuerus. She may have the foresight to know that this rash decision on his part could become the defining moment of his reign. Esther does not want her husband's legacy to be the destruction of the Jews. Like Abigail, Esther is acting out of love without regard to personal consequences. Love for the Jews, love for her husband and his ultimate legacy, and mostly love for the God Who brought her to this point.

> "...let the king and Haman come to the banquet which I will prepare for them, and tomorrow I will do as the king has said."
> Esther 5:8

Once again, Ahasuerus renews his offer to give to Esther anything she petitions of him, up to half of his kingdom. Once again, it may seem to us that Esther has a perfect opportunity to tell the king her request. However, Esther is not trusting in her own wisdom, and something inside her is telling her to wait.

Esther's ultimate request is an even greater cause for concern than going into his chambers uninvited. Esther is intending on asking the king to revoke an order that was written in such a way that it could never be reversed: she is intending on asking the king to go against his own words and come to the rescue of the very people whom Ahasuerus' signature has ordered to kill. Ahasuerus does not know what Esther knows. Considering his volatile temperament, her interference in this matter could easily be misinterpreted and cause his present good mood to disappear quickly.

Will you look up one more verse before we close out for today? Better yet, let's read this one together:

Hatred stirs up strife, But love covers all sins. Proverbs 10:12

Meditate on this little verse throughout your day — "love covers all sins"... your love ought to cover and protect — not expose — the people around you. Let God's love be your cover, and let God's love through you be a cover for the people around you.

Quick prayer: Father, I desire to demonstrate Your love to the people around me... help me to demonstrate Your peace when there is discord, help me to demonstrate Your strength when there is weakness, and help me to know when and how to "step up to the plate" if You need me to stand in the gap for someone in my life!

಄

DAY FOUR: ESTHER 5:7-10

It's so important for you to understand — it is not WHO you are but WHOSE you are! Your view of you will affect almost every area of your life. Ask God for wisdom to know who you are in HIS eyes rather than your own. Our sight is so limited — even when it comes to ourselves!

FRIEND TO FRIEND...

Yesterday we spent so much time with Abigail and David, let's remember what has happened with Esther. Esther invited Ahasuerus and Haman to her quarters for a banquet. They accepted her invitation. Ahasuerus is always in for a dinner, especially when it is about him. Haman is just proud of himself for getting invited at all. Esther prepares the meal for that very day, giving Ahasuerus little time to change his mind. When they were finished eating, King Ahasuerus asked Esther to make her request, repeating his offer that anything she wanted up to half his kingdom would be granted to her.

Ahasuerus is not the only king to make rash, emotional decisions with far-reaching consequences. Mark 6:14-29 relays the history of John the Baptist's tragic death. A rash "heat of the moment" decision is made; at the order of King Herod, Jesus' closest friend is beheaded.

Herod has a history with John the Baptist. In the beginning of this passage, we read that Herod had thrown John in prison. Why was John imprisoned? Some years ago, Herod's brother, Philip, had died. Herod married his brother's widow, Herodias. As Herodias was a close relative, this relationship was considered almost incestuous. John had communicated the truth to Herod, and thereby exposed the king's sin: it was unlawful for Herod to "have his brother's wife" (verse 18). Herod may have been irritated at times by John, but he obviously had a certain amount of fear of him. Herod knew that God was with John. Though Herod protected John, it does not follow that Herod ascribed to John's teachings. Herod revered John as a holy man, but was not interested in giving up his own sins. The respect he had for John did not translate into inspiration to change his wicked lifestyle.

Herodias, Herod's wife, did not have the same sympathy for John that her husband did. She wanted John the Baptist killed, but until now Herod had refused. Herod wanted to protect John, but he also wanted peace with his wife. As a compromise, Herod had put John in jail to placate Herodias. Now Herodias is biding her time.

Sometime after John the Baptist was put in jail and sometime after Herod marries his sister-in-law, Herod has a birthday. Herod gives himself a birthday party, and he is there with all of his officials. When Herodias' daughter comes in and dances for him, lust fills his heart, and he makes an offer to her. Anything she desires will be given to her with only one condition. His rash words, spoken in the passion of the moment, are words which he will come to regret: "up to half my kingdom" (Mark 6:23). After consulting with her mother (who has been waiting for an opportunity to take revenge on John the Baptist), she goes back to Herod and asks for the head of John the Baptist on a platter.

Upon hearing the request, Herod is filled with regret. Though he has protected John in the past (see verse 20), he does not protect him from this. Herod complies with his step-daughter's request. What would cause him to do such a thing? After all these years of fearing John, what caused this change in Herod's attitude toward him? Herod is surrounded by officials who witnessed his promise to Herodias' daughter. For him to refuse her request after telling her that he would give her anything up to half of his kingdom would have been (if you will allow an understatement here) very embarrassing. He goes against his own conscience to protect himself and make sure that he looks good in front of his officials, and afterwards he "was exceedingly sorry" (v.26).

Esther is not like Ahasuerus or even Herod. These kings make decisions in times of great emotion, and both of them have selfish motives. Esther learns of this violent decree against the Jews and does not act out of emotion. She waits three days to take action, and turns to the Lord for direction. Then when she does act, her motives are pure — going into the king's chambers, her attitude is, "If I perish, I perish!" She has no concern for herself because she knows that God will take care of her as she obeys Him. Esther acts out of a passionate concern for her people.

It is that passionate concern that protects Ahasuerus when he makes his offer of anything up to half his kingdom for Esther. Unlike Herodias and her daughter, she will not take advantage of this generous, if misguided and selfish, promise.

> *Then Esther answered and said, "My petition and request is this: If I have found favor in the sight of the king, and if it pleases the king to grant my petition and fulfill my request, then let the king and Haman come to the banquet which I will prepare for them, and tomorrow I will do as the king has said."* Esther 5:7-8

Once again, Esther decides to wait before speaking to the king about the decree against the Jews. Her request is simply that Ahasuerus and Haman join her again for another banquet in her apartment. She takes advantage of his good mood, and asks him to come back tomorrow night with Haman in tow. She promises Ahasuerus that at this next banquet she will tell him the real reason behind these dinners.

Now the dinner with Esther is over, and Haman leaves to go home. What a day for Haman this has been. Singled out to dine with the king and queen, he cannot wait to get home and share the story of this great honor with his friends and family.... specifically how HE was honored by the king and queen!

Haman truly has no clue.

> *So Haman went out that day joyful and with a glad heart...*
> Esther 5:9

"Haman went out that day with a joyful and glad heart". Remember, Haman is a little man with a big position. He is congratulating himself on doing such a fantastic job at the palace. Pleased by such shallow concerns as other people's opinions, it does not take much to raise Haman's spirits. Unfortunately, as man's opinions can make him high, man's opinions can also bring him low. His good mood does not last long.

> *...but when Haman saw Mordecai in the king's gate, and that he did not stand or tremble before him, he was filled with indignation against Mordecai.* Esther 5:9

In spite of the great honor that was bestowed upon him by the king and queen, he allows something small to spoil his mood: he sees Mordecai. His happiness — brought on by man's approval — does not last long. When Haman sees Mordecai and sees that he still will not bow to him, he is filled with indignation again. Of course, when your happiness depends on a man's approval (like Haman feeling important because of his position in the court of Ahasuerus), it is quickly over when a man doesn't approve (like Mordecai refusing to bow to him).

> *Nevertheless Haman restrained himself and went home...*

Esther 5:10a

This time, upon seeing Mordecai refuse to bow to him, Haman restrains himself. Haman is momentarily pacified by his own plans of revenge that are, in his mind, in effect even now. He only has to wait for the appointed time set by his soothsayers (as we read about in chapter 3), and the Jews will be out of his way. Haman is confident that his troubles with Mordecai and anyone else who decides to rebel against him will be over shortly. Haman restrains himself from speaking to Mordecai, and continues on his way home.

When Haman saw Mordecai, he is exactly where he always is: at the king's gates. It is interesting for us to observe what Haman failed to notice. Just three days ago, all the Jews in Shushan were mourning, and Mordecai was right there with them. Wearing sackcloth and ashes, Mordecai could not enter the king's gates because of his mourning. Despite his condition, Mordecai was still outside the king's gates where he could check on Esther. Haman must have been so proud of himself for being able to convince the king to approve his plan of revenge against Mordecai and his people. Because where Mordecai sits in the king's gates is obviously right on his way home, Haman must have seen the mourning; he might even have enjoyed it. (Remember — "Hatred stirs up strife" Proverbs 10:12).

Today, however is a different day for the Jews. Three days ago, they were hopeless and helpless. Today, *their* queen is in the palace acting on their behalf. Mordecai is no longer in mourning, and the fast is over. He is back in the king's gate. The last time Haman noticed Mordecai, he was mourning; and today the mourning is over. Why doesn't Haman see the remarkable difference? Maybe he is so full of himself that he cannot see anything else. He looks at Mordecai and sees only his own hurt ego.

Haman has no idea what is going on.

> *...he [Haman] sent and called for his friends and his wife Zeresh.*
> Esther 5:10

At least for the moment, Mordecai is forgotten. Haman calls for his wife, Zeresh, and all his friends. Now is not a time to worry about some insignificant Jew, is it? No, now is a time to revel in all of his greatness, and Haman takes this opportunity to make sure everyone else is made aware of his greatness as well. Besides, with regards to Mordecai, all he has to do is wait. His plan is in place, and he has no reason to think that everything will not go exactly as he has arranged.

> *Then Haman told them of his great riches, the multitude of his chil-*
> *dren, everything in which the king had promoted him, and how he*
> *had advanced him above the officials and servants of the king.*
> Esther 5:11

As soon as he walks in the door, Haman calls for his friends and for his wife, Zeresh. He has been promoted and honored, and now it is time to enjoy it! He can brag to all his friends, and give them ample opportunity to admire him. He tells them about all *his* money and all about *his* children. He tells them about how the king had promoted *him* and given *him* a position higher than many of the other servants and officials. Just in case all that bragging wasn't quite enough, Haman continues.

> *Moreover Haman said, "Besides, Queen Esther invited no one but*
> *me to come in with the king to the banquet that she prepared; and*
> *tomorrow I am again invited by her, along with the king.*
> Esther 5:12

"Moreover" and "Besides" are two words that mean Haman is not finished yet.... Queen Esther invited only Haman to come and dine with her and the king, so Haman has to share that news as well. He says, "Besides, Queen Esther invited NO ONE BUT ME to come in with the king to the banquet... and tomorrow I AM AGAIN INVITED, along with the king." Did anyone else notice Haman put himself first? The emphasis (or de-emphasis) is mine. In my mind, I imagine that this is Haman's moment, and the key for Haman here is to downplay everyone but himself.

Note the contrast we have in these three personalities. On one side, we have Mordecai and Esther: selfless people who let their promotion come from the Lord, and care only for His approval. They do not wait for accolades from man, and are not working to make themselves look good in the eyes of man. On the other side, we have Haman: selfish and self-serving, he needs other people to think that he is good in order for him to believe it about himself.

One more time: let your self worth come from the Lord. If you are waiting, like Haman, for people to make you feel fulfilled and happy, you are also giving them permission to make you feel empty and miserable. It's a roller coaster not worth the ride.

Look into the mirror of the Word of God (James 1:23-25) to find out who you are in Christ, and walk in it! You are royalty — a daughter of the true KING! Hold your head up, princess — Your Father loves you!

❧

DAY FIVE: ESTHER 5:13-14

We began the week with Esther planning to see Ahasuerus. Now we end the week with Haman planning to see Ahasuerus for a much different reason. It's a blessing and comfort to know that as we obey the Lord, He protects and guides us through perilous times. These are perilous times, don't you agree? Thank God for the anointing — we need it so much!

FRIEND TO FRIEND...

As we have seen demonstrated in Esther this week, a humble and quiet spirit is a great asset. In releasing the need to be considered important by people, a tremendous freedom will be experienced. On the other hand, the Word has a great deal to communicate to us concerning the opposite attitude: pride. In Proverbs 21:24, the Word says that a proud man "acts with arrogant pride". Proverbs 29:23 states that a man's pride will "bring him low". In Proverbs 16:18, it is written that pride comes "before destruction". One passage in particular paints a fairly accurate picture of Haman. Obadiah 3-4 says, "The pride of your heart has deceived you, you who dwell in the clefts of the rock, whose habitation is high; you who say in your heart, 'Who will bring me down to the ground?' Though you ascend as high as the eagle, and though you set your nest among the stars, from there I will bring you down," says the LORD".

Pride brings specific consequences, but we can be encouraged by the specific benefits brought on by the opposite attitude: humility. In Peter 5:5-6, Paul writes that God "gives grace to the humble. Therefore humble yourselves under the mighty hand of God, that He may exalt you in due time, casting all your care upon Him, for He cares for you." To receive grace means to receive favor or blessing. In humbling yourself before God, you are admitting that you are in need of His help. You are admitting that you are in need of His grace. When Esther had to confront the impending destruction of the Jews, she immediately turned to her faith. She humbled herself before the Lord. She knelt before the Lord in prayer, and denied her flesh in a fast. As a result of humbling herself and casting her care upon the Lord, Esther receives the promised grace: Ahasuerus accepts her unannounced visit.

Esther is full of grace and humility, and God's favor is continually upon her life. Haman is full of pride, and he is headed for trouble. Today we find out Haman's next step, and we close this pivotal chapter.

Yet... Esther 5:13

"Yet." A word almost as dangerous as the word "but" which we came across a few chapters ago. After being honored by a private banquet with the king and queen, and an invitation to dine with them again the following night, Haman has received the admiration from man that he craves. Upon coming home, Haman spends all this time bragging about himself, puffing himself up, calling in all his family and friends for his own miniature celebration of himself and his greatness... For someone as conceited as Haman, you would think that this would be considered one of his best days.

And "yet"....

> *So Haman went out that day joyful and with a glad heart; but when Haman saw Mordecai in the king's gate, and that he did not stand or tremble before him, he was filled with indignation against Mordecai.* Esther 5:9

Haman runs into Mordecai — of all the people for him to run into on *this*, his day of days! He restrains himself, but is still filled with indignation at the sight of Mordecai refusing to bow once again. Apparently, the picture of Mordecai standing there in front of him — STANDING not bowing — casts a long dark shadow over his whole little bragging session. After describing the events of his day and the great honors bestowed upon him by the queen, Haman brings his boasting session to an abrupt close with one word: "yet".

> *"Yet all this avails me nothing, so long as I see Mordecai the Jew sitting at the king's gate."* Esther 5:13

"Yet all this avails me nothing..." As long as Mordecai keeps his own position within the king's gate and as along as he refuses to bow to Haman, all of this "honor" that Haman has been experiencing at Ahasuerus' side is nothing to him. Nothing else matters to Haman. "All this avails me nothing", he says. As we discussed before, because he is depending upon approval from man to make him happy, all it takes is disapproval to make him unhappy. It seems that Haman is given to a little drama on top of his conceit. This is a charming combination for any personality.

Haman could use some sound and wise advice at this moment. Unfortunately for Haman, however, he apparently takes his cue from Ahasuerus: like his king, Haman has surrounded himself with people who are as shallow and selfish as he is. Enter Zeresh, Haman's wife.

> *Then his wife Zeresh and all his friends said to him, "Let a gallows be made, fifty cubits high, and in the morning suggest to the king that Mordecai be hanged on it; then go merrily with the king to the banquet."* Esther 5:14a

His wife, Zeresh, and all his friends, tell Haman to build a gallows. After listening to all of Haman's boasting, hearing all the details of the great honor that have come to him, it seems incredible that their first response is to suggest having Mordecai killed. No one suggests that all this fuss over one Jew might seem ridiculous, considering all the other events of the day. All the honor bestowed upon Haman apparently forgotten, his wife presents this plan to kill Mordecai as if it were Haman's only choice.

Once the gallows are built, Zeresh tells Haman to make the suggestion to Ahasuerus that Mordecai be hanged on it. Further than that, Zeresh tells him to "go merrily with the king to the banquet." For any normal person, planning to have someone killed would be inconceivable. To put such a gruesome topic in the same sentence with going happily along to a dinner party seems surreal. Apparently his wife's conversation does not strike Haman as unusual. He seems to understand suggesting to the king that a man be put to death, and then going *merrily* to a dinner. This is the same man that sat down to a drink with the king immediately after plotting to kill an entire nation.

Did you catch that? Haman's wife says, "Just kill Mordecai, and go happily along to your dinner!" What a sad commentary on the value they are placing on human life. One man being put to death is not enough to ruin a good time for Haman. Even the height of the gallows suggested by his friends is ridiculous: 50 cubits is about 75 feet. This figure may be an exaggeration. It may simply represent a number that someone threw out at the moment. However, it could just as easily have been a means of further humiliating Mordecai: at this height, all the inhabitants of Shushan could witness his execution. Haman is first pleased with himself, then this pride causes him to descend even lower. Haman now believes that in order to maintain his high position and the good opinion of his friends, his only choice is to bring Mordecai down.

> *And the thing pleased Haman...* Esther 5:14

Apparently waiting for the appointed date, and taking his revenge on Mordecai at the same time as all the rest of the Jews is no longer an acceptable course of action in Haman's evil mind. As soon as someone suggests a course of action that is more immediate, Haman agrees. Haman is willing to go along with the plan suggested by his friends. Zeresh does not posses the qualities of a godly wife that we see in Esther or even in Abigail. Rather than protecting her husband and steering him away from a bad decision, she encourages him toward this tragic error.

Sadly surrounded by ill-intentioned and foolish people, Haman listens to the only advice he receives. His pride prevents him from stepping back and taking his time in considering the situation. Instead, he desires to appear strong in the eyes of these people.

Needing no encouragement other than what he has received already, Haman makes his decision.

...so he had the gallows made. Esther 5:14

If the Lord has blessed you with godly friends and influences in your life, thank God for them — you might even pray that He would provide you with an opportunity to show these precious people how much you value them! "It is not for you to know times or seasons which the Father has put in His own authority." Acts 1:7

❧

Father, Your love is just right!
If I allow it to, Your love will free me.
Your love will free me to learn the things that You teach me each day,
without worry about the things that I have not been taught yet.
If I can be secure every day in the knowledge that You give,
I do not have to be insecure about the unknown — because nothing is unknown to You!
"Here a little, there a little" is the way that You desire that I grow —
trusting You for every step, and convinced every day that You will teach me today
the very things that I need to know so that I will be best prepared to learn more tomorrow.
Your love will also free me from selfish pride:
as I become confident in you, I will develop the ability to be humble.
I don't have to protect myself or hide my faults:
my shortcomings will ultimately reveal my progress!
Thank you for being my protection, Lord,
and give me strength to trust Your guidance and leave the results entirely in your hands.

ESTHER: CHAPTER 6
Mordecai is honored by Ahasuerus

In Esther 5, Ahasuerus and Haman attend a banquet prepared by Esther especially for them. As soon as the first dinner is over, Ahasuerus tells Esther that any request she makes will be granted to her, "up to half the kingdom". Esther's request is simple: she would like for Ahasuerus and Haman to join her again in her quarters for a banquet the following night. They may think the purpose of these dinners is simply to honor the two of them, but God is working behind the scenes... remember His *providence* is still working! Esther is God's instrument in the palace to rescue the Jews, and she truly recognizes her important purpose in this plan. Mordecai is being used by the Lord outside the palace gates, and he recognizes his vital part in this plan as well.

At the close of chapter 5, Ahasuerus and Haman have just left Esther's first banquet. In regaling his friends and family with tales of his tremendous day, Haman comes to the "fly in the ointment": Mordecai. Seeing Mordecai outside the palace gates refusing to bow was enough to ruin Haman's entire day. When Haman tells his wife and friends, they offer a frightening suggestion: build a gallows and hang Mordecai. Amazingly enough, Haman is "pleased" with the suggestion. As his self worth is dependent on the opinions of other people, does he think the only way to feel better about himself is to kill the one person whose opinions do not stroke his ego?

We have a great contrast in personalities here. On one hand, we have Mordecai and Esther, who are serving the Lord. They are doing their utmost to walk in obedience. Esther and Mordecai know now that they have come to the kingdom "for such a time as this". God is using them, and they are operating in wisdom and in God's providential timing. On the other hand, we have Ahasuerus and Haman, who are serving themselves. They have no idea what is happening in Persia. It won't be long before Ahasuerus and Haman learn what "time" this actually is.

A passage in Ecclesiastes offers a striking parallel to the situation in Persia. In Ecclesiastes 9:14-16, King Solomon relays an event of a "little city". He writes, "There was a little city with few men in it; and a great king came against it, besieged it, and built great snares around it. Now there was found in it a poor wise man, and he by his wisdom delivered the city. Yet no one remembered that same poor man."

Though Persia could hardly be described as a "little city", the men in leadership of Persia could certainly be described as little. Ahasuerus is self absorbed and self serving; Haman is obsessed with promotion and recognition from man. There is one "wise man" whose voice is currently being ignored and forgotten by all in the palace but Esther: Mordecai. Mordecai has continued in faithfulness to his country and to his cousin. His part in exposing an assassination plan and thereby saving the king's life has been all but forgotten. Due to his low position, the king never takes notice of him. The only reason for the attention he receives from Haman is his refusal to bow. Mordecai denies Haman the one thing that Haman desires most from man: public honor. Haman wants to see men physically humbled before him, and Mordecai only bows to One.

Solomon concludes his story with this thought: "Then I said: 'Wisdom is better than strength. Nevertheless the poor man's wisdom is despised, And his words are not heard. Words of the wise, spoken quietly, should be heard rather than the shout of a ruler of fools. Wisdom is better than weapons of war; But one sinner destroys much good' " (Ecclesiastes 9:16-18). Wisdom is more valuable than weapons of war. This is a principle that Mordecai certainly embodies. One sinner destroying much good? That would accurately describe Haman's attempt at destroying the Jews.

Wisdom is truly better than strength. Even if you feel as if your voice is smaller, less popular or quieter than other voices around you, be confident that God will remember you. Do not be motivated by what man thinks; let your self worth come from the Lord. Be guided by the truth that abides in you. As wisdom is a precious and valuable virtue, develop your spirit toward wisdom. The Lord will be your strength!

Esther must be confident that God will remember her this week as she makes her true request to Ahasuerus. She does not ignore Mordecai's warnings. Now it is time to find out the king's response to the same. Her next request will not be another dinner invitation.

ЯR

DAY ONE: ESTHER 6:1-2

The story is moving much faster now! Chapter 6 is a true turning point in our history — events are finally starting to turn back to the Jews' favor. Learn to recognize turning points in your own life, woman of God! God is working on your behalf right now!

FRIEND TO FRIEND...

When we pulled into the parking lot, I stared intently at the building in front of us as if those bricks could offer some clue to my future. I looked over at Michael. He looked handsome in his suit. (Very "pastor like", I thought. Immediately, I wondered inside myself if pastors really had a *look*. If they did, did I want Michael to look like it?) I was wearing my favorite suit and my most uncomfortable shoes. (Now I wondered if it was some sort of unbreakable law of womankind that the best looking shoes also had to be the most painful shoes. Why did I wear these anyway? Didn't I have a pair that matched just as perfectly with my suit and made my feet feel good? Looking down at my feet, I guessed I didn't after all.)

My idle and nervous thoughts were interrupted by the sound of my car door being opened and the feeling of the hot Georgia breeze blowing in. Michael was ready to go inside. Smiling at Michael and stepping out of the car, I wondered why I spent the last thirty seconds wondering what pastors looked like and why pretty shoes were also painful shoes rather than praying about the meeting that was about to take place. (Would I ever learn?) We were planning to leave Florida to become church planters, and this meeting would determine whether we had the blessing of our denomination's Georgia district office.

Michael had started talking to me about his desire to plant a church a little more than two years previous to this meeting. Whenever he mentioned it, I would smile and quote the prophet Nathan's words to David, as David also considered building a house for the Lord: "Go and do all that is in your heart, for the Lord is with you" (2 Samuel 1:3). Doesn't that sound precious and encouraging? I have to be honest; that was the beginning and the end of my encouragement for a while. I never discouraged Michael, but I also never pursued any serious conversation about church planting. I would smile and listen patiently, inside hoping against hope that he was kidding. Every time he said, "Jennifer, I want to plant a church"; I heard, "Jennifer, even though we have three small children, I'd like to quit my job, move to a new state and pastor a church that currently does not exist."

One evening, I went to our room and found a book Michael had been reading about church planting on my night stand. I realized that after a year of smiling and offering pat words, I was going to have to face the fact that God was doing something in my husband. I needed to get busy praying about church planting as well.

As I prayed, the Lord began to reveal to me what I had been afraid to hear: Michael was being called to plant a church. As his wife, I was being called as well. It did not take long for me to realize this was God's will for us. My feelings were confirmed as I began to move beyond mental assent into excitement over the prospect of a new chapter in our lives.

In Luke 14:28-30, Jesus had wise counsel concerning making plans and beginning projects. He told his disciples and the multitudes that surrounded Him, "For which of you, intending to build a tower, does not sit down first and count the cost, whether he has enough to finish it – lest, after he has laid the foundation, and is not able to finish, all who see it begin to mock him, saying, 'This man began to build and was not able to finish.' "

I felt as though we had prayed. I even felt as though we had prayed enough (is it possible to ever pray *enough*?). If the cost was not counted beforehand, it was due to lack of experience and knowledge. Looking back, perhaps we didn't know all that should be included as we were "counting the cost". From a mom's perspective, I thought about my children. Would they be okay with a big move? I didn't really consider myself; after all, I'd learn to be content wherever Michael took us. From a husband's perspective, Michael thought about the entire family: uprooting all of us to go to a situation where the only guarantee was the promise that the Lord put in his heart was daunting to say the least. Beyond his faith, there was no promise of salary, no congregation, no property, no job… there was only a vision: a vision of pastoring a life giving church in his hometown.

Sharing our hearts with the district leadership, we experienced God's favor through these men. Gaining the approval we sought from our new superintendent was the final confirmation we needed to begin the process of church planting. Humbling ourselves before the Lord, we walked out of the meeting ready to begin building.

In Persia, Haman is starting a new project as well: the gallows on which he plans to hang Mordecai. Unfortunately for Haman, he did not "count the cost."

> *Then his wife Zeresh and all his friends said to him, "Let a gallows be made, fifty cubits high, and in the morning suggest to the king that Mordecai be hanged on it; then go merrily with the king to the banquet." And the thing pleased Haman; so he had the gallows made.* Esther 5:14

Haman's friends tell him to build a gallows in his own front yard for the purpose of hanging Mordecai. Led by his wife Zeresh, Haman's friends tell him that he can suggest the idea to Ahasuerus tomorrow and then "go merrily to the banquet". Pleased with the plan presented to him by his friends, Haman forges ahead and has the gallows made.

Apparently the thought occurs to no one, least of all Haman, that this garish request might be refused when presented to the king. Haman has no thought for anything beyond this moment. With no forethought and no consideration for any concern other than his own, Haman begins to build.

In the meantime, we have to take a lesson where we can: it is vitally important to follow the advice of Jesus and "count the cost". This lack of planning on

Haman's part reveals his selfish pride. Haman does not even wait to find out if the king agrees with the building of the gallows. Perhaps he does not think that the king's permission is necessary. Perhaps he does not want to appear weak or powerless in front of his wife and friends. Jesus said that the man who built without counting the cost would be "mocked" when it was found that he could not finish. Be careful that you do not find yourself in a similar situation. Determine you will not be like Haman: consult your King before any decision!

Haman's gallows will be put to use, but not for the purpose he intends. His failure to "count the cost" will turn out to be a tragic error.

While Haman is celebrating with his friends *and* building gallows for the purpose of humiliating and killing a man (does this strike anyone else as a very strange combination of activities?), Ahasuerus is back in his quarters at the palace.

> *That night the king could not sleep. So one was commanded to bring the book of the records of the chronicles; and they were read before the king.* Esther 6:1

For some reason, Ahasuerus is having difficulty falling asleep. After the banquet prepared for him by his wife, he returns to his own quarters where he tosses and turns. He calls for one of his servants to come to him and read to him from the chronicles of his reign. (It comes as no surprise that Ahasuerus would enjoy a story about his favorite character: himself!)

Even in a king losing sleep, we can see God's providence at work. Psalm 127:2 says that the Lord gives sleep. If the Lord can give sleep, then He can also take it away! Perhaps Ahasuerus' insomnia can be attributed to the Lord keeping him awake for a specific purpose: there is an event that Ahasuerus needs to re-discover.

Before Ahasuerus is reminded of a certain incident, let's take this opportunity to remember it ourselves.

> *In those days, while Mordecai sat within the king's gate, two of the king's eunuchs, Bigthan and Teresh, doorkeepers, became furious and sought to lay hands on King Ahasuerus. So the matter became known to Mordecai, who told Queen Esther, and Esther informed the king in Mordecai's name. And when an inquiry was made into the matter, it was confirmed, and both were hanged on a gallows; and it was written in the book of the chronicles in the presence of the king.* Esther 2:21-23

You remember that some time ago, Mordecai had uncovered a plot to assassinate the king. He overhears two of the king's servants, Bigthan and Teresh, making plans to "lay hands on King Ahasuerus". Armed with this information, Mordecai immediately sends word to Esther. Esther tells Ahasuerus of the plan to kill him. Giving credit where credit is due, she even tells the king who uncovered the dark plan: Mordecai. After the story is confirmed, Bigthan and Teresh are hanged on the gallows.

"And it was written in the book of the chronicles of the king." In God's providence, the Lord made sure that Mordecai's name and actions were recorded. Mordecai's loyalty, though seemingly forgotten at one time, is being brought to light once again.

Immediately following Mordecai's intervention in this assassination plot, Ahasuerus gives someone a promotion. However, it is not the person that came to his rescue.

> *After these things King Ahasuerus promoted Haman, the son of Hammedatha the Agagite, and advanced him and set his seat above all the princes who were with him* Esther 3:1.

"After these things" (3:1) is referring to the assassination plot uncovered by Mordecai, yet Haman is the one celebrated and promoted. Mordecai, the man who had just saved the king's life, is ignored.

Part of recognizing God's providence at work is learning to see Him in the details. At the end of chapter 2: "and it was written in the book of the chronicles in the presence of the king." As the assassination attempt was unsuccessful, Ahasuerus lived through this drama once. As the details of each day were recorded in the chronicles, it became Persian history. Now, on a sleepless night as his servant reads it back to him, he re-lives the event in his mind.

Little did Ahasuerus know that this chapter in his life would turn out to be so important. Of course, neither did Mordecai!

God knew, and in His *providence* had this detail exactly in place. The importance of this detail would be revealed at exactly the right moment, to exactly the right person.

> *And it was found written that Mordecai had told of Bigthan and Teresh, two of the king's eunuchs, the doorkeepers who had sought to lay hands on King Ahasuerus. Then the king said, "What honor or dignity has been bestowed on Mordecai for this?" And the king's servants who attended him said, "Nothing has been done for him."*
> Esther 6:2-3

Ahasuerus is read the story of the assassination plot that had taken place some five years earlier. It seems random: why did the servant pick out *this* specific story, *this* specific day, *this* specific event? These histories were long and sometimes tedious. He could have read any story.

Easy to explain in one word: providence!

Your Heavenly Father keeps you continually — your "every day" is important to Him! Thank Him for His presence in your life, and do your best to recognize Him in every circumstance!

℘

DAY TWO: ESTHER 6:3-5

God is in the details — the minutia, the day-to-day that we can easily pass off as common. Find joy in a regular, routine, seemingly dull event today — and praise God for His great interest in YOU! You are the apple of His eye!

FRIEND TO FRIEND...

Our happiest days are easy to remember: a birthday, a wedding, a first day of school, a graduation. Even sad days are nearly impossible to forget, however hard we might try to erase them from our memories: a tragedy, a funeral, a heartbreak. Offering sometimes rare opportunities to show our true colors, such days as these bring out our best or expose our worst.

In between these days, heartwarming and heartbreaking, we have "everydays" when nothing out of the ordinary seems to happen. You got up and went to work, had lunch with a girlfriend, finished a little laundry or cooked a meal for your family. The sun shone on your face, and God was good. Perhaps a little rain came, but God sustained you. It is these "everydays" that we tend to overlook, these days that are too readily forgotten. It is in these "everydays" that it might become easy to overlook God's goodness. Psalm 118:23-24 comes to mind again, as it seems to so many times in my life like a familiar theme, "This was the Lord's doing and it is marvelous...this is the day that the Lord has made..." God is in the "everydays".

Through the days you will not be able to forget, as well as the days you will not be able to remember, God is working. Big events and little happenings, it is all "the Lord's doing" and "it is marvelous"! In an event that may be easily forgotten by man, God never forgets. In His providential power, a common day becomes an extraordinary circumstance for change. A king's sleepless night might seem like a small event, but God is in the details.

In Persia, King Ahasuerus has had a rough night. Unable to sleep, he calls for a servant to read to him from his book of chronicles. Upon hearing the history that the servant chose to read, Ahasuerus is reminded that Mordecai saved him from an assassination attempt some years ago. For some inexplicable reason, Ahasuerus has been able to forget that there were once people who had planned to kill him.

Then the king said, "What honor or dignity has been bestowed on Mordecai for this?" Esther 6:3a

Ahasuerus wants to know what honor has been bestowed on the man who saved his life. The way in which Ahasuerus worded this question is in keeping with his selfish style: he does not ask, "What did *I* do to honor this person?" Ahasuerus asks what has been done, as if honoring Mordecai might have been someone else's responsibility entirely. Even considering the familiar wording, this question seems a little out of character for Ahasuerus. For what may be the first time, he seems concerned for someone other than himself. Making this even more unusual, Ahasuerus seems concerned about someone other than himself receiving recognition.

And the king's servants who attended him said, "Nothing has been done for him." Esther 6:3b

The servants answered the king, "Nothing has been done for him." Nothing had been done for Mordecai. If Ahasuerus did not remember anything else about the incident, it is no surprise that he does not remember how it was concluded. However full of himself Ahasuerus is, even he knows that Mordecai should have been honored for this selfless deed.

So the king said, "Who is in the court?" Now Haman had just entered the outer court of the king's palace to suggest that the king hang Mordecai on the gallows that he had prepared for him. Esther 6:4

Haman has just walked in to the palace gates. He is coming with a single purpose in mind: to suggest to the king that Mordecai be hanged. The last time Haman brought a plan to the king (the order to kill all the Jews), he presented his request in such a way as to make it very easy for the king to consent to his evil plan.

Once again, Haman has made it very easy for Ahasuerus to agree with this new plan: the gallows are already being built at no expense to the king, and Mordecai can be executed at little or no inconvenience to the king. Of course, it does not enter his mind that Ahasuerus might refuse. Why should it? Certainly Ahasuerus would not be looking for a way to *honor* a Jew, considering that he already agreed to Haman's previous decree. It was not too long ago that the king agreed to utterly destroy all the Jews in Persia, so why should he care about killing one of them just a little early?

Ahasuerus' memory may be short, but it is not *that* short.

The king asks his servants what has been done for Mordecai. When he learns that nothing has been done for him, Ahasuerus' first question is, "Who is in the court?" As is his pattern, Ahasuerus is looking for someone to give him advice. We have yet to see him make a decision on his own. Now Ahasuerus is looking for the first available person to help him decide how to honor Mordecai. When the servants reply to his question, Ahasuerus is most likely pleased to find out that Haman is so close by. Now his closest advisor can help him decide how to honor Mordecai.

The king's servants said to him, "Haman is there, standing in the court." And the king said, "Let him come in." Esther 6:5

On his way into the king's inner court, Haman is missing some important pieces of information. He does not know what a restless night the king has passed. He does not know that Ahasuerus has been reminded of how he was rescued from an assassination attempt. He does not know that the king has just learned that Mordecai was the rescuer. Haman does not know, that even at this very moment, Ahasuerus is trying to decide how best to honor Mordecai for saving his life.

The one piece of information that Haman does have is the same piece of information that is going to lead to his destruction: Haman knows that Mordecai is a Jew. Armed with only this piece of knowledge and his prideful anger, he is going to Ahasuerus to ask that Mordecai be put to death immediately.

And the king said, "Let him [Haman] come in." Esther 6:5

All the "blanks" are about to be filled in for Haman.

We do not always have all the answers — and that's okay! Thank God that we are not like Haman or Ahasuerus... we trust the One Who does have all the answers! Sometimes it has to be enough to trust in God's knowledge. He is able!

ॐ

DAY THREE: ESTHER 6:6

Pride comes before a fall... Father, help us to look to You every day. You are our source and our strength — help us to keep You first in our lives!

Friend to friend.... In the familiar story of Jesus and the woman at the well, a Samaritan woman meets Jesus at the well in the center of town. Though Jews and Samaritans were not generally friendly, Jesus was no common Jew. He opens a dialogue with her by asking for a drink. When she seems surprised that a Jew would ask a Samaritan for a favor, Jesus tells her, "If you only knew what a wonderful gift God has for you, and who I am, you would ask me for some living water!" (John 4:10 TLB). In other words, Jesus was telling her that He was not merely talking to a Samaritan, He was talking to a woman in need. She was not merely talking to a Jew, she was talking to her Savior. If she understood Who He was, she would be asking Him to fulfill her needs, not the other way around.

Jesus explains to this woman, "whoever drinks of this water will thirst again, but whoever drinks of the water that I shall give him will never thirst. But the water that I shall give him will become in him a fountain of water springing up into everlasting life" (John 4:13-14). This unnamed woman may have thought she was thirsty for water but through the simple conversation recorded over the next few verses, Jesus was able to reveal her true desire: she wanted acceptance and salvation from the Messiah. Used and left empty by men, she wanted change in her life. A sip of water from the well would provide momentary relief for her physical need, but her true need would remain unfulfilled.

She had a choice. She could take the water from the well, and leave Jesus alone. She could return to the empty shell of a life that she led with some man who used her like the other men in her life had used her. It wasn't pretty, but at least it was familiar. Knowing what she had settled for and also knowing what greatness was possible in her life, Jesus looked into her heart. The deciding moment; the moment between clinging to the familiar and letting it go for the hope of something more must have created excruciating suspense for our Lord. While His love was a gift to her, her free will was also a gift. She had to choose to change her life. Sometimes it's just easier to stick with what you know. As she ran away, imagine the joy in His heart as He heard her immediately tell the first people she saw: "Come, see a Man who told me all things that I ever did. Could this be the Christ?" (John 4:29). Now that she knew the right question to ask, she would find the right answer.

Like this woman at the well, we have a choice: we can try to fill ourselves with the temporal and transitory, or we can allow the Lord to fill us with something that will last. Taking a drink from "this water" at the well may have been easier for the Samaritan woman; but a break from the familiar, an acceptance of what she could not create for herself, would change her life forever. The temporal will not satisfy; only Jesus can fulfill your every need. What you can do for yourself will not last; what Jesus does for you is forever.

Haman is about to be given a choice of sorts. Ahasuerus has a question for him. Wrongly convinced he can be satisfied by what he can create for himself, he gives an answer.

His answer will change his life, but first let's hear the question.

> *So Haman came in, and the king asked him, "What shall be done*
> *for the man whom the king delights to honor?"* Esther 6:6a

Haman loves the attention that he receives from the king, and welcomes any opportunity he gets to be close to Ahasuerus. When he is summoned, he comes. He is probably looking forward to having more fantastic stories about himself to tell his wife and friends. Haman is becoming fairly predictable. It did not take long for his character to be revealed to us. For Ahasuerus, however, discovering Haman's true colors will take a little longer. Ahasuerus asks him, "What should be done for the man whom the king delights to honor?"

Now Haman thought in his heart, "Whom would the king delight to honor more than me?" Esther 6:6b

He considers it in his heart, and decides that it must be him on whom the king wishes to bestow honor. Haman must be delighted to hear this question. Of course, who could Ahasuerus wish to honor more than Haman? Haman cannot imagine anyone more deserving than himself to be honored by the king. This morning is going even better than Haman had anticipated! Already invited into the king's quarters this morning, already invited to a second banquet with the queen tonight, and now Ahasuerus is planning on honoring him? Yesterday was nothing compared to this great day: imagine the boasting that will be going on in Haman's home tonight! Haman's pride will become his downfall.

The Word says that God "resists the proud" (James 4:6). In one of his letters, Paul warns young Timothy to "withdraw" from a proud person (1 Timothy 6:3-5). With such serious warnings (the knowledge that God will not be drawn to a prideful person should be taken as a warning to the believer), we need to focus on what qualities should be developed in us. With every warning, there is an encouragement or instruction, and James 4:6 is no exception: "He gives grace to the humble".

The Father's love for us is unconditional and everlasting. No matter what your course of action, no matter what your attitude, God's love for you never changes. The Word says that He resists the proud, but never does it say that He does not love them. Though you can always be confident of God's love, it will take a deliberate effort on your part to daily live in His presence. As you love the Lord and submit to His love for you, purpose in your heart to do your utmost to please Him.

If pride is not pleasing to the Lord, what qualities are pleasing to Him? For an example, 1 Peter 1:7 tells us that the "genuineness of your faith" is "much more precious than gold". A genuine faith readily recognizes the sovereignty of God and is quick to become humble before Him. Another way to please God might be found in 1 Peter 3:4. Here. Paul conveys that it is your inner person, the "beauty of a gentle and quiet spirit which is very precious in the sight of God". A quiet spirit does not flaunt itself; a gentle spirit puts the needs of others before its own. Purpose in your heart not only to resist the proud — resist becoming proud yourself. Psalm 10:4 states that the "wicked in his proud countenance does not seek God; God is in none of his thoughts." Let go of your pride, and begin to make pleasing your Heavenly Father a joyful discipline.

Driven by his selfish pride, Haman is only interested in pleasing himself... and is he going to fail miserably. The king cannot sleep. Rather than a musician or some other form of entertainment, the king calls for a chronicler to help him pass the time. The chronicler chooses the story of the assassination, some five years past, just out of the blue... Ahasuerus cannot figure out how to honor Mordecai, the man who saved his life. At the very moment that the king is seeking advice, the servants notice Haman approaching the palace.

A series of mere coincidences? No, this is a carefully laid plan orchestrated by our Father. God is faithful. All knowing and all seeing, in His providence, events are carefully and purposefully planned.

Refuse the temporal; trust in God's providential plan for you.
He will fulfill your every need along the way!

ℵ

DAY FOUR: ESTHER 6:7-11
God made a great sacrifice for you, the greatest sacrifice. Though it may seem small in your eyes, purpose to make your life a sacrifice for Him. How can you "decrease" so that Jesus in you might "increase"? (John 3:30)

FRIEND TO FRIEND...
In 2 Samuel 24, we have an account of David's census in Israel. Though the reason is uncertain, it is clear that God did not want this census to be taken and was greatly angered by David's ordering this counting. Following the census, David realizes his mistake and repents. The Scripture tells us his "heart condemned him" (2 Samuel 24:10). Through the prophet Gad, God gives David three choices: seven years of famine on the land, three months being pursued by his enemies, or a plague that will last three days (see 2 Samuel 24:13). Heartbroken by the consequences of his own evil choices, David pleads with Gad, "Please let us fall into the hand of the LORD, for His mercies are great" (2 Samuel 24:14). In other words, "Let God do what He determines is most appropriate; I have faith in His mercy."

God sends a plague. In those three short days, some seventy thousand men are struck down as the angel of the Lord passes through. When the angel approaches what is called the threshing floor, a wide open space or barn area, the Lord stops the plague with three simple yet powerful words: "It is enough..." When David realizes the plague has ended, Gad speaks to him again. He tells David to build an altar to the Lord on this threshing floor. In the midst of horrifying destruction and almost incomprehensible loss of life, David is instructed by the Lord, through the prophet Gad, to create a place of worship. David is instructed to worship. His sin has caused these deaths, his disobedience has caused this destruction; he is surrounded by evidence of his shortcomings and reasons to be in desperate mourning, and God tells him to *worship*. Surely, this was meant to be a sacrifice of praise.

David does not hesitate to follow the Lord's instruction this time. As he approaches the threshing floor, the owner of this area sees him coming. As King David and his servants come, Araunah falls before him. Humbled by the presence of the king, his action signifies a willingness to serve. When David tells Araunah that he would like to buy the threshing floor and whatever materials or tools that will be needed to build an altar, Araunah tells David, "Let my lord take and offer up whatever seems good to him. Look, here are oxen for burnt sacrifice, and threshing implements and the yokes of the oxen for wood. All these, O king, Araunah has given to the king" (2 Sam 24:22-23). A generous offer, to be certain. Araunah's generosity could be motivated two ways on this day. First, he could be loyal to the king and desires to serve David. Secondly, he could have been affected by this plague as well. Among the seventy thousand men killed could have been family, friends, workers or servants of Araunah. He knows that one of David's primary purposes in coming to worship is so that the plague will "be withdrawn from the people" (2 Samuel 24:21), and Araunah has an equally urgent desire to see the plague come to a quick end.

Whatever the reason for Araunah's generosity, David's answer is clear and decided: "No, but I will surely buy it from you for a price; nor will I offer burnt offerings to the LORD my God with that which costs me nothing" (2 Samuel 24:24). David refuses to offer to the Lord *that which has cost him nothing*. As the praise is meant to come as a result of sacrifice, the material, the substance that makes the praise possible, must also be a result of sacrifice.

In refusing to make an offering to the Lord that cost him nothing, David is also refusing to create a solution or reward for himself. If this plague is to end, it must be at the Lord's discretion, not at a sorry attempt to manipulate. When the plague does end, David will not be able to take credit for the relief; he will have to say, "I worshipped the Lord, I trusted His mercy... thanks be unto God." David is demonstrating a principle that is as timeless as it is true: that which costs us nothing will eventually mean nothing to us.

Haman is not operating in the light of such wisdom. He has been asked how a man should be honored by the king. Without any attempt to earn any honor, he tries to create something for himself. Even if Haman were to receive this honor that he describes to King Ahasuerus, it would not be enough for him. Only God can fill you up! When you try to fill yourself with something that you can do for yourself, you will always come up empty. It will never be enough. What is truly needed is something that only God can provide. Be careful every day that you are looking to God as your true and only source. Develop a desire for the everlasting in your life. Trust God to provide for you.

It is important to note the end result of David's worship and return to obedience. 2 Samuel 24:25 says, "the Lord heeded the prayers for the land and the plague was withdrawn from Israel".

Let's return to Persia and find out how Haman answers Ahasuerus.

What shall be done for the man whom the king delights to honor?
Esther 6:6

Haman's mind is reeling trying to come up with a suitable way to honor the "man whom the king delights to honor". He easily became convinced that this honor is coming to him. Since Haman depends on man to promote him and make him feel worthy, this is a fantasy come true: he now gets to determine his own fate (or so he thinks). He does not have to think long to come up with an answer.

And Haman answered the king, "For the man whom the king delights to honor, let a royal robe be brought which the king has worn, and a horse on which the king has ridden, which has a royal crest placed on its head. Then let this robe and horse be delivered to the hand of one of the king's most noble princes, that he may array the man whom the king delights to honor. Then parade him on horseback through the city square, and proclaim before him: 'Thus shall it be done to the man whom the king delights to honor!'"
Esther 6:7-9

Haman comes up with a good one! First, he deserves to be clothed in royalty: "let a royal robe be brought". Not just any robe, however: one that has been worn by the king himself. Next, he should have a horse, "on which the king has ridden", that has the royal crest on its head. Any man deserving so great an honor from the king should not have to walk. All of these items should be delivered to him by the most noble prince that serves the king. Haman is thinking that being shown honor by the most noble prince in the kingdom would certainly inspire honor from everyone else. Lastly, but surely one of the most important aspects of this plan, all of this should be done *publicly* and *loudly*. The noble prince should parade him through the city square while he shouts before him: "Thus shall it be done for the man whom the king delights to honor!"

Notice that Haman has no interest in earning any of this honor. Remember that this entire time Haman (even though no one has confirmed this) is convinced that he is describing the honor that is coming to him. He does not ask what he as done to receive it, or show any humility in receiving it. Haman does not thank Ahasuerus for this honor. He does not give any thought to any thing other than this great honor that *he* is about to receive. He wants to be wrapped in a robe belonging to the king. In other words, he desires other people to identify his position as being on the same level with Ahasuerus. He wants to ride through the town with a man shouting out his greatness. It should come as no surprise that Haman wants a man to proclaim this honor; Haman demands affirmation from man constantly. He wants all of this to be literally handed to him.

Haman is looking to fill himself with something that he can create for himself. For example, this reward that he came up with to honor himself. As mentioned earlier, that which costs us nothing will eventually mean nothing to us. Even if Haman were to receive this honor he describes to King Ahasuerus, eventually it would not be enough for him.

Back at the palace, Haman has suggested his idea of honor to Ahasuerus. Apparently reveling in his moment of fantasy, Haman has all but forgotten his true purpose this morning: to ask that Ahasuerus allow him to hang Mordecai on the gallows that he built yesterday in his front yard.

> *Then the king said to Haman, "Hurry, take the robe and the horse,*
> *as you have suggested, and do so for Mordecai the Jew who sits within*
> *the king's gate! Leave nothing undone of all that you have spoken."*
> Esther 6:10

Ahasuerus loves Haman's idea. He tells Haman to "hurry" and carry out this plan! However, Haman had not considered that it is Ahasuerus' wish to honor Mordecai. Haman is completely taken aback when he hears the object of King Ahasuerus' delight. Who is the most noble prince that, according to Haman's own plan, that is supposed to lead this parade in Mordecai's honor? Haman. To make sure that this plan is carried out in full detail and glory, Ahasuerus charges Haman to "leave nothing undone of all that you have spoken."

From his fantasy world of glory from the king, Haman is brought back to reality with a sudden shock: *Mordecai* is the man whom Ahasuerus wishes to honor? With his return to reality comes a return to his senses. Haman remembers now what he had momentarily forgotten: his design this morning was to ask Ahasuerus to execute Mordecai. Now, he finds Mordecai is to be honored. To make it worse, it is Haman who must publicly honor him.

Ahasuerus is unaware of the personal conflict between Haman and Mordecai, but there are several people in the city of Shushan who are not ignorant of their history. When Mordecai first refused to bow to Haman, he was questioned by other officials as to the reason. They reported this reason back to Haman. Now Haman must parade Mordecai around in front of the same people that witnessed

Mordecai's "disrespect" to Haman. It is more than just officials who know of the conflict: do not forget that the Jews in Shushan have been praying and fasting for Esther to rescue them. They know the source of the conflict. Haman must parade Mordecai before the Jews as well. Can you imagine anything more embarrassing for Haman than this scenario?

After all his boasting to his family and friends, all the great things that had happened to him at the palace turned out to be "nothing" (Esther 5:13). Once again, Haman cannot see anything good in the situation. He does not notice that in his own plan he asked King Ahasuerus to choose his "most noble prince" to carry out the honor. Ahasuerus chose him, signifying Haman as the most noble prince. Haman does not care. As long as someone else is receiving glory, he cannot be happy.

Haman has no one to blame but himself here. His situation was created by HAMAN for HAMAN. When we try to create something for ourselves, it always turns out to be wrong.

> So Haman took the robe and the horse, arrayed Mordecai and led him on horseback through the city square, and proclaimed before him, "Thus shall it be done to the man whom the king delights to honor!" Esther 6:11

Haman has not made wise decisions in the past, but even he knows better than to disobey an order given by the king. Haman collects the articles that he thought were intended for him. He knows exactly where he will find Mordecai: sitting in the king's gate, as he has every day since Esther's being taken to the palace years ago. He dresses Mordecai and parades him through the city square, the center of activity, shouting before him, "Thus shall it be done for the man whom the king delights to honor!"

Changing one letter to a capital makes an amazing difference in that sentence: "Thus shall it be done for the man whom the **King** delights to honor!" For every good thing that the Lord has for you, the devil has a counterfeit. Let's look at Haman's plan one more time before we close for today.

Haman asked for a robe and crown: "the Lord will give you a crown of righteousness" (2 Timothy 4:8).

Haman asked for a noble prince to be made low before him: "Jesus humbled Himself to a degree that we cannot possibly understand in order to save us from death" (Philippians 2:8).

Haman asked that a man proclaim his greatness loudly: "the Lord will rejoice over you with singing" (Zephaniah 3:17).

"Thus shall it be done" for the *woman* that the King delights to honor as well!

Let your promotion come from the Lord, woman of God! He delights in blessing you!

DAY FIVE: ESTHER 6:12-14

Sometimes the only way to survive any day is a deliberate faith in God. Trust God to keep you and order your steps — ask Him to steady you so that you will not become emotional at every turn... there is a great difference between emotion and passion! Learn to discern the difference between the two in your life.

FRIEND TO FRIEND...

Paul offers valuable instruction in Philippians 2:3-4: "Let nothing be done through selfish ambition or conceit, but in lowliness of mind let each esteem others better than himself. Let each of you look out not only for his own interests, but also for the interests of others." Paul's words are not easy; it is a habit that must be practiced. Putting other people first does not always come naturally, and it becomes increasingly more difficult on our worst days.

Invariably, it is on my "bad days" that my focus is entirely on me: how someone wronged *me*, interrupted *me*, or ignored *me*. On those days, it takes the Holy Spirit to remind me that I must look up "from whence comes my help" (Psalms 121:1). I must take my focus off of myself and get it on the Lord. Where does your help come from? In Psalms 121:1-2, the psalmist writes, "I will lift up my eyes to the hills – from whence comes my help? My help comes from the LORD, Who made heaven and earth." In order to receive the help available to you, you must first give up your pride and take your eyes off of yourself.

When Michael and I first married, I began to notice a pattern: when one of us was "down in the dumps", the other went right down as well. If it is true that misery loves company, we were becoming good at keeping each other's misery company! As the months passed, we realized misery also breeds misery. Solomon offered the wisdom that we needed in Ecclesiastes 4:9-10, "two are better than one, because they have a good reward for their labor. For if they fall, one will lift up his companion. But woe to him who is alone when he falls, for he has no one to help him up." I realized that every time I went "down in the dumps" along with Michael, he was left with no one to "help him up", and vice versa. We purposed early on that when one of us was "down", the other would encourage and comfort *without* joining the "pity party". If it is needed, we can remind each other to "look up". In this case, two are better than one. To maintain any healthy close friendship, both must be willing to "esteem others better than himself".

Haman's sight is so limited that he cannot see anyone but himself. His point of reference always begins and ends with himself. Haman's decisions are made based on his feelings alone, without regard for anyone else. Unfortunately when

Haman's "pity party" begins, he does not have the benefit of the Holy Spirit or even a good friend to remind him to "look up". Let's find out how Haman and the people around him respond to his "bad day".

Yesterday, Haman enters the king's gates with the intention of having Mordecai hanged. When he goes to King Ahasuerus, he discovers Ahasuerus wants to honor Mordecai. To make it worse, Ahasuerus makes it Haman's responsibility to see to it that Mordecai is honored in the very manner in which Haman had wanted to be honored himself. Causing great embarrassment to Haman, he has to publicly honor Mordecai.

> *Afterward Mordecai went back to the king's gate. But Haman hurried to his house, mourning and with his head covered.*
> Esther 6:12

"Afterward Mordecai went back to the king's gate." No ceremony, no bragging, no throwing himself a party for the honor bestowed upon him by Ahasuerus and Haman. In sharp contrast to the personalities of Ahasuerus and Haman, Mordecai is not distracted from his purpose because of flattery from men. The honor may be appreciated, but not important enough to cause him to sway from his original purpose. God is his source, and he goes back to where we usually find him: the king's gate. Mordecai is faithful to God and faithful to Esther as well. Besides, he knows the conflict is not yet over. Esther has one more banquet for the king and Haman.

Haman, however, is in a much different emotional state. As soon as he finishes with Mordecai (and this was a different kind of "finish" than he was originally intending), he covers his head and mourns. Haman goes home to his wife utterly defeated. The fact that he had to participate in someone other than himself receiving honor was what brought on his mourning. Haman did not lose anything or suffer any tragedy. Haman was not demoted, he was not disgraced in front of the king; and other than his pride, he was not hurt. Haman is an emotional man and his mood is dependent on other people. By his standards, this was not a good day.

Haman's day is not going to get any better from here.

When Haman told his wife Zeresh and all his friends everything that had happened to him, his wise men and his wife Zeresh said to him,

> *If Mordecai, before whom you have begun to fall, is of Jewish descent, you will not prevail against him but will surely fall before him.* Esther 6:13

Haman goes home and tells his wife, his family, and all his friends about what has happened. The chronicler does not tell us what he says, but we can imagine the tragedy that it became through Haman's tendency to exaggerate!

The last time Haman's wife Zeresh gave advice it did not turn out well. This time she does not have good news, but she is exactly right. She tells Haman that he cannot prevail over Mordecai if Mordecai really is of Jewish descent. "If" is a strange word to place in that sentence — there is no question of Mordecai's heritage at this point. Zeresh may be trying to soften the blow to Haman, but at this point there can really be no denying that Haman's time of favor with the king is coming to a close.

Zeresh is also referring to the long conflict between the Agagites and the Jews. She understands that this conflict did not begin with Mordecai refusing to bow to Haman. We have already discussed the conflict between these people, and we already know Haman is an Agagite. Remember that "Agag" refers to a person rather than a place — King Agag of the Amalekites.

In Exodus 17:15-16, the Lord swore that He would be at war with Amalek from generation to generation. The Lord cannot be defeated! Even though Zeresh and Haman are not believers, they know their history. Through their history, Zeresh is able to predict their future. She tells Haman that he cannot win over Mordecai. Unfortunately, Haman is unable to find a sympathetic ear; all of his friends are in agreement with Zeresh. Even his "wise" men cannot tell him any differently.

Reading this same verse in the Message translation is interesting. Haman's wife tells him, "If this Mordecai is in fact a Jew, your bad luck has only begun. You don't stand a chance against him — you're as good as ruined." Not exactly what Haman was hoping for from his "helpmate". Haman is "down in the dumps", and Zeresh is going down with him.

If it is possible, Haman's wife has just encouraged him toward an even more dangerous place emotionally than he was in before. Haman's wife confirms for Haman the very thing he had begun to fear in chapter 5: in order to keep his high position and friends/family's good opinion, he must bring Mordecai down. In essence, Zeresh tells her husband something like this: "Haman, there is no way you can win against Mordecai. You only have one option if you want to come out on top: as he is the competition, you must eliminate him."

Beyond these spiteful words is another darker and more discouraging message: "Get used to this feeling of defeat and humiliation that you are experiencing now because this will become the theme of your life. There is no way for you to become any greater or better than you are today. You will never enjoy higher promotion or greater success than you have already attained." Horrible words to hear from anyone, let alone the one person in his life who should have been dedicated to his success and well-being. Unfortunately, it becomes worse.

In casually suggesting Mordecai's murder, Zeresh's meaning to Haman was this: "In order for you to maintain your current position, you must not allow anyone to surpass you. It is impossible for you to improve, so you must do what is necessary to maintain the appearance of high position. If someone seems to be achieving, kick him down. Kill him. Do whatever it is you have to do to keep the look of your high office. It wasn't your talents that got you here, Haman, and it won't be your talents that keep you here. Mordecai is not the last threat to your position; he is merely the first. You've already begun to fall before him. Kill him now before you fall any further."

Father God, help us. If you have come to a place where you feel as if the only way for you to succeed is by stopping the progress of others, you are in a dangerous place. If the only way for you to feel good about yourself is to make others feel badly about themselves, you have adopted a "Zeresh" attitude. Consider one more time: Haman was not being demoted or humiliated. He has not lost his standing with Ahasuerus in any way. Nothing has happened to Haman; Mordecai is having a good day. Actually, it has nothing to do with Haman, yet he goes into mourning over Mordecai receiving honor from the king.

While Haman's friends are still talking to him, they are interrupted.

> *While they were still talking with him, the king's eunuchs came, and hastened to bring Haman to the banquet which Esther had prepared.* Esther 6:14

Perhaps in the midst of his wife's discouragement, Haman had momentarily forgotten that he was supposed to be at the palace for dinner. The chronicler does not tell us if the reminder of this banquet with the king and queen improves Haman's mood. In the middle of talking to his friends and family, Ahasuerus' eunuchs hurry to take him to the banquet Esther has prepared for him and the king.

Proverbs 4:7-9 offers us the perfect benediction for the week: "Wisdom is the principal thing; Therefore get wisdom. And in all your getting, get understanding. Exalt her, and she will promote you; She will bring you honor, when you embrace her. She will place on your head an ornament of grace; A crown of glory she will deliver to you."

❧

For You meet him with the blessings of goodness; You set a crown of pure gold upon his head. He asked life from You, and You gave it to him --Length of days forever and ever. Psalm 21:3-4

❧

Father, Your love is perfect!
If I allow it to, Your love will free me.
Your love will free me from having to wonder if I am valued, treasured,
celebrated...
I do not have to create honor for myself,
and I do not have to lower myself by settling for something that man can give.
You do meet me with the blessings of goodness
(blessings that I could never create for myself);
and You are able to set a crown of pure gold on my head -
to encompass, protect, envelop me
(all the things that I could never do for myself).
If I wait for Your blessings,
and refuse any man-made counterfeit,
I know that You will bless me.
I can be secure in the knowledge that my glory is from You, and I love You.

ESTHER: CHAPTER 7
Esther Makes Her Request

When we left Esther last week, she was hosting banquets for Ahasuerus and Haman, and she was waiting on the Lord to release her to make a very important request. Try to put yourself in Esther's place. Time is ticking on an order to destroy all the Jews in the provinces of Persia, and Esther's purpose has been revealed to her: now she knows that she has come to the kingdom "for such as time as this". Her words and actions in the next few hours could save the Jews. Even though this must have been a very emotional time for her, Esther has patiently waited on the Lord and deliberately followed the direction He gave.

When we left Haman last week, he had just finished following Ahasuerus' order to parade Mordecai through the town, proclaiming honor over him. Afterward, he was complaining to his family and mourning over "what had happened to *him*" (Esther 6:12). It is remarkable that Haman considered these events to be about *him*; when in truth, the events were about Mordecai. Mordecai was honored by the king, and Haman thinks that the day was all about Haman. Having to honor Mordecai brings out a great deal of emotion in Haman, yet Mordecai seems unaffected. While appreciative for the honor that the king bestowed on him, Mordecai goes back to his own business without ceremony. After he is recognized throughout the city as the one "whom the king delights to honor", he goes back to the king's gates. He is not distracted by the praise of man.

In continuing on his set course, Mordecai sets a great example for us. He has now experienced criticism from man (when he refused to bow before Haman), and he has also received praise from man (in the honor from Ahasuerus). When praise comes, recognize that it came because of the good things the Lord placed inside you. From the correct point of view, it becomes apparent that the praise really belongs to Him. Give all the praise back to the Lord. Proverbs 18:16 says "A man's gift makes room for him, and brings him before great men". As Mordecai's gifts have caused Ahasuerus to honor him, at times your gifts will cause men to honor you as well. However, do not allow yourself to become "puffed up" when man recognizes good in you. Every good thing comes from above! Continue to be faithful; refuse to become distracted from your purpose because of man's praise. Just as easily as praise can fill you up, rejection or criticism can bring you down. Do not allow either to distract you from your purpose in God.

At this critical point, it is important to recognize a few specific qualities in Esther's character. Faith is not an accident of circumstances: it is a lifestyle. Esther demonstrates this point beautifully throughout the entire history. Let's look at a few examples of her faithfulness, and also look at a few things we need to understand about living a life of *faith*.

Esther was faithful in spite of her circumstances. Esther's faithfulness did not begin at the moment that she was called upon to step in on behalf of the Jews. Esther was taken from her home and her cousin in order to learn the customs of Ahasuerus' palace. Through a year of beauty preparations, she was given absolutely no guarantee of a favorable outcome. Even a "favorable outcome", being chosen queen, would come at a tremendous cost. However, her faithfulness is not determined by circumstances. Like Esther, we must not look to our circumstances to determine our actions. Circumstances change. God, in Whom our faith lies, never changes. We must look to God and be faithful regardless of what seems to be ahead. Be encouraged: *where* you are does not determine *who* you are!

Esther practices her faithfulness. She began with submission to authority and graduated to becoming a person of authority herself. Once Esther demonstrated her willingness to act on behalf of the Jews, the Lord trusted her with the most important and possibly the most difficult mission so far: going into the king's chambers uninvited. Like Esther, we must willing to start out with the small things. We must prove ourselves to be trustworthy in small situations so that we will be trustworthy in big situations. Do not allow foolish pride to discourage you or convince you otherwise: the day of small beginnings is your training ground. Submit to the Lord completely during these times. Do not resist His training. Be encouraged: the Lord can use you and train you at the same time.

Esther allows her faith to work by love, and she is not afraid of personal sacrifice. Beyond her love for God, it is her love for her people that drives her to obedience. As she is confident in God's love for her, she is released to love her people without concern for her own personal welfare. When Esther is ready to make her request to the king, she is prepared for whatever happens. She is trusting the Lord, and she is willing to follow the course He placed before her regardless of the outcome. Like Esther, you must operate in love to a point where you would be willing to sacrifice your own needs for the good of others. Paul wrote, "I would gladly spend and be spent for the sake of your souls" (2 Corinthians 12:15). Be encouraged: as you take care of others, God will take care of you.

Because of the qualities the Lord had placed in Esther, she experienced favor and promotion with man. Ahasuerus selected her from thousands to be his queen. Just like Esther, the Lord has placed good things in you. When people recognize these beautiful qualities in you, praise the Lord and point it all back to Him. When people fail to recognize these beautiful qualities (and unfortunately, sometimes they will), praise the Lord and be content that you are a treasure to your Creator. He loves you so much!

Esther is not the only one in the kingdom on "pins and needles": Mordecai and the Jews that have been praying for her are waiting to hear what is going on in the palace between Esther and Ahasuerus. In a time of great stress, anxiety, and emotion for the Jews, they are about to realize that God placed the right woman in the right place at the right time... all a matter of His providence.

DAY ONE: ESTHER 7:1-2

God always honors obedience and faith! Take your example from Queen Esther this week — as you pray to discern His will for your life, determine in your heart that you will give yourself over to it completely.

FRIEND TO FRIEND...

Shortly after our move back to Georgia, I had dinner with a good friend. Sitting across the table from Noelle at our favorite Chinese buffet, a proverb came to mind; "there is a friend who sticks closer than a brother" (Proverbs 18:24). Noelle was certainly that kind of friend. Another quote seemed to describe our friendship well, not from the Bible, but a favorite nonetheless, "Oh the comfort, the inexpressible comfort of feeling safe with a person; having neither to weigh thoughts nor measure words, but to pour them all out, just as they are, chaff and grain together, knowing that a faithful hand will sift them, keep what is worth keeping and then, with the breath of kindness, blow the rest away."[1] A friendship such as this is a gift, made more precious for me by the often necessity of having to be guarded as the "pastor's wife".

As we chatted, we began to notice a few things seem to "line up". Noelle was sensing a change in her spirit, a possible unrest about her current ministry. Even though she was happy at her full time church position, she felt as if the Lord was beginning to stir her to pursue something new. Michael and I had just experienced a change ourselves; we were beginning to lay a foundation for our new church that would be starting in just a few months. Noelle's roommate would be moving soon, and she had an opportunity for an apartment nearer to her parents. Coincidentally, it would also be nearer to the desired location of our church plant.

Finally, one of us said aloud, "Wouldn't it be awesome if the Lord put us in ministry together?" The other agreed whole-heartedly; it was something that both of us had considered on our own. We smiled as we considered the great benefits of working together. We thought of all the ways that she could be a blessing to our church body, as well as all the ways that the Lord could grow us together...

While it was fun to day-dream, we had to come back to earth sometime. Finally, Noelle asked me, smiling, "Jennifer, are you really *feeling* it?" I knew exactly what she meant; she and I often talked about the importance of hearing a "rhema" word (a personal, individual spoken direction) from the Lord before taking any step. She was asking me if I felt as if the Lord had told me that she would work with us. Because Noelle was a friend with whom I could be completely honest, I could admit the truth: "No, Noelle, I'm not feeling it. You?" Again with a smile, because the Lord always confirms His word, she answered, "No. But in the natural, wouldn't it be perfect? I don't know why, but I just can't get a peace in my spirit about it." I understood her again. As much as I wanted to minister with her, I had not heard from the Lord about it either.

We talked then about how funny it was sometimes, serving the Lord. We exchanged thoughts on how easily someone could miss God by trying to follow signs, rather than hearing His voice. Sometimes certain events may seem to come together in our lives, serving as confirmation and helping us to choose the right path. Other times, certain events may seem to come together in our lives as a result of coincidence, and could just as easily serve as distractions from our true path.

Signs are not meant to be followed; signs are meant to follow us as believers (Mark 16:17). Signs are not meant to direct; signs are meant to be discerned (Matthew 16:2-4). Noelle could have followed the signs and come to work for us. However, we were not looking for a sign, we were waiting for a *word*. Certain events were coming together in our separate lives, but they were just that: events in our separate lives. It was not to be interpreted as anything more than that. In this realization, there was no sadness. There was contentment that we were following the Lord. There was confidence that we were hearing His voice. There was comfort in the knowing that as we continued to seek Him, He would continue to guide us. Happy to be sheep who knew His voice (John 10:4), we returned to "graze" at the Chinese buffet.

In Acts 16:6-10, while on one of his missions trips, Paul had an opportunity to preach the Word in Asia. He tried to go into Mysia, Bithynia, and then to Troas, but the "Spirit did not permit" (Acts 16:7). As Paul considered preaching in these cities in Asia Minor, the Holy Spirit changed his course, and forbid him to preach there at this time. While considering entering another city in this area, Paul received a "rhema" word from the Lord: a vision of a man in Macedonia pleading with him to come and help. Paul discerned that this was the Lord's guidance. While there may have been signs in favor of his entering Asia, Paul was not waiting for a sign. He was waiting on the Holy Spirit to guide him. When he received a word from the Lord, he changed his course.

Later, in 2 Corinthians 2:12, Paul writes of this same missionary journey. He describes coming to a crossroads when the door to preach the gospel in Troas was opened to him "of the Lord". An open door could be considered a pretty strong sign. Even though Paul clearly recognizes that it was the hand of the Lord opening the door, his decision is made in verse 13: "I had no rest in my spirit." When the door was opened to Paul, that was not sign enough to go forward. Paul prayed and sought the Lord, and he could not find peace about ministering in Troas. He went in another direction entirely.

2 Corinthians 2:14, Paul writes, "Now thanks be to God who always leads us in triumph in Christ". Always is a powerful word, but Paul knew that following the Holy Spirit's direction always leads to victory. You can be assured of victory as you discipline your heart to hear *and obey* His voice! Paul prayed for the *right* door to be opened, and it was. Placing a higher value on God's guidance than on seeking signs, Paul waited on the Lord. When he received the word he was waiting for, he did not hesitate to obey.

An open door for Paul could have been interpreted as a "sign". You have had "open doors" in your life as well. However, we are beyond waiting for "signs" that could just as easily be coincidences. Just because a "door is opened" to you, it may or may not follow that you are to go through it. Seek wisdom from the Lord, not from happenings around you.

Esther receiving favor at her unannounced arrival in the king's chambers could have been interpreted as a sign. Ahasuerus repeatedly asking her to make her request known to him could have been interpreted as a sign. Esther being given assurance that her request would be met could have been interpreted as a sign. However, Esther is not waiting on a sign, she is waiting on God's direct guidance. By the time of this final banquet for Ahasuerus and Haman, she will have it.

So the king and Haman went to dine with Queen Esther.
Esther 7:1

Constantly trying to draw attention to himself, Haman was bragging to his friends and family only yesterday about the honor shown to him by the king. Today, he is moaning to his family and friends about the honor shown to Mordecai by the king. Positive attention or negative attention, Haman thrives on it. (Remember, this little "pity party" was interrupted by the king's servants; Haman's presence is required at the second banquet.)

The king and Haman attend Esther's banquet. While Haman had been looking forward to this dinner, his mood may be dampened by the events of the day. Do you remember Haman's mood after the first banquet? Even with all the honor that he had received, the "fly in the ointment" was Mordecai's refusal to bow. Quickly go back to Haman's words in Esther 5:13:"Yet all this avails me nothing as long as I see Mordecai sitting at the king's gate." Imagine how he must feel tonight after he has had to parade Mordecai through the town.

While Haman has been impatient and driven by irrational emotions, Esther has shown a tremendous amount of patience in her quest to save the Jews. Though she had to have been emotional — her people have been condemned to death by her own husband — Esther was not driven by emotion. She was driven by the purpose God placed in her heart.

> And on the second day, at the banquet of wine, the king again said to Esther, "What is your petition, Queen Esther? It shall be granted you. And what is your request, up to half the kingdom? It shall be done!" Esther 7:2

Apparently Ahasuerus is still pleased with his wife, and his spirits are high. Once again he declares that whatever her petition is, it shall be granted — up to half of his kingdom. Esther has heard this speech before — last night he told her the exact same thing, and she did not make her request at that time. Clearly, it is not Ahasuerus' good mood that inspires Esther to action. She is waiting for the Lord to tell her that the time is right. It does not always follow that you are to walk through a door simply because it is open.

As Paul was assured of victory through Christ, Esther has this assurance of victory inside her. She knows that God's intention is to save the Jews from annihilation. Esther recognizes that this purpose would be accomplished with or without her. Most importantly, Esther realizes that God desired to work this out *through* her, and she submits to His plan.

Remember how she prepared?
She wanted to please God!
Remember how she fasted?
She wanted to purify the vessel so the Lord could use her!
Remember how she waited?
She wanted to operate in His timing!
Remember how she trusted?
She went to the king without an invitation!
Esther has completely surrendered herself to the will of God. Esther knows inside herself that *this* is the door that the Lord has opened to her. She is ready, and will not miss this opportunity. Remember that being faithful is not a one-time act, or a coincidence. Faithfulness must be practiced every day. Being prepared for the challenges that will come your way is no accident. Preparedness is a result of

being faithful to the Lord through the heartwarming times as well as the heart-breaking times.

Esther was confident of the Lord's hand on her life. She knew that as she was faithful, the Lord would deliver her.

Do you have that knowing inside yourself?

When the Lord calls you to action, make sure that you are ready as Esther was! The only true way to be prepared for the situations that come to you in this life — both good and bad — is to daily walk out your faith in God!

❧

DAY TWO: ESTHER 7:3-4A
There is no "muscle" more important for you to "exercise" than your faith!
The Word says that the Lord gives us faith as a mustard seed (Matthew 17:20).
Thank Him for the seed, but don't stop there: a seed should grow!

FRIEND TO FRIEND...

My "mother-in-love" ("in-law" sounds too technical a term for someone with whom I enjoy such a close relationship) has a "green thumb". She has a knack for growing just about anything, and has a beautiful yard that speaks volumes of her skills in this area. I appreciate it all the more due to my absolute inability to grow anything. This fact is demonstrated by my yard that speaks volumes about my *lack* of skills in this area! I appreciate the time that goes into gardening, and the knowledge that comes before one can grow anything with success; I just don't possess that knowledge myself.

I do know a few things, though. A garden can suffer just as much from lack of attention as it can from the wrong kind of attention. To make anything worth-while grow, conditions must be almost perfect. You must have the right kind of soil and seeds. You must know what to plant, when to plant it, and where to plant it. Too little sunlight could destroy it; too much sunlight could destroy it. Too little water could dry it out, too much water could drown it. You also have to be able to tell the difference between plants and weeds, being careful to uproot one and not the other. A delicate balance must be found; and my poor, neglected yard is my fault: I just don't make the time to find it.

Sitting on my front step this morning having these thoughts, my son Tyler came out to join me. A welcome interruption in my solitude, I looked at him and realized that I was tending seeds. Three of them, in fact: my children. Like seeds in a garden, they have to be carefully and gently tended to if they are to grow properly. Like a successful gardener must acquire the right knowledge and tools, a successful parent must acquire the right knowledge and tools. This knowledge does not always come easily; we must depend on the ultimate Parent for guidance, and daily put into practice what He teaches.

Aware of the fact that my children have been given to me for a specific reason, I trust God to work through me to teach them, guide them, lead them by example to the place where they can discover God's will for their lives. My relationship with my children requires time, just as my relationship with the Lord requires time. As the seeds are affected by the time that the gardener spends in learning and working in the garden, my children's lives are affected by my relationship with the Lord and spending time with Him. These are my three little seeds, and I have to do all I can to see that they grow.

As a result of recognizing this responsibility, my relationship with the Lord becomes in part about understanding that what God is doing *in* me is not only *for* me. This fact makes it much more vital for me to keep growing in God. My walk with the Lord will impact my husband, my sons, my daughter, and anyone else within my sphere of influence. My relationships with the Lord and with His people require daily attention and practice as well.

Just as my successes with God will have a positive impact on other people in my life, my failures will have a negative impact on other people in my life. It would not only be selfish, it would be foolish to believe that any direct repercussions to my actions would affect only me. As people who are aware of God's providence, we understand that what God is doing in us is not only for us. Your walk with the Lord does not impact only you, but the people around you as well. As the Lord planted a seed in you, you can plant seeds in the people around you.

Practicing faithfulness to the Lord and to what He is calling you to will be a benefit to the people in your life as well as preparation for whatever comes next. Committing yourself to the process of serving the Lord will ensure that you are prepared for each day. In His providential care, He will place you exactly *where* you should be, *when* you should be, and *with whom* you should be; if you obey at each step. As you grow closer to the Lord, you will begin to place a higher value on the impact that you have on other people.

Esther has been faithful throughout this entire process. When she was first brought to the palace, she submitted to the beauty preparations (Esther 2). When she first became queen, she used her influence to give honor to Mordecai and rescue the king from assassination (Esther 2). When she was given authority by God, she laid it back down on the altar and agreed to use it to rescue her people (Esther 4). When she sought favor with Ahasuerus, she found it and waited for God's timing to speak (Esther 5). Esther is willing to take risks on behalf of her people. Her closeness to her God gives her the clarity she needs to recognize the impact that she is able to have on her people. Her faithfulness has been practiced.

Faithfulness is not something that happens accidentally. It is something you must practice every day. Esther has been faithful since the first day. It is because of her faithfulness that she can be trusted in such a precarious and dangerous situation for the Jews.

Let's return to Persia and to Queen Esther's banquet. At the "banquet of wine" after the meal, King Ahasuerus and Haman are relaxing in Esther's chambers. Ahasuerus tells Esther once again to make her request. "Up to half my kingdom" was not the phrase Esther had been waiting to hear, though the king did say it. In fact, Ahasuerus makes this promise to her *three times* (Esther 5:3, Esther 5:6, Esther 7:2). She is waiting on an opening from her true King. Since the moment Mordecai and Esther realized that saving the Jews from annihilation was their purpose, they have been waiting for this time. After fasting, praying, and obeying the Lord, Esther discerns this is finally the right time to speak to Ahasuerus.

Esther now makes her request to the king.

> *Then Queen Esther answered and said, "If I have found favor in your sight, O king, and if it pleases the king, let my life be given me at my petition, and my people at my request."* Esther 7:3

Esther requests that her life be given to her. Imagine Ahasuerus' profound surprise and possible confusion over his wife making such a request. He is probably accustomed to hearing such requests from strangers or criminals, but from his wife? Ahasuerus probably cannot imagine any reason for Esther to ask for her life to be spared. Ahasuerus has been willing to give her anything she requested, limited only by his own wealth. Power, money, jewels, the favor of the king, he is able to provide any natural desire Esther may have. Ahasuerus has even honored her with his presence at her banquets. Living under his roof, under his protection, what danger could possibly come to her? What could have happened that made Esther feel as if her life was in some sort of danger? What could possibly put such a fear in his queen's heart?

While Ahasuerus is still trying to put together some reason for Esther's unusual request, she continues.

> *"For we have been sold, my people and I, to be destroyed, to be killed, and to be annihilated."* Esther 7:4a

Even now, Esther could have continued in the secrecy that has kept her from revealing her heritage. She could have asked only that her life be spared, and Ahasuerus would have used all his power to assure her of her safety in the palace.

However, Esther is not only thinking of herself. In the selfless quality that we have seen become a hallmark of her personality throughout the book, she also asks for the lives of her people. In doing so, she reveals her heritage and exposes herself to Ahasuerus. Esther can do this without fear because she is confident in her God.

Given that Ahasuerus is the one who signed the decree against the Jews, he could have betrayed Esther upon learning that she was a Jew. Certainly he could have justified going back on his word to give her "half his kingdom" once he learned that she was Jewish. He could have gone back on his word based on what could have seemed to him to be a great deception; his own wife never told him that she was a Jew. Considering how easily Ahasuerus is swayed by man's opinion, Haman's presence could have been an encouragement in and of itself to break his promise to Esther. Considering Haman's hatred for the Jews and the king's own part in the ordered annihilation, Ahasuerus might have broken his promise to Esther.

Even with all these factors to consider, Esther has assurance of victory in her heart from the Lord and does not turn from her purpose now. This determination comes from years of faithfulness to God. Like tending to a seed inside her, she has prepared and practiced for this time. Esther continues in her request to Ahasuerus.

Esther explains to Ahasuerus that she and her people have been sold — "to be destroyed, to be killed, and to be annihilated" (Esther 7:4a). In Esther 3:13, we read Haman's decree.

> *And the letters were sent by couriers into all the king's provinces, to*
> *destroy, to kill, and to annihilate all the Jews, both young and old,*
> *little children and women, in one day...* Esther 3:13

Notice that Esther has chosen the *exact* words that Haman wrote into his decree. She tells Ahasuerus the truth without embellishment. Esther is not exaggerating the situation, or trying to make it seem more dramatic than it already is.

Esther teaches us by example here, as Mordecai has done before her: when we are in any kind of trouble, we should strive to magnify our God rather than our problem!

While you are growing your "seed of faith", you will be accomplishing another objective without even trying — your difficulties will become minimized! Whatever you give the most time to will become the most important aspect of your life. Refuse to give time to your troubles; concentrate your thoughts on the Lord!

☙

DAY THREE: ESTHER 7:4B-5

In order for your "seed of faith" to grow, you will need plenty of obedience!
Do your best to stay in God's will!

FRIEND TO FRIEND...

I couldn't get past them. I thought about them all the time. How could I hide them? Even if I covered them with a bandage, I would have to explain the bandage. There was simply no concealing something that is on your hands: five disgusting warts on my right palm. Everyone had a theory or a home remedy, of course. Cover them with duct tape overnight. Bury a washcloth in your front yard. (What?) Growing more and more frustrated by every ridiculous piece of advice I heard, a friend finally told me, "It's a virus. If you don't want to go to a dermatologist, just wait. They'll go away by themselves." Well, how long would that take? The answer was not welcome: "Only about two years."

Now I was even more irritated. I told my friend, "I don't have to wait two years. I don't even have to wait two days. My God is a Healer and He is stronger than warts or any other virus." I proceeded to curse the warts. Raising my right hand and pointing to the nasty warts with my left index finger, I shouted every verse about healing that I could think of on the spot. While my friend rolled her eyes, I prayed aloud that God would heal my warts. After my tirade, I praised God for healing the wart-causing virus and refused to look at them for the rest of the day (a feat that took some effort after being fixated on them for so long).

Sound a little silly? Sound like too big an effort over something so trivial? Sound like what you might expect from a vain eighteen year old? Maybe, but let me tell you what happened the next morning. Waking up, I went to the sink to brush my teeth and wash my face and hands. I saw those warts and one more time said quietly (humbly?), "Father, thank You for healing me." As I lathered the soap and let the warm water run over my hand, a wart rolled off my palm as if it were something completely unattached to my skin. Another, then another, until all of them were gone.

I know it sounds unbelievable. (If I had buried a washcloth in the front yard, would that make it easier to believe?) Over the years, I have had to face so many obstacles that were much harder to overcome, infinitely more difficult than a few warts. So many heartbreaks, so many hardships, so much that the Lord has brought me through, that it may make those warts seem ridiculous to even discuss.

Even though it was years and years ago, I still think of it from time to time. I remember how young I was then, not only in years, but in my faith as well. I think of it as a personal encouragement, a sort of "faith-builder" from the Lord to me. During a hard time, the Lord will bring those warts to my remembrance. "If I cared about *that*, Jennifer, don't you think I care about *this*?" Now remembering those ridiculous warts and smiling through my difficulty, I begin to rest in His love again. I am soothed by His faithfulness, and comforted by the fact that He is unchanging. I don't know how He does it, but I know that He does. That is more than enough.

Isaiah 28:10 tells us how we are to learn the word of the Lord: "For precept must be upon precept, precept upon precept, Line upon line, line upon line, Here a little, there a little." Learning requires a process. A baby cannot understand how to speak until she is spoken to often. She learns by example, and by the process of learning a few words at a time. A child cannot learn to read until she understands that each letter makes it own sound: the process of sounding out words, until those words are connected to the spoken word that the child already knows. The Lord is laying a foundation in you — teaching you the things that you need for today, and thinking forward: He knows that the information that you acquire today will help you learn the things that you will need to learn tomorrow. Baby steps.

God knew I had to grow my faith. Before I could believe Him to heal my children or heal my community or provide for our family or build a church, I had to be able to believe Him to heal my little warts. Here a little, there a little. That healing was laying a foundation. It takes time to lay a foundation, and the Lord tells us in Isaiah 28:16, "whoever believes will not act hastily". As difficult as it may be at times, do not try to get "ahead" of the Lord. Growing, like obedience, is a process! What we learn today will be valuable tomorrow, as long as we are committed to the process.

As the process is learned, one aspect begins to stand out: God is bigger. Bigger than warts, bigger than disease, bigger than financial struggles, bigger than any obstacle that we have to overcome. Esther has committed herself to the process, and she now knows her God is well able to care for her and her people. She knows that He is bigger than Haman's threats or Ahasuerus' short-sightedness. Having made her request, she is unafraid to offer the further explanation that the king is now asking of her.

> *"Had we been sold as male and female slaves, I would have held my tongue, although the enemy could never compensate for the king's loss."* Esther 7:4b

"Had we been sold as male and female slaves, I would have held my tongue"... Esther tells Ahasuerus that she would not have troubled him with this situation if they had merely been sold into slavery. Esther wishes the king to know that she the only reason for her interference in this matter is because it is life and death.

The Jewish people have lived through difficult times before this. They know as well as Esther does that they can depend on the Lord no matter what the circumstances. There is a big difference between being made slaves and being put to death. In slavery, they might have had some hope of being made free again. In slavery, they would have the opportunity to be faithful to God while waiting for their release. In slavery, they would live, even if they were never released. However, this decree is final: it means certain death for the Jewish people:

Esther further points out that "the enemy" (signifying to Ahasuerus that only one man is behind this terrible action against her people) could not make up for the losses that the king will suffer. Though losing the Jewish people would be a tremendous loss to the kingdom, Esther is not referring to the loss of the Jewish people. Such an argument would be fruitless, as she is aware that Ahasuerus does not really value people. Esther is referring to the loss of the taxes the Jewish people pay into the king's treasury. In the long run, these taxes would far outweigh the ten thousand talents of silver that Haman has offered to the king for allowing this decree to be carried out (Esther 3:9).

Unlike Haman, who acted without full knowledge or understanding, Esther has waited for the right moment and is operating in wisdom; she is armed with all the information that is necessary for success in the task placed before her.

Compare Esther's request to Haman's in chapter 3 or even to Memucan's advice way back in chapter 1. Memucan told Ahasuerus in Esther 1:16-17, "Queen Vashti has not only wronged the king, but also all the princes, and all the people who are in all the provinces... the queen's behavior will become known to all women, so that they will despise their husbands..." Remember what Haman told Ahasuerus about the Jews? "There is a certain people scattered and dispersed among the people in all the provinces of your kingdom; their laws are different from all other people's, and they do not keep the king's laws. Therefore it is not fitting for the king to let them remain" (Esther 3:8). Both of these men greatly exaggerated the situations, and then twisted their words to make it seem as if their only concern was for the king's benefit while they were selfishly considering their own positions.

Esther does not do either. Esther tells Ahasuerus nothing but the truth. She tells him honestly that if the situation were anything other than death for the Jews, she would have remained quiet. In order to make him understand her motive here is only to save her people, Esther goes as far as telling him that she would have stayed silent if the situation were different. She tells him that even though putting the Jews into slavery would cause the rest of the kingdom to suffer (financially), she would have remained quiet. Maybe she is showing him that she would have trusted God to provide for Persia through such a hardship. She does not flatter him, or play word games to represent the situation as anything other than it truly is. In a calm, honest, matter-of-fact manner, Esther presents the situation to Ahasuerus, and then leaves it to him.

Esther is exposing the situation to Ahasuerus. In doing so, she is not only revealing Haman as the enemy of the Jews, but she is exposing her own heritage. Esther is also giving Ahasuerus an opportunity to avert this terrible tragedy. Esther knows God can work in Ahasuerus' heart. While it may look as if she is trusting Ahasuerus, she is really trusting God.

Now that Esther has finally made her request to Ahasuerus, she has only to wait for his reaction. Once again, Esther does not have to wait long.

> *So King Ahasuerus answered and said to Queen Esther, "Who is he, and where is he, who would dare presume in his heart to do such a thing?"* Esther 7:5

When Esther quoted Haman's own words to the king ("to be destroyed, to be killed and to be annihilated" v. 4), she may have been hoping to spark some memory in Ahasuerus, or maybe give him some idea of what she was telling him. No surprise here: Ahasuerus does not get the hint. Ahasuerus wants to know *who* this enemy is, *where* this enemy is, and *how* this enemy dares to come against the queen and her people. Clearly, Ahasuerus has no idea who "this enemy" is. These questions also suggest that Ahasuerus is ready to take action against "this enemy".

As he listens to the queen make her request, I wonder if Haman recognizes who "this enemy" is....

At any rate, the suspense for Ahasuerus and Haman is about to end: Esther is done waiting. The king has asked Esther several questions about "this enemy", and Esther is ready to answer.

You are assured of victory, woman of God! However, you must do your part — and then trust that God will add His "super" to your "natural"!

❦

DAY FOUR: ESTHER 7:6-7

Faith and obedience. Discernment and timing. Father, help me to be wise to Your plans for me!

FRIEND TO FRIEND...

John wrote in 1 John 4:18, "There is no fear in love; but perfect love casts out fear." Fear can be the root of so many problems in our lives, but God is greater than fear. In His love, you can be released from fears that may keep you from achieving success in life. Fear of lack? Philippians 4:19 tells us that God is able to provide all our need. Fear of failure? Philippians 4:13 encourages us that we are capable of anything so long as we depend on the strength of Christ. Fear of rejection? Ephesians 1:3-6 speaks to our being chosen and accepted by God Himself.

Fear such as these can determine our decisions and cripple our progress in God. Once you allow yourself to become controlled by it, fear can alter the way you view your life, people, and the world. Allow the Lord to release you from any fear that you may have in your life. Allow His "perfect love" to cast it out. Ask Him to reveal your fears to you, so that you may effectively pray through and seek the Lord for strength to let go of fear in your life.

Paul wrote of fear to his young friend Timothy, and this truth is applicable to our lives today: "For God has not given us a spirit of fear, but of power and of love and of a sound mind" (2 Timothy 1:7). If you are operating in fear, you may be sure that you did not receive that fear from the Lord. Have you ever noticed that the Lord always offers a trade? Notice this as well: we continually receive the sweet end of His exchanges. In place of fear, we can receive power, love, and a sound mind. Isaiah 61:3 names a few as well: "beauty for ashes", "joy for mourning", and the "garment of praise for the spirit of heaviness". Matthew 11:29-30 names even more "trades" from which we can benefit: rest for our labor, easy yokes for our hardships, and light burdens for our heavy loads. The requirement for us is that we have to be willing to lay down something in order to receive something from the Lord!

Sadly, Haman operates in a constant state of fear that is fed by his negative wife and fueled by his own selfish motives. Today, like some twisted prophecy which he has unwittingly made over himself, some of his worst fears are going to be realized. As Esther has at last revealed her request, she is now ready to reveal the reason behind it.

> *Queen Esther answered and said, "If I have found favor in your sight, O king, and if it pleases the king, let my life be given me ...and my people..."* Esther 7:3

Upon hearing Esther's request for her life and for the lives of her people, Ahasuerus may have felt confusion and concern. The concern turns to strong emotion when he realizes that his wife is in fear for her life. Ahasuerus wants to know why she feels this way. He questions his queen, and expects answers. Though he does not yet know who this enemy is, he is ready to take action against him.

Do not overlook another presence in the room: Haman, who is sitting here listening to the exchange of words between the king and queen. He is probably experiencing some strong emotions of his own.

"Who is he, and where is he, who would dare presume in his heart to do such a thing?" Esther 7:5

Ahasuerus is determined that Esther's enemies are his enemies as well. His response to her request shows Esther that he is on her side. However, Ahasuerus may have been completely unprepared for Esther's response to his questions.

And Esther said, 'The adversary and enemy is this wicked Haman!"
So Haman was terrified before the king and queen. Esther 7:6

Esther tells the king that the enemy and adversary is Haman. Ahasuerus is clearly stunned by the accusation *before* he finds out who is the perpetrator of this heinous crime. He cannot imagine someone being evil enough and BOLD enough to make such an attempt on the life of the queen and her people. Now that he knows the antagonist is his own "right hand man", Ahasuerus could be feeling doubly angry; angry at Haman, but possibly angry at himself as well.

Haman is described as "terrified before the king and queen". It is no surprise that Haman is full of fear. For as long as we have known him, his actions could easily be translated as motivated by fear. Fear that Mordecai's refusal to bow to him could "spread" to other Jews in the kingdom. Fear that Ahasuerus will not recognize him an reward him publicly. Fear that the only way for him to seem better in the eyes of those around him is to put other people down.

Perhaps now Ahasuerus realizes that he has been the somewhat unwitting accomplice in this crime. He certainly knew his part in the decree against the Jews, but at the time he was not aware that he was condemning his own queen to death. Now Ahasuerus and Esther are united in their purpose to save the Jews.

Then the king arose in his wrath from the banquet of wine and went into the palace garden... Esther 7:7a

Ahasuerus "arose in his wrath" and left the banquet. He went outside (and we may have the first ever example of King Ahasuerus *leaving* a party). Ahasuerus wants to clear his head, and try to wrap his mind around the events of the evening. For once, he leaves the "banquet of wine". Ahasuerus is going to deal with this situation while *sober*. This is another little detail that the Lord worked out, one that we may not have considered before: King Ahasuerus will be sober when he makes a decision regarding how to deal with Haman. Notice that when he made his decision about Vashti, he came to regret it. He knew that because of the influence that alcohol had on his mind, he did something he would not normally have done. In the past, Ahasuerus has been influenced by alcohol, but this time he is in his right mind. This is an important detail!

Another important detail here: not only is Ahasuerus dealing with this situation sober, he is dealing with it *alone*. He does not call for his seven servants, or his most trusted princes. Finally, it appears as if Ahasuerus is going to do something right. For once, we can take positive example from Ahasuerus: there are moments when being alone is a tremendous benefit.

Sometimes our tendency may be to surround ourselves with people during times of difficulty. We may seek to have people hold our hands up, as Aaron and Hur did for Moses (Exodus 17:11-12). Sometimes you need people around you, and that is not wrong. However, it is also important to know and experience that your own faith can sustain you. Sometimes the best way to handle a situation is to get alone with the Lord. There are times when it is most appropriate for us to be *alone*. Just as there are moments in your life to seek advice, there are moments to be alone with your God.

Jesus, our greatest example, recognized the value in being alone to draw strength. He went *alone* to a desert place when He found out that John had been beheaded (Matthew 14:13). He went *alone* to the garden to pray before His crucifixion (Matthew 26:36). When Jesus perceived that He was about to be taken, He went alone to pray (John 6:15). He went *alone* to the cross.

Of course, Ahasuerus' design is not to be alone with the Lord, but our providential God has His own design on this moment.

> *...but Haman stood before Queen Esther, pleading for his life, for he saw that evil was determined against him by the king.* Esther 7:7b

Haman turns to Esther to beg for mercy. His reaction is certainly not unexpected. As Ahasuerus has stormed out of Esther's quarters in a rage, Haman must think that his only recourse and only hope is to throw himself on Esther's mercy. The thought of begging for Esther's help may not have seemed entirely wrong to Haman at this moment. Of course, he should consider the most recent revelation that the queen herself is included in the group that Haman wanted destroyed. It seems ironic that upon hearing the queen plead for her life before the king, now Haman is pleading for his life before the queen. Unfortunately for Haman, begging Esther for mercy was not his biggest mistake today. When he did not follow Ahasuerus out of the queen's quarter's, Haman made a tragic error: he was left alone in the queen's quarters with the queen.

Let us consider Haman's last few days. On this very day, Haman has been humiliated before Mordecai. He has been in mourning. His own wife has told him that he will not prevail against Mordecai the Jew. Standing in his front yard, he has a monument to his own stupidity and false pride: a gallows fifty feet high. The very thing that he built to destroy Mordecai has become an embarrassing and blaring symbol of his defeat to everyone to whom was bragging just two nights ago.

As soon as Ahasuerus leaves the queen's chambers, Haman is left alone with Esther. Considering the custom of the times, he should have followed Ahasuerus out. The male servants who tend to Esther have had to become eunuchs because of their contact with the queen. There could never be any question of the queen's virtue. Haman should have known better than to be alone with Esther, but he is not in his right mind. Haman is terrified of the king who is now filled with wrath against him, and probably just as terrified of the queen who exposed him as her enemy. His mind is probably spinning at how fast circumstances have changed for him. Yesterday Haman felt honor above any other official in the kingdom, and today he is exposed as "Public Enemy Number One". The only thing on Haman's mind at this moment is saving himself.

One more detail to notice from verse 7: Haman sees that Ahasuerus has determined evil against him. He sees the *determination* in Ahasuerus, and he knows that this is a situation in which it will be completely fruitless to talk to Ahasuerus. For possibly the first time, Haman does not even consider talking to Ahasuerus. He does not attempt to persuade him to another opinion, as he has been able to do in the past. Haman knows that his days of favor with Ahasuerus are over. As his last resort, as his only resort, he goes to Esther. He must know that his chances of convincing her to help him are very slim. After all, she is the one who exposed his crime to Ahasuerus in the first place. Furthermore, she is a member of the group that Haman had desired to see destroyed as a result of his decree. Mistakenly thinking that his chances are better with the queen than with the king, Haman stays in the queen's quarters.

Haman has grossly misjudged the situation.

Father, thank you for being MORE THAN ENOUGH in my life — help me depend on you completely. Help me follow You in every situation. You are worthy of my trust, and I love You!

⁂

DAY FIVE: ESTHER 7:8-10

Father, I know that the only way for me to see where my help comes from is to look UP — to get the focus off of myself and on to YOU! You are my inspiration, and the reason that I continually look up!

FRIEND TO FRIEND...

1 Samuel 16:7 says that "the LORD does not see as man sees; for man looks at the outward appearance, but the LORD looks at the heart." I find encouragement there (if you knew how awkward and clumsy I am, you would better understand my love for that verse!). With the encouragement of those words, comes an im-

portant life truth: man looks at the outward appearance. Having discussed often
the importance of allowing your self worth to come from the Lord, we must now
determine a balance. While it is not important to please man, it is important to
demonstrate your belief in Christ and walk out your faith before people as well
as God. Sometimes this will bring you compliments, sometimes it will bring you
criticisms; but it will always serve you well to protect your reputation.

Your reputation goes before you. Though it is most important what God thinks
of you, it is also important what man thinks of you. Make sure that the way you
live your life is indicative of the gift God gave to you in His only Son, Jesus Christ.
In 2 Corinthians 9:15, Paul writes, "Thanks be unto God for His indescribable
gift!" Though some of the people around you may be at a loss to describe the difference in you, they should see something remarkable.

A few verses demonstrate the importance of guarding your reputation. Proverbs
22:1 tells us that a "good name is to be chosen rather than great riches, loving
favor rather than silver and gold." Your reputation is more valuable than great
riches, and it should be protected and valued. In Galatians 5:22, Paul lists what he
calls the "fruit of the Spirit": love, joy, peace, patience, kindness, goodness, faithfulness, gentleness and self control. "Fruit" is a sign on the outside that something
is going right on the inside. Do your best to see that your life bears this precious
fruit of the Spirit!

Even Jesus describes the importance of bearing "good fruit" in your life. He
tells a parable to illustrate this point in Luke 6:43-45,

> For a good tree does not bear bad fruit, nor does a bad tree bear good
> fruit. For every tree is known by its own fruit. For men do not gather
> figs from thorns, nor do they gather grapes from a bramble bush. A good
> man out of the good treasure of his heart brings forth good; and an evil
> man out of the evil treasure of his heart brings forth evil. For out of the
> abundance of the heart his mouth speaks.

Every tree is known by its fruit. What does the fruit of your life reveal about
you? Your Father has placed gifts in you as well. Are you developing those gifts
so they may be seen by men? No, do not seek the praise of men for yourself, but
that "they may see your good works and glorify your Father in heaven" (Matthew
5:16). Your good works should point to the good that the Lord does in you! Your
fruit will speak for itself, and the reputation that you guard will guard you when
you need it. Esther has continually demonstrated the "good fruit" of her life to
Ahasuerus, and today she needs his favor more than ever.

Haman's anxiety over the developments of the evening cause him to forget his
"palace etiquette". When Ahasuerus leaves the queen's quarters, Haman does not
follow him out, but rather stays with Esther to plead with her for his life. This is

yet another example of Haman focusing on himself. Esther has practiced being governed by the Lord and not her emotions. She has practiced faithfulness and selflessness in every situation. In contrast, Haman has practiced his conceit and continues to be motivated by the opinion of man. Now that he has lost Ahasuerus' good opinion, it seems that there is nothing left for him to do but beg. Now his sole concern is to save his own life. However, lacking in wisdom, he has not placed himself in a position to receive help from anyone.

> *When the king returned from the palace garden to the place of the banquet of wine, Haman had fallen across the couch where Esther was. Then the king said, "Will he also assault the queen while I am in the house?"* Esther 7:8

Ahasuerus comes back into the room to find Haman "fallen across the couch", probably on his face before Esther. Ahasuerus, consumed with wrath, immediately assumes Haman is attacking the queen because she has just exposed him as a "wicked adversary". Take note of the fact that there is no question of Esther's innocence. Because Ahasuerus knows Esther's character and has been witness to her faithfulness over her years in the palace, he does not consider for a moment that she is doing anything wrong.

As we discussed earlier, Esther's "fruit" reflects the gifts which her Heavenly Father placed inside her.

> *As the word left the king's mouth, they covered Haman's face.*
> Esther 7:8b

"They" refers to the servants that attended Esther and her guests at the banquet tonight. By covering Haman's face, they were signifying an understanding of Ahasuerus' response upon finding Haman in this compromising position. No longer worthy to be see the king or be seen by him, Haman is marked for execution. As the queen's position cannot be compromised, Haman's error cannot go unpunished.

> *Now Harbonah, one of the eunuchs, said to the king, "Look! The gallows, fifty cubits high, which Haman made for Mordecai, who spoke good on the king's behalf, is standing at the house of Haman."*
> *Then the king said, "Hang him on it!"* Esther 7:9

Harbonah suggests to the king that Haman be hanged on the gallows that he had built for Mordecai. The irony! The honor that Haman dreamed up and meant for himself in chapter 6 is given to Mordecai. The plan that Haman had concocted to kill Mordecai is now going to be used to kill him. Ahasuerus agrees immediately to the suggestion, and orders that Haman be hanged on his own gallows.

> *So they hanged Haman on the gallows that he had prepared for Mordecai. Then the king's wrath subsided.* Esther 7:10

Haman is hanged, and only seeing him dead causes Ahasuerus' anger to subside.

Though this evening has brought some measure of victory, let's not overlook a major detail: the instigator behind the decree against the Jews has been eliminated, but the decree is still in effect. Now the hope is that even though Ahasuerus' anger toward Haman for his action against Esther has diminished, his anger for what Haman decreed against the Jews will still be strong. Hopefully that anger will stir him toward action on their behalf.

Esther's work is not yet finished. She must speak to the king again.

Proverbs 4:23-24 says, "Keep your heart with all diligence, For out of it spring the issues of life." Guard your heart, woman of God — if life can spring from it, then so can death if we are not diligent. Your true character will not always be hidden! Thank God for the treasures that He has placed in you, and continue to do your best to develop into the jewel that He means for you to become!

❧

I will lift up my eyes unto the hills, from whence cometh my help. My help comes from the LORD, who made heaven and earth. Psalm 121:1-2

Father, Your love is my help.
If I allow it to, Your love will free me.
Your love will free me from the need to focus on any "thing":
on my problems, on my circumstances, or even on other people.
I can be released to focus on You,
and in You I will be able to see
my answer, my healing, and my needs met.
I can be free from the worry that I might be "let down";
because as I keep my gaze fixed on You,
I realize something truly amazing:
your gaze is fixed on me!
You never sleep, you never slumber, and you never let me go!
My help comes from You,
and my focus is constantly on You.

❧

---

1.   Dinah Maria Mulock Craik, The Gold of Friendship: A Bouquet of Special Thoughts, (USA, The C.R. Gibson Company, MCMLXXX), p. 2.

ESTHER: CHAPTER 8
The Jews are Saved

Even though she has accomplished a great deal, Esther's work is not yet done. She has shown great courage and demonstrated her great faith by going to the king uninvited. She has also shown boldness and confidence as she exposed a man who is so close to the king. Now Esther must continue to trust in the Lord and in the favor He has given to her. Now is the time to speak to the king about the decree. Even though Haman is no longer a threat, the decree against the Jews is still in effect. Her first victory is tremendous, but it is not enough. Esther must see this through to the end.

It's a funny little verse, but it will serve: "...for him who is joined to all the living there is hope, for a living dog is better than a dead lion" (Ecclesiastes 9:4). A lion is often a symbol of strength in the Bible, while in many instances in the Bible, being referred to as a dog is a terrible insult. However, in this verse, Solomon says that even a live dog is better than a dead lion. Can I tell you what I take from this verse? God has done great things in my past, but that is where they are: *in my past*. I have to continue pressing forward. If all I do is look backward, then I may find that all I have years from now is a "lion graveyard".

Psalm 126:3 offers an expression for past victories: "the Lord has done great things for us, and we are glad!" Remembering past triumphs can be a source of encouragement, particularly in times of struggle. However, it is not healthy to dwell on the past. As you rejoice in what the Lord has brought you through, look forward to what success He still has in store for you. What is God doing in you TODAY? Celebrate *that* and submit to it!

Esther can look to her past experience as a testimony to God's faithfulness. Throughout her life, and obviously throughout her years in the palace, He has been faithful. He certainly would not have brought her so far to leave her now. Esther must continually leave these experiences where they belong: in her past. Esther must continue to press forward. It is a good lesson for us as well. Take this example from Esther this week: thank God for what He has done in your past. At the same time, look forward to what He is doing in your present and what He will do in your future. Refuse to become content with "just enough" when the God you serve is capable of "more than enough". God is not through with you yet!

DAY ONE: ESTHER 8:1-2

Father, thank You for what You are doing in me today — help me to celebrate the NOW that You have given to me!

FRIEND TO FRIEND....

It was a little ridiculous. Okay, it was A LOT ridiculous. We weren't that far away, we were really happy with our new location, and it had only been a week. I just wanted to see our old house. The Saturday after the move, Michael was busy working in the yard. He could easily see the kids riding their bicycles in the cul-de-sac. I would just do a little "drive-by".

On the way over, I remembered Lindsay's reaction to seeing the "for sale" sign in the front yard. The move was not a surprise; we had talked to the children about it. I supposed that seeing the sign made it more real for her. We had been in Florida for all of Lindsay's "remembering days", and the only move she remembered was the one to Georgia. In that particular move, she had to leave her little friends and her church. Her five-year-old mind couldn't really understand that this move was different: she would still be in the same school, at the same church, involved in the same activities. In her own little way, this move from one house to another in our same community had been a "move of faith" for her; she was having to trust Mom and Dad to tell her the truth and act in her best interests, even when she did not understand.

Pulling into our former subdivision, I passed the pool, and then a favorite neighbor's house. This sweet couple had brought over dinner for us the day we moved in. It was a welcome treat after being on the road from Florida for so many hours, and then spending the morning of the move in an attorney's office for closing. Turning the corner, I saw "our" house. Though the new owners were not outside at the moment, I could tell some work was going on. It appeared that they were in the midst of moving plants, bringing in new furniture, sweeping sidewalks...the same things we were doing in our new house today. I could see cans of paint on the driveway, and a ladder. It was certainly no surprise that they were painting; I imagined that Lindsay's vivid pink walls would be the first to go! It was an exciting time, transforming a house into a home, and I smiled for the new couple.

In the front yard, I could see a big white... wait. What was that? No, they didn't. They couldn't have. Really, they wouldn't have. I had to slow down so I could see it better. Yes. The big white piece in the front yard was my custom bookshelves, and it was apparent that the bookshelves were on the way to the dump. They had been built in, so getting them out must have been some work... I loved those bookshelves. Eight feet high, they went almost up to the ceiling. Cabinets underneath the adjustable shelving, and moulding to match the rest of the room; they looked as if they belonged there. The carpenter did a beautiful job, and they were my favorite part of my living room.

I remember when I had finally saved enough money to have those shelves built. I couldn't wait to see them installed. Upon moving to this house, I had not been able to unpack all my books because I didn't have a place to put them. The day the shelves were finally finished, I carried my boxes of books up from the garage. Opening each box and taking the books out, I had to open a few pages of many of them right then, as if I was reuniting with old friends. I sorted them and put them in my own kind of order on the shelves, arranging some by category, arranging some by height, arranging some by memory... Once I was done, I loved how the books and the shelves looked. I just sat in there and admired them. Moving my favorite chair in between my shelves and my big picture window created a perfect setting for a quiet read.

Now my bookshelves were in the front yard. Scrap wood.

Heartbroken at first, I turned around and went home. When I told Michael, he wasn't surprised at all. He told me, "You know why they did that, don't you? When you had those shelves built in, you covered up the cable outlet."

The cable outlet? Was he for real? The cable outlet. I thought about my shelves. Jane Austen used to live there, and Charlie Shedd. Emily Bronte and Elisabeth Eliot. Margaret Runbeck and Catherine Marshall. All my biographies (I love a true story); and my own stories, journals and photo albums...treasures. Now they were ripped out, and for what? SportsCenter?

Michael brought me out of my melodrama and back to reality. "Jennifer, they did not rip out Jane Austen. *You* moved her *here*. Go inside and read a book if you want. Besides, SportsCenter is awesome." I had to laugh at myself. I did go inside; and started to make plans for my new bookshelves.

Jesus had advice regarding our treasures here on earth. He said, "Do not lay up for yourselves treasures on earth... but lay up for yourselves treasures in heaven, where neither moth nor rust destroys and where thieves do not break in and steal. For where your treasure is, there your heart will be also" (Matthew 6:19-21). It is not wrong to have material things, but it is wrong if your greatest treasures, those items closest to your heart and most important in your life, are tangible and temporal.

We are told that earthly treasures can be stolen or destroyed. Jesus does not tell us how to protect these "earthly treasures". There is no way to protect or preserve forever what is man-made. He tells us to replace them with treasures in heaven. There's our exchange again. If we will release our earthly "treasures", God will give us treasures in heaven where man cannot ever take them away. We carry these God-given treasures in our hearts and in our spirits.

At the end of the day, my lost bookshelves weren't really that great a loss. They weren't even my bookshelves anymore. My reaction was obviously disproportionate. Besides, my joy was not found in those bookshelves. They were paint, wood and nails, and easily replaced. Pretty silly, really, and petty. I had more valuable treasures in my life and in my heart.

If we give man the power to control our happiness (a great treasure indeed), then we are also giving man permission to destroy our happiness. In Persia, by placing such a high value on the opinions of men, Haman placed the responsibility of his happiness in the hands of men. He failed to realize that what is created by men can be destroyed by men. The potential to lose was great, and ultimately Haman's losses were tremendous.

> *So they hanged Haman on the gallows that he had prepared for Mordecai. Then the king's wrath subsided.* Esther 7:10

In chapter 7, Esther requested that the king give her the lives of her people as well as her own life. In response to this unexpected request, King Ahasuerus demands to know the identity of the man who put his queen in danger. When Haman is exposed as this enemy, Ahasuerus has him hanged. Then, his "wrath subsided". Ahasuerus does not understand yet that Esther is not finished with her request. If you can, imagine how Ahasuerus must be feeling at the moment. His wife, who has "obtained grace and favor in his sight" (2:17) has had her life and the lives of her people threatened by his own closest advisor.

In order to process this series of events, Ahasuerus excuses himself to the garden. Here, he can clear is head and be alone for a few minutes. When he does return to Esther's quarters, he finds Haman across Esther's couch and thinks that Haman is physically attacking her. Enraged, he orders Haman's death at that very moment. Ahasuerus may have misunderstood the scene before him upon returning to Esther's quarters. Haman most likely was not attacking Esther, but merely kneeling before her to beg for mercy. Whatever the situation, the end result would have been the same; it was highly inappropriate for Haman to have any physical contact with the queen whatsoever.

It is a very emotional time for him, and Ahasuerus is probably feeling a little more attached to Esther as a result of this excitement and stress.

> *On that day King Ahasuerus gave Queen Esther the house of Haman, the enemy of the Jews.* Esther 8:1a

In these times, it was customary for the king to keep the property of a traitor. However, in this case, Ahasuerus gives Haman's house to Esther. Perhaps he means it as a sort of consolation for the evil which Haman had intended for her. Of course, this transfer of property could not have made up for the fear that Haman had placed in the hearts of the Jews, but Ahasuerus is showing great honor to Esther in this gesture.

Much information previously hidden has been brought to light in Persia. Esther's Jewish heritage has been revealed. Haman has been exposed as the enemy of the queen and the Jews. However, there is still one more important piece of information for Ahasuerus to learn.

> *And Mordecai came before the king, for Esther had told how he was related to her.* Esther 8:1b

Esther explains to Ahasuerus that Mordecai is her cousin. Before these banquets, Ahasuerus had not seen Esther for a month and was unaware that she was a Jew. For Esther to explain her relationship with Mordecai to King Ahasuerus probably required a fair amount of explaining! As Ahasuerus had no clue about Esther's heritage, it is a great possibility that he had no idea that she was an orphan being raised by her cousin in Persia before she was queen. Having so much new information to process, Ahasuerus seems to be handling it well.

> *So the king took off his signet ring, which he had taken from Haman, and gave it to Mordecai; and Esther appointed Mordecai over the house of Haman.* Esther 8:2

Apparently before Haman died, he was stripped of every honor that Ahasuerus had bestowed on him during his life. Ahasuerus removes his signet ring and gives it to Mordecai. Do you remember this signet ring? The last time Ahasuerus gave this ring away, it was to enable Haman to put his evil plan into irreversible law. Now Mordecai is given the *ring* that once belonged to Haman and the *position* that once belonged to Haman. To complete this reversal of fortune, Esther gives Mordecai the *property* that once belonged to Haman.

As Ahasuerus takes away everything that had once belonged to Haman, it is important for us to recognize that Haman not only lost material possessions, he lost something even more valuable. Haman has been working to please other people, he attempted to find his self worth from man's opinion of him, and he allowed his moods to be determined by the actions of others. As Haman received promotion and "honor" from man, man was able to take it away. Haman valued above anything else what man could give, and he lost everything because of one important truth: in giving Ahasuerus permission to make him feel worthy, he was unwittingly giving Ahasuerus permission to make him feel worthless. It is a mistake we can easily make in our own lives, if we are not grounded and secure in our Father's love.

Can you imagine how Haman's wife, friends, and family feel now? As they are not mentioned, we can only speculate. Even though Zeresh predicted Haman would not triumph over Mordecai, she probably did not expect that her husband would be hanged in front of her on the very gallows that SHE had suggested he build. She has to feel somewhat responsible, considering her advice to Haman over the past several days. Maybe she can see now how wrong she has been.

Fortunately for us, hindsight is 20/20. With the privilege of reading this history in its entirety rather than living through day by day as Mordecai and Esther, or even Haman and Zeresh, we can see beginning to end, how God's providence was at work, and how one person's actions or words can make a tremendous impact — for good or evil.

Whatever the intention of man, God's "intended end" will come to pass! Father, help me to recognize today as the gift that it is! Help me to handle what "treasures" You have placed in my hands with grace and wisdom.

⁂

DAY TWO: ESTHER 8:3-6

In Ecclesiastes 7:8 it is written, "The end of a thing is better than the beginning" — that is so true! Make sure that you hang on until the end — don't give up! God is with you, and He will stay with you!

FRIEND TO FRIEND...

While the Word of God instructs us and encourages us to wait upon the Lord, our society does not favor waiting on much of anything. People want answers and solutions *now*. People want favor and prosperity *now*. People want healing and *peace now*. Even our kitchens reveal our impatient nature: pre-made peanut butter and jelly sandwiches in the freezer, pre-packaged lunches in the pantry, and a microwave sitting on the counter. Nothing wrong with convenience (I'm actually describing my kitchen!), but when we begin to allow our human nature to determine how long we are willing to wait on the Lord, we have moved into dangerous territory spiritually. His timing and our timing are not the same.

For us, Esther's struggle has lasted a few days or even a few weeks. For her, it was much longer. Before she even became queen, she was taken (possibly by force, certainly not by choice) from her home and only family (2:2). She spent a full year in beauty preparations (2:12), unsure of the outcome of that year. Can you imagine? How many times during that year might Esther have prayed for some circumstance that would release her from the palace and this emotionally challenging process?

Once Esther finally did become queen, she was in completely new territory. Immediately following the coronation party, her new husband called for another round of virgins to be brought to the palace (2:19). This was probably not the welcome to her new marriage that she had envisioned. Dealing with a unpredictable and moody husband, Esther had the added stress of having to keep her spiritual identity a secret (2:10, 2:20).

Like an infomercial announcer saying for the hundredth time, "but wait, there's more", Esther's new life seems crowded with worry and strife. Some months after she is crowned, an attempt is made on her husband's life. Though Esther is able to avert this crisis, she must endure seeing another man benefit from Ahasuerus' gratitude: rather than Mordecai, it is Haman who receives promotion and favor. Even through this, Esther keeps silent.

Now there comes the weight of being made responsible for stopping a decree, written in such a manner that it can never be reversed (3:12). This irrevocable decree commands the destruction of her people, with whom she cannot openly identify, and she is somehow supposed to put a stop to it and save the Jews (4:8). The king goes days, weeks, months without asking for her, but she is expected to speak to him in a timely manner about his own decree. Every excuse Esther tries to offer comes up short. Mordecai gives her an encouragement and a warning, as if he can identify with her in this most difficult position: "if you remain completely silent at this time, relief and deliverance will arise for the Jews from another place, but you and your father's house will perish. Yet who knows whether you have come to the kingdom for such a time as this?" (4:14). An important task had been set before her; one filled with even more stress.

Following the realization that she must accept this mission as her God-given purpose, Esther begins a time of concentrated prayer and fasting (4:16). Prayer is always necessary, fasting is oftentimes necessary, but bringing the flesh under submission is not often easy. Sometimes, it can even be stressful.

Finally, Esther determines to obey (4:16). Once the decision is made to obey the Lord and follow through with His purpose for her, she must face the uncertainty of going into the king uninvited (5:1). More stress. She receives favor from Ahasuerus, but now had the stress of waiting through these two banquets for a release from the Lord to speak of the wicked decree (5:8, 7:1). The triumph over Haman's decree must have been bittersweet for Esther, causing more stress and inner turmoil. Though he was killed (7:10), any death, even that of an enemy, is not truly a cause for joy. Haman's removal did not remove the entire problem; the Jews are still facing imminent danger, and Esther is still responsible for their lives.

She must feel some level of weariness, but even though she must be experiencing emotions, she is not being controlled by them.

Being tired is being human; it is not a lack of faith. Feeling sad or any other emotion is a feeling; it is not a mirror of the truth. Experiencing trials is a part of life; it is not a sign that God has abandoned you. Sometimes you can pray every prayer and feel victory rise up in your spirit and still wake up to the same circumstances the next morning. Does this mean that your prayer was not heard? Does it mean that your victory was not real? No, it just means that you must continue to stand confident that God is working whether or not His hand is seen. Sometimes the battle is long, but all the time God is faithful.

Having done all... stand... Ephesians 6:13

If all you can do is stand, then just stand. God knows you are tired. He does not condemn you for your tiredness. God knows that you feel as if you are almost at the end. He does not judge you for your feelings. God desires your faithfulness and praise through the circumstances. He knows there are times when all you have is a sacrifice of faith and praise. Just bring it to Him. Lay it all at His feet: "Lord, I'm broken, but I'm coming. Lord, I don't understand, but I'm following. Lord, I'm weary, but I'm standing..." Precious daughter, you will be received and restored.

Thankfully for Esther, the end of her battle is in sight. The evening banquets with King Ahasuerus and Haman are over. Esther has exposed the enemy of the Jews, and made her request to the king. Haman is killed, Mordecai is promoted, Esther is honored by the king... but it is not over. Esther returns to speak to the king.

Now Esther spoke again to the king, fell down at his feet, and implored him with tears to counteract the evil of Haman the Agagite, and the scheme which he had devised against the Jews. Esther 8:3

Esther, falling at the feet of Ahasuerus, crying and pleading, begs the king to counteract the decree against the Jews. What we have studied in a few days or weeks, Esther lived through for over a year. These months have been arduous, stressful, and charged with emotional highs and lows. It is no wonder that Esther "implored Ahasuerus with tears" (8:3). Considering what she has endured, her tears are not remarkable. What is remarkable is the fact that these are the first tears which the historian records. What is remarkable is that she has continued to persevere. The battle has been long, but Esther has remained consistent and faithful. That is remarkable.

Even though Haman is dead and his property has been turned over to Esther (and by extension to Mordecai) as restitution for the evil intended against them, the decree is still in effect. The Jews are still set to be destroyed on the "thirteenth day of the twelfth month" (Esther 3:13). With the danger still imminent,

Haman's property is little consolation to Esther. Read Esther 7:10b again: "the king's wrath subsided". Ahasuerus' anger has passed, and most likely so has any motivation he may have had to extend his aid. Esther and Mordecai know that making Ahasuerus aware of the situation is not enough; he must be persuaded to revoke this decree.

Surely at this point, Esther could have stopped acting on behalf of the Jews. Even if this decree was still to be carried out, Esther could have stopped her intervention and been confident that no one would come into the palace to kill Mordecai and her. If Esther had been interested only in saving herself or Mordecai, then there would be no reason to return to the king's chambers regarding this matter. However, Esther is an extraordinary woman and is not swayed from her original purpose: that "relief and deliverance will arise for the Jews" (Esther 4:14). Relief and deliverance *for the Jews*: Esther realizes what God is doing through her is not only for her. She recognizes her part in God's providential plan, and will not be moved in her determination to see her purpose fulfilled.

The historian does not tell us exactly the setting in which this particular conversation took place, but the next verse suggests that the king is back in his quarters.

And the king held out the golden scepter toward Esther.
Esther 8:4a

Perhaps he is resting and thinking about what has transpired over the last few days. Perhaps now that his "wrath has subsided", Ahasuerus has completely put the situation out of his mind. Perhaps he is thinking that killing Haman and turning his property over to Esther is enough to make amends for the terrible decree.

Whatever Ahasuerus' thoughts are, Esther goes to his chambers. For the second time, she has gone to him uninvited. For the second time, she has found favor and he extends his golden scepter to her, indicating to her that she is welcome. Another great example of the proverb: *"The king's heart is in the hand of the Lord, Like the rivers of water; He turns it wherever He wishes."* (Prov. 21:1). God's favor is still strong on Esther's life.

So Esther arose and stood before the king Esther 8:4b

When Esther realizes that she is welcome, she rises and addresses the king as an equal. Esther wants the decree against the Jews revoked, but she is aware that Ahasuerus had given his signet ring to Haman to seal this order, which made the order impossible to reverse. Maybe Ahasuerus is regretting his part in this scheme. Right now it is very easy for Ahasuerus to blame this entire situation on Haman. Let's not overlook the fact that Ahasuerus could have avoided this by showing a little backbone at the time that Haman presented the idea of destroying the Jews. By giving the power to Haman, Ahasuerus himself made this decree irreversible.

Esther, like we said before, has experienced some relief in this situation. Her life, as well as Mordecai's, may be saved even though the decree against the Jews is still in effect. Surely no one would be bold enough to come in to the palace and kill the queen and her highly honored cousin. However, Esther's relief is not a signal that her task has been completed. An important but simple lesson for us in this: if any situation has driven you *in* to your "prayer closet", do not allow the relief of that situation to drive you *out*!

Esther has remained true to her purpose, and intends to see this situation through until the Jews can feel assured of their safety once again. This will be her final request of the king.

> *So Esther arose and stood before the king, and said, "If it pleases the king, and if I have found favor in his sight and the thing seems right to the king and I am pleasing in his eyes, let it be written to revoke the letters devised by Haman, the son of Hammedatha the Agagite, which he wrote to annihilate the Jews who are in all the king's provinces. For how can I endure to see the evil that will come to my people? Or how can I endure to see the destruction of my countrymen?" Esther 4b-6*

Esther asks Ahasuerus, "*How can I endure to see the destruction of my countrymen?*" What a difference from her statement to Mordecai just a few chapters ago; *"any man or woman who goes into the inner court of the king, who has not been called, he has but one law: put all to death....I myself have not been called..."* (Esther 4:11). There is no fear in her now. God has been faithful, and she knows that He will continue to be faithful!

After all that has happened, Esther is showing the king that she is driven by her passion for the Jewish people. Her motive is to rescue her people, not only to have her own life spared. God seeks out our motives and knows our hearts. Our obedience is more meaningful if our hearts are pure before Him.

Since we began with Ecclesiastes 7:8, let's finish the verse before we close for today: "The patient in spirit is better than the proud in spirit." We have certainly seen this truth demonstrated in Esther and Haman — how will you demonstrate it in your life?

※2

DAY THREE: ESTHER 8:7-8

When the Lord puts a task before you, follow through wholeheartedly! Determine to show yourself trustworthy to your Heavenly Father!

Friend to friend...

I remember Jacob and Tyler's little fingers trying to button their first buttons. Deliberate and determined, they worked until finally that button made it through the buttonhole. Given, many times the button made it through the wrong buttonhole, but it was a beginning. Though it would have been simpler and quicker had I just done it for them, I let them struggle for a little while before I intervened. I believe that my sons would have been discouraged on some level if I had come in and done it for them as soon as I noticed they were having difficulty. They would have wondered, "Why can't she just let me try?" Learning to button their buttons did take a little while, but they learned through the struggle. We struggled through weeks of shirts with buttons in the wrong holes, but they got it all together eventually. Now they button their own shirts with great ease! In this way, the struggle was of benefit to them.

I remember when my daughter first learned how to write her own name, as it turned out to be a little struggle for both of us. Lindsay was so excited and proud of herself that she found the first writing instrument that she could as soon as she got home from pre-school that day: unfortunately for me, it was a ball point pen. Determined to practice, she wrote her name all over her bedroom walls. She crawled under furniture and climbed on top of furniture to make sure every possible spot was covered. When her handiwork was finished, she came to find me. She was proud of herself and wanted to give me an opportunity to admire her newly acquired skill. I forced a smile and chose my words carefully, realizing that I had never asked Lindsay *not* to write on her walls. After that, I made sure that she had markers, crayons, pencils, and plenty of paper ready for any future urges to practice! Learning to write her name was not easy (on her or on my walls!), but the struggle was good for her. Today she writes a beautiful hand.

Your Heavenly Father will allow you to struggle in the same way. In His wisdom, He knows that from your struggles will come strength *if* your response is right. Even when we are faced with adversity, God is continually in control. Isaiah 54:17 is a very familiar passage to many believers, stating that "no weapon that is formed against you shall prosper". It is encouraging to know that there is no weapon of any sort anywhere that can destroy us while we are under God's protection. However, it is the previous verse which truly gives Isaiah 54:17 meaning in our lives. Isaiah 54:16 states,

> *"Behold, I have created the blacksmith who blows the coals in the fire, who brings forth an instrument for his work; and I have created the spoiler to destroy. No weapon formed against you shall prosper, and every tongue which rises against you in judgment you shall con-*

demn. This is the heritage of the servants of the LORD, And their
righteousness is from Me," says the LORD.

"This is our heritage": success, to be certain, but also to endure the fire that comes
from the weapon. At the same moment in which we are promised the success, we
are promised the struggle. You cannot truly experience one without the other.

God is in control of every situation. He even tells us that He "created the
blacksmith...who brings forth an instrument for his work". It is not only that He
knows your trial; He created the situation by which you are being tried. Anything
that comes to you is filtered through His hand. It is a tremendous encouragement
to know that God is in control — even of the struggles and trials that come to
you. The creation can never be more powerful than the Creator! There will never
be any situation that comes to you that you are not able to handle if you fully trust
the Lord. The Lord Himself guarantees you of that fact.

Do not misunderstand: God is not the author of confusion, strife, lack, or sickness. You have an enemy roaming about, "seeking whom he may devour" (1 Peter
5:8). You have an enemy who is trying to steal, kill and destroy you (John 10:10).
Satan is the "god of this world" (2 Corinthians 4:4), and therefore the devil is
the force behind such struggles as these. However, God has provided a means of
refuge and healing, hope and peace in Jesus. "I have come that they may have life,
and may have it more abundantly" (John 10:11).

He also warns us there will be times when He will send us out as "sheep in
the midst of wolves", but He will send us out. Like it or not, you will struggle
at times. In this life, we are not exempt from trials, but (praise the Lord!) we are
promised divine protection. Matthew 10:19-20 are absolutely incredible: "But
when they deliver you up, do not worry about how or what you should speak. For
it will be given to you in that hour what you should speak; for it is not you who
speak, but the Spirit of your Father who speaks in you." Part of your responsibility
in responding to your struggle is taking advantage of the opportunity to obey God
and glorify Him through it.

Esther is our example of being sent out as a "sheep among the wolves". As she
has gone to the king again, uninvited, she must trust the Lord to give her the right
words. Ahasuerus absolutely has to be convinced to counteract the evil decree
against the Jews. She is determined to follow through. Ahasuerus listens to her
request, and makes his answer.

> *Then King Ahasuerus said to Queen Esther and Mordecai the Jew,*
> *"Indeed, I have given Esther the house of Haman, and they have*
> *hanged him on the gallows because he tried to lay his hand on the*
> *Jews." Esther 8:7*

Ahasuerus, true to form, begins his reply by making a little speech about himself and all the great things that he has already done. He gave Haman's house to Esther. He had Haman hanged on the gallows for the Jews' sake. We know from our experience with Ahasuerus that he does not really like to make decisions. Remember when he gave Haman a free hand to carry out his plot against the Jews? Remember when he let Memucan decide for him what should be done with Vashti? He broke from his pattern to determine Haman's fate quickly and without advice, but that moment has passed. Considering Ahasuerus' history, his reply to Esther is no surprise. After he reminds of her all that he has already done, Ahasuerus makes his answer.

> *"You yourselves write a decree concerning the Jews, as you please, in the king's name, and seal it with the king's signet ring; for whatever is written in the king's name and sealed with the king's signet ring no one can revoke."* Esther 8:8

Basically, Ahasuerus tells them that he has already done enough. Rather than doing something himself, he gives them the authority to follow though with whatever they want done next. Ahasuerus tells them to write another decree concerning the Jews. He tells them to write it in the king's name, and seal it with the king's signet ring. This way, it can never be revoked. (This is the same offer that he made to Haman a few chapters ago!) This way, Ahasuerus will not have to take any further responsibility.

Ahasuerus thinks that he gave Mordecai and Esther this authority. However, we know Ahasuerus' heart is in the hands of the Lord (Proverbs 21:1). God used Ahasuerus to give this power to Esther and Mordecai. Unlike Haman who abused his authority, Mordecai and Esther have shown through their consistency and faithfulness that they can be trusted with this power. Pray that when the time to accept some authority comes in your life, He will find you trustworthy as well!

Authority is defined one way as "freedom from doubt; belief in yourself and your abilities". Esther must have been freed from doubt — but her belief was in the power of the Lord, from Whom she received her authority! You can experience this same confidence as you trust the Lord, and move ever forward in your God-given authority!

※

DAY FOUR: ESTHER 8:9-13

God is in control — you do not need to worry! Leave yourself in His hands and endeavor to follow Him closely every day!

FRIEND TO FRIEND...

When I go through a struggle, I have to remind myself...

The struggle is not necessarily a punishment. When we are experiencing difficulty in any area, it is initially a good idea to look inside. I ask myself if I did anything, made any mistake, committed any sin that might have produced such a trial. Sometimes, I find that I did bring it on myself. Good or bad, there are consequences to our actions. For a very simple example: at school, my daughter's teacher has her students sit out for a few minutes of recess if they do not turn in their homework. If Lindsay does not do her homework, she has to suffer the consequences of that decision, and that day at school will be uncomfortable: recess is a big deal when you are in the third grade. It does not have anything to do with God; Lindsay failed to complete an assignment and there are consequences. This is a situation that she created herself; her little struggle is not a punishment from the Lord.

Having been in youth ministry for so many years, sadly Michael and I saw several teenagers go through unplanned pregnancies. This is a serious struggle for a teenage girl, but is it a punishment from God? No, it isn't. A young couple makes a mistake and goes too far, breaking an important commandment (Exodus 20:14, 1 Corinthians 7:1). God did not force them into it, and He did not cause the mistake to be made. Sex outside of marriage is wrong, and there are serious and unfortunate consequences for making that decision; but those consequences are not punishments from the Lord. The consequences are *consequences*. God is not punishing these young people; they made a choice and have to face the consequences. God loves them and desires to see them restored. He is there with all the resources and love they need in order to come into a right relationship with Him again.

What do you do now, after you discover it was your mistake that brought on difficult times and struggles? You pray. You might shed a few tears. You ask for forgiveness, and God gives it to you freely (1 John 1:9). Now you tell yourself that you are suffering a consequence, not enduring a punishment from God. He loves you; you are His most precious and treasured creation. You seek His help, His guidance, His direction and you receive it. He helps you to get back on a right road. Are the consequences still in effect? Probably, but they are just that: consequences. You make choices, you live with those choices, and God is still good and loving, kind and generous.

Sometimes, when I am in a battle, I look inside myself and am not able to find any mistake that I made to create these hardships in my life. Sometimes, many times, a trial is not the result of something that we did wrong. Sometimes we struggle because we have to live in an imperfect world. I remember seeing a good friend in the hospital with a serious ailment. Over our many visits, she seemed strong and surprisingly upbeat considering the seriousness of her situation. One afternoon, however, as we sat there talking, she suddenly burst into tears. Absolutely terrified and heartbroken, she told me, "I keep wondering why God is doing this to me. I keep asking myself and God what I did to deserve this. What did I do wrong?"

Her tears broke my heart as well. I was able to explain to her that she had done nothing wrong. She had not committed any act that resulted in her present situation. For my friend in the hospital, it was simply a result of living in an imperfect world. She needed to hear that God was not the author of her struggle (John 10:10), that she was not enduring an arbitrary punishment for some unknown sin. She needed to hear out loud and often that God was her healer and her strength. The struggle was not brought in order to teach her some sort of lesson. However, even through a situation that He did not design, God in His generosity and wisdom was able to teach her how to trust Him more, and was able to bring her into a closer relationship with Him as a result. God was able to turn a bad situation around for her good (Genesis 50:20, Romans 8:28). After some time, His healing was manifested in her life, and she is in perfect health today.

While it is right and appropriate for us to turn inward when we are facing a battle, other times there is simply no correlation between the hardships we are enduring and the decisions that we made. God does teach us, but He is a gentle and loving father. As a parent myself, I know that there is no way I would break my son's arm and then tell him, "Son, I am trying to teach you something through this pain. You figure out what the lesson is, and don't make this mistake again." Never. God would not do such a thing to His children; that would be cruel, and God is never cruel. Sometimes the struggles that we have to endure are nothing but consequences of living in this fallen world.

In times of struggle, I also have to remind myself: God can be glorified through my response as well as my rescue. I went through a time in my life where I felt that if I did not experience a quick and miraculous ending to every battle I faced, I interpreted that as my own failure to operate in faith. I viewed lengthy battles as failures, as if they were caused by some lack of faith on my part. This caused me to feel shame and caused to me to hide my struggles.

God does not mean for us to feel ashamed as a result of any struggle. He means for us to become stronger and better in Him. I learned I could glorify God in the midst of hardships by remaining faithful to Him in the process. When I was younger, I had mistakenly thought that God could only be glorified in my success and ease. Now I know that God can be glorified in my response to the battle as well as my relief from the battle.

One more: the duration of the struggle is not a reflection of God's concern. Some struggles will end as quickly as they began. Praise God for those times.

Some battles last longer. We have to keep in mind that God's timing is not our timing. What seems prolonged to us, even excruciating slow, may not be long to the Lord. He knows exactly what you need and when you need it; trust Him to give guidance through the battle and give victory at the right time. Trust that "no weapon formed against you shall prosper" (Isaiah 54:17), and know that while God is not the author of your trial, He is the author of your peace. Through one, you can experience the other.

Esther did not create the stressful climate in Persia. Though the battle has been long and extremely difficult, God is being glorified through Esther's graceful response to the hardship. Notice: she is not being punished for Ahasuerus' weakness. God is not being mocked as a result of His people's trial. This struggle has gone on for many months, yet Esther's faith has not waned, nor has she grown weary in the fight. God has remained faithful to her, and His favor will remain strong in her life as she approaches Ahasuerus once again.

> *"You yourselves write a decree concerning the Jews, as you please, in the king's name...."* Esther 8:8

Ahasuerus has made his reply to Esther's final request. In a nutshell, he tells them, "If anything else needs to be done, you do it. I have done enough." Ahasuerus, though he may be feeling as if his responsibility to the Jews is over, he gives Mordecai and Esther the authority to continue their aid to them. In doing so, he must not really believe that he has done all that anyone could do for the Jews, but he does not sense an urgency for any further personal involvement. Maybe he wonders why his interest in this situation should be continued at all, seeing as the queen is safe and her enemy executed. In observing Ahasuerus, we know that he is not really concerned with too much that goes on in his kingdom; his greatest concern is for himself. Now that matters are cleared up in the palace, it appears that he is beginning to lose interest.

> *So the king's scribes were called at that time, in the third month, which is the month of Sivan, on the twenty-third day; and it was written, according to all that Mordecai commanded, to the Jews, the satraps, the governors, and the princes of the provinces from India to Ethiopia, one hundred and twenty-seven provinces in all, to every province in its own script, to every people in their own language, and to the Jews in their own script and language.* Esther 8:9

Having been given a purpose from the Lord and now permission from Ahasuerus to carry it out, Esther and Mordecai get busy writing the new decree for the Jews. Esther sends for all the king's scribes, and Mordecai dictates a new decree to all the Jews. For the remainder of this lesson, we will refer to the original decree written by Haman as "Haman's" letter or decree, and the subsequent decree written by Mordecai as "Mordecai's" letter or decree.

Mordecai obviously knew what he was doing. He sent his decree out to everyone who received a copy of Haman's decree. He had the king's courier's go out "on horseback, riding on royal horses bred from swift steeds". Mordecai understood that he was in a race against time, and he knew exactly where to send his decree *quickly*. Part of Mordecai and Esther submitting to the *purpose* that God had for them was submitting to the *process* and the *preparations*. Due to his faithfulness to be at the palace gates daily, Mordecai had information. During all of those days, Mordecai was continuing in faithfulness to God. As Esther was submitting to preparations inside the palace, Mordecai was submitting to his own preparations outside the palace. The knowledge of when Haman's decree was sent, to whom it was sent, and the exact contents of his decree comes in handy to Mordecai. At the moment that it is needed, he has all the information he needs.

Mordecai's decree went out in the third month on the twenty-third day. According to Esther 3:12, Haman's decree went out in the first month on the thirteenth day. Just two months and ten days after Haman's decree, Haman is executed and a new decree to counteract his plan is issued. Keeping this information and knowing how to handle it is now revealed as vital to the Jews' salvation; Mordecai was patient during these crucial two months. Remember, Haman had left a period of about eleven or twelve months in between issuing his decree and carrying out the destruction. At the time Mordecai's decree goes out, there are about nine months to go before the original order is to be carried out.

> *By these letters the king permitted the Jews who were in every city to*
> *gather together and protect their lives — to destroy, kill, and annihi-*
> *late all the forces of any people or province that would assault them,*
> *both little children and women, and to plunder their possessions,*
> *on one day in all the provinces of King Ahasuerus, on the thirteenth*
> *day of the twelfth month, which is the month of Adar.*
> Esther 8:11-12

Because of the way Haman's decree was written, it could not ever be reversed. The best that Mordecai and Esther could do was to give the Jews permission to defend themselves against the coming attack. Did you notice the wording? The Jews are now allowed to "destroy, kill or annihilate all" the forces of people who would assault them. Look at Haman's decree in Esther 3:13.

> *And the letters were sent by couriers into all the king's provinces, to*
> *destroy, to kill, and to annihilate all the Jews, both young and old,*
> *little children and women, in one day, on the thirteenth day of the*

twelfth month, which is the month of Adar, and to plunder their
possessions. Esther 3:13

The same words: destroy, kill, and annihilate. The same day: the thirteenth day of the twelfth month.

Even though we read earlier that the inhabitants of the city of Shushan were confused by the order to destroy the Jews, there must be people in the provinces who do not feel kindly toward the Jews. Even considering what happened to Haman when he was exposed as the enemy of the Jews, Esther and Mordecai must feel that there are people will still follow the first decree, otherwise there would have been no point in pursuing a means of defense against it.

If Haman's decree to destroy the Jews confused some people, imagine what they must think of this new order written by Mordecai. As both decrees were signed by Ahasuerus and sealed with his signet ring, both decrees must have seemed to have come from Ahasuerus himself. So, in the minds of the people, the king first orders the Jews to be destroyed; then two months later, he gives them permission to defend themselves against that same attack by any means. It may seem to the subjects of Persia as if the king is setting them up for a war in their own country, against their own country.

A copy of the letter was issued as a decree, and published all over the cities so every Jew would know about the new decree and be ready to defend themselves against the attack. They still have time to prepare themselves. Do not forget that God is in control of this entire situation. God has carefully orchestrated all of these events to work in favor of the Jews.

A copy of the document was to be issued as a decree in every province
and published for all people, so that the Jews would be ready on that
day to avenge themselves on their enemies. The couriers who rode
on royal horses went out, hastened and pressed on by the king's com-
mand. Esther 8:13-14a

The decree has been written; now it is time to get it out to the people of the kingdom. The king's scribes are called for, and they write out the new decree in all the languages spoken in the provinces of Persia. Mordecai signs Ahasuerus' name and seals it with Ahasuerus' ring. The fastest horses go out to deliver these letters carrying glad tidings for the Jews!

Your faith will stand trial at some point in your life — rejoice in the knowledge
that you will overcome as you put yourself in God's hands! He loves you so much
— and He knows that you can grow stronger in the struggle sometimes!

୨୧

DAY FIVE: ESTHER 8:14-17

Out of the struggle will come change as well as strength... This morning, I was thinking about a piece of sandpaper. It may feel rough, but it will make an object smooth... Allow the Lord to smooth out your "rough edges" — however He may choose to do it!

FRIEND TO FRIEND...

I went back to work when my youngest started kindergarten. As I had been at home and away from teaching for so many years, I did not feel ready to take on a classroom of my own. I decided to take a position as a teacher's assistant in a kindergarten class. The first challenge was work clothes. Looking into my closet, I had plenty of super-casual for everyday with the babies and housework. I also had plenty of suits and heels for Sunday mornings at church. Neither was appropriate for school with a noisy, messy group of 5 year olds.

I needed to buy new clothes, but I also needed to economize. After all, we had been a single-income family for a long time. Shopping at my favorite store, I hit a great deal: five pairs of pants on the clearance rack, and all were my size (a feat in itself; finding pants long enough for my 5'11" frame is not always the easiest task!). One small problem: all five pairs were exactly the same. Same cut, same brand, same color. I decided to purchase all five pairs anyway, and make the best of it. I bought two button down shirts, two pairs of loafers (one brown, one black) and went home to take inventory once again. Looking again at the closet and digging deeper in dresser drawers, I came up with three more button down shirts, a brown belt, and a black belt. Five pairs of pants, five shirts, matching shoes and belts... looked like my first week of school wardrobe!

Day one, I spilled glue on my shirt. Day two, it was tempera paint on the pants. Day three? Well, those mustard packs in the cafeteria are nearly impossible to open. I was successful on the third try, but got more mustard on my clothes than on my hot dog. By day four, I had given up. Kindergarten was going to be a mess! That weekend, I tried my best to get the stains out, and went on with the same five outfits the next week. I figured that if my clothes were going to be destroyed anyway, I would just wear them out. Besides, what five year old would notice what I was wearing, and what adult would care?

Surprisingly, I made it all the way until January of that school year before my pattern was discovered. One morning, a precious little girl came in and said, "Mrs. Spivey, I like your shirt." The boy behind her in line followed her compliment with, "It's kind of the same shirt you wear every day." I cheerfully explained to him this it was the shirt I wore every Thursday and was one of the same five outfits that I wore every day to school. The children laughed at having discovered something. The teacher and I laughed that it had taken them so long to pick up on my "school uniform". After that day, it became an inside joke of sorts between the children and me. They would come into class in the mornings and ask, "Is this your Monday shirt? Is this your Tuesday shirt?" One Wednesday, a little girl even came wearing an outfit that matched mine! Though I left that position several years ago, I saved one pair of those pants. They have become a sort of symbol of that happy year, and the memory always brings me a smile.

In Bible times, what a person wore often reflected his or her identity. In Mark 10:46-52, we have an account of a man named Bartimaeus. Bartimaeus was a blind beggar who was desperate for a way out of his personal darkness. Upon hearing that Jesus of Nazareth was coming through his hometown of Jericho, he began to cry out to Jesus (Mark 10:47,48), "Son of David, have mercy on me!" Though he was discouraged by his circumstances and by the people around him, Bartimaeus' faith was bolstered as Jesus came nearer. Finally, he heard the words that he had been longing to hear, "Rise, [Jesus] is calling you" (Mark 10:49).

Bartimaeus' next action is worth our notice. Before he began walking toward the sound of the Master's voice, the Bible tells us that he threw "aside his garment" (Mark 10:50). So many times in the Bible we see examples of a person's dress reflecting their identity. When Bartimaeus went to "throwing aside his garment", he was truly throwing aside his identity as a blind beggar. Bartimaeus, before even receiving his healing, had confidence in Jesus' ability to heal him. His faith did not go unnoticed or unrewarded. Jesus, in His infinite wisdom knew why this man had come to Him. Even so, He asked Bartimaeus to confess his need: "Teacher, that I may receive my sight" (Mark 10:51b). "Go your way; your faith has made you whole"(Mark 10:52). Bartimaeus received his sight immediately. When Bartimaeus was healed, he threw away the clothes that had identified him as a blind man. He came into the presence of the KING and he walked away changed.

The account of Bartimaeus' healing is more than just a story to read. It is an example of what should happen when we come into contact with Christ. It is an encouragement of what is possible when we truly experience the presence of God. We should enter His presence and be changed by His power.

In Ezekiel 46:9, the people were instructed on how to enter and exit the temple. "But when the people of the land come before the LORD on the appointed feast days, whoever enters by way of the north gate to worship shall go out by way of the south gate; and whoever enters by way of the south gate shall go out by way of the north gate. He shall not return by way of the gate through which he came, but shall go out through the opposite gate."

The people were instructed to come in by the south gate, and exit by the north gate. If they entered by the north gate, they were to exit by the south gate. They were never to exit the temple through the *same* gate they used to enter the temple. The people were literally required to exit in a different way than they had entered. Imagine entering your church next Sunday morning with a purpose in your spirit; "I will leave differently than the way I came in"... not a literal, physical difference like choosing an alternate door; but a spiritual difference. You entered mournfully; receive joy from the presence of the Lord and leave jubilantly. You entered wearily; receive peace from the presence of the Lord and leave rested. When you come before your KING, come with an attitude of expectancy that *you* will be changed. Every time you come into His presence, determine to receive what the Lord has for you, and *be changed* as a result of your contact with your King!

I stopped wearing my "teacher's assistant clothes" when I stopped being a teacher's assistant, but my spiritual "garments" were the most important change of my life. Bartimaeus stopped wearing his "blind beggar" clothes when he stopped being a blind beggar, but imagine the glorious garment that identified his change! What is it that you need to put aside in order to receive your new identity from the Lord?

Today in Persia, Mordecai is undergoing change; an outward expression of his inward faith. The Jews in Persia will experience change as well. Let's read and rejoice with them as they begin to celebrate their newfound victory.

> *The couriers who rode on royal horses went out, hastened and pressed on by the king's command. And the decree was issued in Shushan the citadel.* Esther 8:14

The decree is going out, and the royal couriers have been commanded by the king to hurry. They are being "hastened and pressed on" by the king to deliver this important message. The very day that Haman meant to be a day of destruction for the Jews will instead be a day of triumph for them. Now they have nine months to prepare to defend themselves against anyone who may still be planning on obeying Haman's decree, sent out a little over two months ago.

Let's take a look back and remind ourselves of the emotional climate in Persia in the last two months. First, there has been an enormous change in Mordecai. When he first learned of the decree, even his outward appearance reflected his inner turmoil.

> *When Mordecai learned all that had happened, he tore his clothes and put on sackcloth and ashes, and went out into the midst of the city. He cried out with a loud and bitter cry.* Esther 4:1

Mordecai went into the king in one way, and left in another way entirely: clothes changed, position changed, demeanor changed. Though he always possessed assurance of victory in the Lord by faith, now he has tangible confirmation. His connection to Esther has been revealed, and he has been given the authority he needed to fight Haman's decree. Now his outward appearance reflects his inner joy.

> *So Mordecai went out from the presence of the king in royal apparel of blue and white, with a great crown of gold and a garment of fine linen and purple...* Esther 8:15

When the decree goes out, Mordecai goes out from the presence of the king. Now, leaving the palace, Mordecai is honored and promoted. He is wearing a royal robe, a great golden crown, and a purple garment. This would be an immediate signal to the Jews in Shushan that their petitions had been heard and answered by God.

Speaking of the Jews, there is a great change in their demeanor as well. Just a few chapters ago, upon hearing Haman's decree, they were beyond discouraged.

> *And in every province where the king's command and decree arrived, there was great mourning among the Jews, with fasting, weeping, and wailing; and many lay in sackcloth and ashes.* Esther 4:3

Depending on God to work through Queen Esther to bring about their rescue, their hopes are confirmed as they see Mordecai. After they see their faith has been met, they express their jubilation.

> *...and the city of Shushan rejoiced and was glad. The Jews had light and gladness, joy and honor.* Esther 8:16

In contrast to their prior feelings, the inhabitants of Shushan are now rejoicing. They are full of light and gladness, joy and honor. (Do you have those feelings when you feel certain you are in the will of God?) Things are not exactly perfect for the Jews yet. An attack is still coming, but now they are certain the Lord is on their side, and they have no reason to fear.

> *And in every province and city, wherever the king's command and decree came, the Jews had joy and gladness, a feast and a holiday. Then many of the people of the land became Jews, because fear of the Jews fell upon them.* Esther 8:17

We certainly have become accustomed to events and situations being turned "upside down" in the book of Esther. Where it was a pitiable position to be a Jew in Persia only a few short months ago, now it is an enviable position; so much so that people are converting to Judaism! Just a few months ago, it was the Jews who were in great fear, now it is people who are not Jewish who have something to fear. Though this reversal may have come as a surprise to some, God has had this plan in His mind from the very beginning. The Jews may seem to be the "underdog" now, but we'll soon find out who ultimately comes out on top.

One more before we close out the week, and we'll read this one together:

"But God has chosen the foolish things of the world to put to shame the wise, and God has chosen the weak things of the world to put to shame the things which are mighty; and the base things of the world and the things which are despised God has chosen, and the things which are not, to bring to nothing the things that are, that no flesh should glory in His presence. But of Him you are in Christ Jesus, who became for us wisdom from God — and righteousness and sanctification and redemption — that, as it is written, "He who glories, let him glory in the LORD." 1 Corinthians 1:27-31

It may seem backward, but in the absence of your understanding, you must trust the Lord. He does not require your strength or wisdom or gifts to bring you success: He requires your faith!

Thinking better of it, I realize that "upside down" was not exactly the right term. For lack of a better one, I'll borrow a silly little word that I remember one of my sons saying to me when he was very little: things in Persia are being turned "upside *right*"!

Are things upside down in your life? Things that once made sense do not make sense anymore... maybe plans that seemed right have fallen through... Do not allow confusion to turn your heart from the Lord — trust Him to turn things "upside right" for you!

❧

"Blessed be the name of God forever and ever, For wisdom and might are His. And He changes the times and the seasons; He removes kings and raises up kings; He gives wisdom to the wise and knowledge to those who have understanding. He reveals deep and secret things; He knows what is in the darkness, And light dwells with Him."
Daniel 2:20-22

Father, Your love is a gift.
If I allow it to, Your love will free me.
Your love will free me from being afraid
of the struggles and trials that may come my way.
Because of your love, I am able to recognize
that seasons and times are in Your hands.
When I need wisdom, I trust You to give it.
When I need knowledge, I trust You to give it.

Your love will free me from being afraid that change will not come —
whether it be a change in my circumstances, or a change in me.
You reveal secrets, and in You is the light that I need in order to see.
You are all I need,
and I love belonging to You!

৯২

---

1.   Dr. Augustus Hopkins Strong, Systematic Theology, p. 420.

ESTHER: CHAPTER 9
The Jews Overcome their Enemies

Esther has boldly gone to the king. Demonstrating a principle we can learn from her, as well as in the New Testament, she follows her faith with action. James, the brother of Jesus, writes, "Thus also faith by itself, if it does not have works, is dead. But someone will say, 'You have faith, and I have works.' Show me your faith without your works, and I will show you my faith by my works" (James 2:17-18). This verse is a challenge, a sort of "wake-up call" to anyone who thinks that faith alone is enough. Your faith should not be without good works. "Works" ought to be a natural progression from faith; the all-important next step. Esther demonstrates this principle to us beautifully. She believed the Lord, and her belief stirred her to action. Esther's faith in God's word over her life gave her the confidence to take the next step, and the next step, and the next step...

Jesus offered several parables about seeds and sowers, but one in particular seems to stand out today. He said the kingdom of God is "like a mustard seed which, when it is sown on the ground, is smaller than all the seeds on earth; but when it is sown, it grows up and becomes greater than all herbs, and shoots out large branches, so that the birds of the air may nest under its shade" (Mark 4:31-32). Consider Esther's life for a moment. Before she came to the palace, she may have seemed small, unimportant, or even unnoticed. A tiny seed. However, when the Lord placed her, *sowed* her, into the palace at the right time, she became "greater than all". Esther's influence, like the large branches of that now-grown little mustard seed, became far reaching and life changing. Through her obedience, the Jews were able to find relief and peace, like the birds of the air nesting in the shade of a mighty tree.

In another passage, Jesus says the "kingdom of God is within you" (Luke 17:21). That little seed with tremendous potential is already inside you. You received this gift at the point of salvation. Through God's providence, partnered with your obedience, you have an awesome responsibility to see that seed planted into the right ground at the right time. God will provide the direction and protection you need to flourish; you have to provide the obedience and commitment necessary to see harvest come. When the harvest does come, you will be amazed to find that the growing was not only for you; God will use the harvest produced in you to strengthen the people around you. People will find rest and peace, a place to grow and find "shade" in you. Ultimately, they will be drawn to the One who truly provides that rest. When you are able to see this kind of fruit spring from your life, even one changed soul will make all your struggle in waiting for the harvest to come absolutely worthwhile.

Where are you in this cycle? Are you the seed waiting to be sown? Wait no more. Recognize that it is God Who is waiting for you. He has already invested a great deal: His entire kingdom is in you! Seek His direction and see that you are sown into good ground. Are you the young sprout whose green, pliable branches are being threatened by the heat of the sun? Refuse to give up. Refuse to give in. Find your strength in the Lord. Feed yourself on His Word and depend on His strength to grow you into a mighty tree. Are you already the mighty tree? Evaluate your purpose. Are people finding rest and retreat in your testimony? Is your faith (are your branches) strong enough to carry someone weaker than yourself?

Of course, a huge tree could be a roadblock as easily as it could be a refuge. Are you a help or a hindrance to the people who might find peace in your strength? What is your next step? Pray that the Lord would reveal it to you even this week. As Esther, Mordecai and the Jews are experiencing victory in Persia, I am praying that you will too experience personal victory.

Here's the true challenge: your big victory will not come without big risk. Thank God for the gift of faith. Thank God for His promise that He will always lead us to triumph in Christ Jesus (2 Corinthians 2:14). With that promise serving as our "safety net" this week, let's follow our heroine's example, and work to ensure that our faith is reflected in our actions.

❧

DAY ONE: ESTHER 9:1

As the Lord trusts you with victories, He may also trust you with trials. Remember that the strength to face either with grace comes from the same place inside you. Pray that God will give you this strength!

FRIEND TO FRIEND...

In Proverbs 17:11, Solomon writes "an evil man seeks only rebellion." (1 Samuel 15:23 describes rebellion as being comparable to the "sin of witchcraft".) Proverbs 17:11 also tells us the consequence for the evil man seeking rebellion: "a cruel messenger will be sent against him". Certainly this is what happened to Haman. In his rebellion against God and God's chosen people, he received a "cruel messenger": one that brought the news of his own destruction.

Surely the evil man described in this verse is not entirely alone in the world. What of the good men that happen to be in the vicinity of the "evil man who seeks rebellion"? *Nothing.* No word is spoken in this verse about them because there are no consequences to the good man who happens to witness evil, unless the good man gives into the temptation as well. In this truth you can find the freedom that you need to serve the Lord without worrying about what will happen to you as a result of someone else's shortcomings. Look at Esther and the Jews in Persia: though there was a struggle and though there were hard times, at the end of the day they were not punished or judged for Haman's rebellious and hateful nature.

Our application here is this: you must be faithful to God and successful in God *while living in this world.* You may be working with people who do not share your exact set of beliefs. You may be living with people who do not share your exact set of beliefs. You may even be worshiping with people who do not share your exact set of beliefs. The challenge and the necessity for us is to continue being faithful to God regardless of what people may do. A person with a different set of values than yours does not affect or change your values in any way. A different set of values does not have the power to change your values in any way; unless *you* give it that power. Your faith in God is not determined by the actions of man. Refuse to be swayed by the actions of others.

Your reflection is found in the word of God (James 1:22-25), not in people. James 1:27 gives us direction for Christian living in this age: "keep yourself unspotted from the world". The Living Bible translates the verse in this way: the "Christian who is pure and without fault, from God the Father's point of view, is the one...who remains true to the Lord-not soiled and dirtied by his contacts with the world." We will come into contact with the world. while we are inevitably forced into contact with the things of this world, we must find a way to maintain our integrity and effectiveness as believers.

Just as important as being submissive to God, is being submissive to the government under which we live. In Mark 12:17, Jesus tells us to give to "Caesar that which is Caesar's". It is important for us to obey the laws that govern our country. Excepting for the most extreme situations, following the laws of our country will not interfere with following the laws of God. For example, we pay taxes to our government and we pay tithes to our churches. One does not interfere with the other. We have freedom of speech as every other citizen does; we can use our freedom of speech to "cry out and shout... for great is the Holy One of Israel" (Isaiah 12:6)! Trust God to provide a way for you to be successful in Him without being rebellious to the governmental authority in your life.

Esther, as always, offers a wonderful example for us. Living among non-believers, Esther maintains her faith *and* makes a powerful impact on the people around her. To be honest, if it were possible to live in this world and not come into contact with any non-believer, would you? Hopefully, your answer is a resounding "no"! The Word instructs the believer to "let your light so shine before men, that they may see your good works and glorify your Father in heaven" (Matthew 5:16). Find a balance between affecting the fallen world you live in and not letting it affect you.

Let's return to Persia now and watch as Esther continues to make an impact in her world. We will also witness how God creates a situation in which the Jews can be saved and not be rebellious to the very government that put the decree against them in place.

During the time recorded in chapter eight, Esther made a final request of Ahasuerus and asked that he reverse the decree. Unfortunately for Esther and the Jews, the king had been persuaded by Haman to write the decree in such a way that it could never be reversed — not even by the king himself. Though Ahasuerus could not reverse the order to utterly destroy all of the Jews, he did give the Jews permission to defend themselves against the impending attack. Using a tremendous amount of wisdom and foresight, Mordecai writes out the new decree and has it published to all the people in all the provinces.

Our chronicler "cuts to the chase" with the beginning of this chapter. Though we were some months away from the attack on the Jews at the end of chapter eight, now we skip right to the day when Haman's decree against the Jews is supposed to be carried out.

> *Now in the twelfth month, that is, the month of Adar, on the thirteenth day, the time came for the king's command and his decree to be executed. On the day that the enemies of the Jews had hoped to overpower them, the opposite occurred, in that the Jews themselves overpowered those who hated them.* Esther 9:1

This verse is describing the day in which the Jews were to be destroyed by their enemies. This battle was not a surprise to the Jews or to their enemies; both groups had several months to prepare for the fight. Both sides had a royal decree as well: one to attack, and the other to defend against the attack. God, in His great wisdom and grace, has provided a way for the Jews to defend themselves without being rebellious to the government. Please consider that there is no mention that the Jews considered any alternative means to defend themselves before Mordecai's decree. Had it not been for the second decree, the Jews would have certainly been destroyed.

God will provide a way for you to be successful in Him without being rebellious to the authority in your life. Even though Ahasuerus is not a godly individual, he is the authority in Mordecai's and Esther's lives. Earlier in the study, we discussed how God knew exactly where the Jews were at this moment in history. Furthermore, God was the One who had them sent to Persia in the first place. (For a reminder, go to Jeremiah 29). God knew the king in Persia. God knew the circumstances in and the spiritual climate in Persia. Mordecai and Esther were there by providential design. God created a situation in which the Jews could be saved without being rebellious. He can do the same for you!

Consider your own personal circumstances. God, in His infinite wisdom, knows exactly where you are. He is omnipresent: everywhere at once. Beyond knowing where you are, He is there with you. God also know exactly what you are going through. He is absolutely and completely aware of your situation. Jesus promises never to leave us (John 14:18); let that knowledge encourage you. Good times and bad times alike, you are never without His presence. In Psalm 139:7-8, the psalmist describes two extremes. He writes, "where can I flee from Your presence? If I ascend into heaven, You are there; If I make my bed in hell, behold, You are there." Never changing in His concern for His people, God is able and willing to do for you today what He did for the Jews so long ago. He loves you, He refuses to leave you... How much more of a reason could you need to trust Him?

Let's take a look back at the Jews in Persia.

> *And in every province where the king's command and decree arrived, there was great mourning among the Jews, with fasting....*
> Esther 4:3

The Jews first response was to take their fear to God. Upon receiving the news of the first decree, they did not begin plotting their best defense against the coming slaughter. Self-defense was not on their minds. They turned to the Lord and fed their faith rather than their fear. This attitude was also taken by the psalmist in Psalm 59:16. He writes, "But I will sing of Your power; yes, I will sing aloud of Your mercy in the morning; for You have been my defense and refuge in the day of my trouble."

Even Esther is convinced that this decree will be carried out to Haman's satisfaction (the destruction of the Jews) unless the Lord intervenes. Her response is the same as that of the rest of her people: she turns to the Lord.

Then Esther told them to reply to Mordecai:

> *"Go, gather all the Jews who are present in Shushan, and fast for me; neither eat nor drink for three days, night or day. My maids and I will fast likewise."* Esther 4:15-16

Another easily applicable truth also found in the psalms: "I called on the LORD in distress; The LORD answered me and set me in a broad place. The LORD is on my side; I will not fear. What can man do to me?" (Psalm 118:5-6). What can man do? Absolutely nothing.

Esther will not lead a rebellion. She knows that the Jews will not rebel against the government, even to save their own lives. They are in unity. Mordecai, Esther, and the rest of the Jews trust the Lord to be their defense. Remember Esther's bold statement in chapter 4 verse 16: "If I perish, I perish!" Do not overlook this powerful and important aspect of their faithfulness to God: the Jews are more willing to *die* while *in* the will of God than to *live* while *out* of the will of God. Rebellion is not in God's will.

Do you have that same determination? Would you rather die than be out of the will of God for you? It is a big question, but one you may have to answer within yourself. What is the "bottom line" in your life? Encourage yourself with the word of God!

The Lord is your defense, and He will make a way where there seem to be no way. God will defend you and keep you no matter what comes into your path. Of course, we have to understand the meaning of the word "defend". "Defend" is a verb, an action word, that literally means to resist some sort of attack, or protect someone from some sort of harm. The very term suggests that there is danger for you to be defended against. Once again we see our twin truths: the warning and the promise, the direction and the encouragement. In promising His defense, the Lord is also gently reminding us that there will be an attack. We live in an imperfect world. Thankfully, we serve a perfect God!

One last verse before we close for today; a precious promise from the heart of our precious Savior. Because faith comes by "hearing and hearing by the Word of God" (Romans 10:17), read it aloud if you can:

> *"Indeed the hour is coming, yes, has now come, that you will be scattered, each to his own, and will leave Me alone. And yet I am not alone, because the Father is with Me. These things I have spoken to you, that in Me you may have peace. In the world you will have tribulation; but be of good cheer, I have overcome the world."*
> John 16:32-33

Be of good cheer: regardless of your circumstances, Jesus has already overcome the world! In Him, you will overcome too! Keep these words in your heart today and meditate on them : you are an overcomer!

God's faithfulness is enduring to all generations — that includes you! Show Him that you are grateful for His faithfulness to you by being faithful to Him. Show your faith by your works!

DAY TWO: ESTHER 9:2-5

If God be for you, who can be against you? Have no fear, woman of God!

FRIEND TO FRIEND...

Ecclesiastes 4:9-12 reveals important truths about relationships and unity: two truly are better than one. Specifically, look at verse 10: "if they fall, one will lift up his companion." This is our job as believers together. If someone around you falls, the needed and appropriate response is to pick him or her up. It is not for us to judge when someone makes a mistake or takes an inappropriate action. It is for us to offer our assistance and allow the Lord to work through us to strengthen that person. You should to be conscious of the need for you to remain in a position from which you can be a support and strength to them. It is not for us to "fall" with them. Even if you do not "fall" into the sin you see someone commit, adopting a critical or judgmental attitude is a downward "fall" in itself. Leave the judging to God; offer your help and make it your business to "lift up" your companion.

The same idea is echoed in the New Testament in James 5:19-20. James writes, "if anyone among you wanders from the truth, and someone turns him back, let him know that he who turns a sinner from the error of his way will save a soul from death and cover a multitude of sins". We are to lift each other up and help each other turn from sin and error. Though a natural response may be to remove yourself from the situation and criticize from the sidelines, fight that urge. Take the higher road. As we learned earlier, you will not be judged for the actions of another person. However, you will be judged for your own: don't be afraid to reach down and come to the rescue.

As you allow your strength to help others, do not become prideful; there are times when you must allow the strength of others to help you as well. For some reason, this is an area where many Christians experience difficulty. Among believers there should be no room for jealousy or competition. There is no reason for you to feel threatened by another believer's gifts. If you can overcome a fear in this area and push yourself through to a place where you can receive from another believer, you will find tremendous blessing and power.

Recognize also that it is always of utmost importance for you to stay in unity with the people serving God around you. You are not always in a position to help; you are always in a position to serve alongside. Ecclesiastes 4:11 brings to mind a most comforting picture: "if two lie down together, they will keep warm; but how can one be warm alone?" We are not meant to be alone. Even in the very beginning, the very first thing that God did not describe as good in His creation was the fact that Adam was alone (Genesis 2:18). Learn how to let your gifts flow with the gifts of the people around you.

I have a good friend who has a wonderful voice and true anointing to lead people in worship. People are drawn to Jennifer's talent, and as she dedicates this talent to the Lord, they are drawn to Him. I am blessed by her gift as well. I have wondered what my response to her would have been had we met as younger women. I am ashamed to admit that I may have been jealous of her! In college, I was a music major, and spent a great deal of time practicing voice and piano. I really thought at one time that my ministry would be music. Years later, I have traded my dreams and goals for what the Lord has ordained for me. Ultimately I found that His dreams were truly a better fit and I have found such tremendous joy in serving Him in a different way than I had expected when I was young.

When Jennifer sings at our church, I have a much different view than I may have had when I was young and immature: I love it! I am not jealous of her; I am glad we are on the same "team". In 1 Corinthians 12:20, Paul states that in Christ "there are many members, yet one body". While it's true Jennifer is a much better singer than I am, her gifts do not take anything away from mine at all. Her success is my success because we are serving the same God: we are both members of the same body. We are on the same "team" serving the same God. There is no need for discord; there is great cause for joy in our separate gifts! If we were all singers, who would preach? If we were all missionaries, who would minister here at home? There are so many "positions" to be filled within the body of Christ. Laboring together and in harmony with each other's gifts is what makes it all work.

In Matthew 18:19-20, Jesus gives us a promise concerning unity: "where two or three are gathered in My Name, I am there in the midst of them." Another promise in Psalm 133:3 says it this way, "For [where there is unity] the Lord commanded the blessing — life forevermore." Where people are gathered together for a singular purpose in the name of the Lord, God commands His blessing, promises His presence, and reveals His power.

In Persia, the Jews have claimed this promise and acted in unity against the attack. In spite of Mordecai's decree giving the Jews permission from the king to defend themselves, there are still people in Persia determined to follow the first decree ordering the destruction of the Jews on the appointed day. However determined these enemies are, it will not be enough to defeat a people who had the power of the Almighty God on their side. In Esther 9:1, the Jews overpowered their enemies. Esther 9:2 gives a little insight into how they were able to defeat their enemies, and at the same time demonstrates a life principle.

The Jews gathered together in their cities throughout all the provinces
of King Ahasuerus to lay hands on those who sought their harm.
And no one could withstand them, because fear of them fell upon all
people. Esther 9:2

The Jews "gathered together in their cities.... to lay hands on those who sought their harm." They worked together. It was through their unity that they were successful: unity in purpose, unity in their faithfulness to God, unity in the fight... Unity is a very powerful tool. It would have been very difficult for the Jews to defend themselves had they all stayed in their homes, or adopted an "every man for himself" attitude. Their strength was in their UNITY, and the word of the Lord is proven true again: "there the Lord commands His blessing — LIFE forevermore" (Psalm 133:3)! The Lord's blessing was *commanded* in the place of *unity*.

Fear of the Jews had fallen on all the people by now. If the enemies of the Jews had underestimated the Jews before, they realize their mistake at the end of this fated day. "No one could withstand them"... Not a single person in the kingdom was able to withstand the power of the Lord in His people. No one can come against you either, woman of God. The Lord is on your side!

And all the officials of the provinces, the satraps, the governors, and
all those doing the king's work, helped the Jews, because the fear of
Mordecai fell upon them. For Mordecai was great in the king's pal-
ace, and his fame spread throughout all the provinces; for this man
Mordecai became increasingly prominent. Esther 9:3

The Jews were not alone in this battle. In God's generous way, He caused the officials and all the men working for the king in the different provinces to come to their aid. Though God was on their side, making the support of men unnecessary, this aid probably served as a confirmation to the Jews that they were on the right course. We do not seek signs; our faith alone must be evidence enough of God working on our behalf, but this confirmation must have offered tremendous relief and peace to the Jews.

While we know it was the Lord causing these kingdom officials to assist the Jews, what natural reason did these unbelieving men have to help? As verse 3 tells us, Mordecai is feared by the other kingdom officials, and recognized throughout the provinces. In verse 4, we read that his fame is spreading all over Persia. Because of his presence in the palace, the other kingdom officials are starting to offer help to the Jews. It is apparent now that he was placed in the right place at the right time. In God's providence, the timing was perfect. Perhaps they think if the king notices their help to the Jews, they will receive favor as well. What they do not know is that Mordecai's favor is coming from the true *King*!

Thus the Jews defeated all their enemies with the stroke of the sword, with slaughter and destruction, and did what they pleased with those who hated them. Esther 9:5

"Thus" is a word that means "*in this way*". In this way, the Jews defeated all their enemies: together!

It truly is good and pleasant when we live together in unity...Like the Jews working together in Persia so long ago, it is important for you sometimes to make decisions based on what is best for the group — not only what is best for you. You'll find that ultimately a decision made with selfless motives is the best decision!

⁂

DAY THREE: ESTHER 9:6-11

God means for you to be victorious! That is a true comfort! However, He also means for you to be continually aware of where your help comes from — do not trust the victories, and do not allow a victory to cause you to trust in yourself. It is only as you continue to follow Him that you will continue to be successful!

FRIEND TO FRIEND...

Mordecai has received promotion from Ahasuerus and favor with the people of Persia, Jew and non-Jew alike. As we read in Esther 9:4, Mordecai's fame is spreading all over Persia, to every province. Notice that Mordecai did not have to seek out this position; he obtained it by his faithfulness. It is also important to notice that Mordecai does not use his position to seek out revenge. He does not abuse his newfound power in any way. Just as he has been faithful with whatever God entrusted to him throughout his entire life, he is faithful with the authority that has been entrusted to him now. Like Esther has done during her time on the throne, now Mordecai continues to demonstrate submission and faithfulness to the Lord Who gave him this authority.

In Luke 16:10, Jesus offers an important insight: "He who is faithful in what is least is faithful also in much." If someone is trustworthy over a few things, they will also be trustworthy over many things. By the same token, if someone cannot be trusted with the small things, they will not be faithful with the larger things either. This principle proved unfortunately true in Haman's life. When he received his promotion from Ahasuerus, his pride started to swell and his heart conceived evil plans. This was most likely a reflection of how Haman lived. The authority given to him by Ahasuerus did not make him evil; he had been practicing being evil his entire life. Haman was not trustworthy, and giving him more authority only proved to highlight this characteristic in his life.

On the other hand, consider Esther and Mordecai. Esther and Mordecai had always maintained a pure heart before the Lord. When their promotion came, they recognized it as from the Lord. They continued in the same faithfulness which they had been practicing their entire lives. The positive response which they had received from Ahasuerus did not make them "good". Esther and Mordecai dedicated their lives to the Lord and tapped into the potential for good that He places inside all people. They continually dedicated their gifts to the Lord. Esther and Mordecai were trustworthy in all things.

Being trustworthy is such an important trait, and one that should be developed in the life of every believer. One effective way to cultivate this quality is to remain humble before the Lord. What does being humble have to do with being trustworthy? A humble person will be quick to give credit to the Lord in the midst of victory and joy. A humble person will effectively point others to the Lord and not take credit for him or herself. A humble person will faithfully represent the goodness of God to believers and non-believers alike. The ability to faithfully represent the Lord is a prime example of being trustworthy in the gifts with which He has entrusted you.

Victories are described in the Word of God over and over again. Many different situations, many different people, many different times, God proves He can always make a way. However, in all the myriad ways that God works to bring about triumph for His children, one aspect is always the same: victory comes from and belongs to the Lord. 2 Samuel 23:10 says that "the LORD brought about a great victory that day". 2 Kings 5:1 tells us that "the LORD had given victory". In 1 Chronicles 11:14, "the LORD brought about a great victory". 1 Chronicles 29:11 tells us that "Yours, O LORD, is the...victory". 1 Corinthians 15:57 states "thanks be to God, who gives us the victory through our Lord Jesus Christ". Begin being trustworthy by giving all the glory to God.

For me, just reading the first few verses of chapter nine did not really give a clear picture of what the Jews truly accomplished on the day that was set for their destruction. We know that they were victorious, but the chronicler does not tell us how many people came against them — only that *all* the people who did come against them were in fact defeated. All 5? All 50? We haven't learned that... yet. If you were rejoicing with the Jews yesterday over their victory, just wait until you read the rest of the account! We learned that the Jews destroyed all of their enemies, and did what they pleased with the plunder. Today, we'll get into a little more detail about this victory; and see how Esther, Mordecai, and the Jews continue to handle it.

And in Shushan the citadel the Jews killed and destroyed five hundred men. Esther 9:6

Five hundred. Let that number sink in for a minute. That is an overwhelming number for one city. Five hundred men. That is an overwhelming number for one DAY. Five hundred men. This represented a tremendous victory for the Jews. However, for every victory we win, we must understand the struggle from which it came. A minimum of five hundred people in Shushan alone were against the Jews. The struggle had been great, but the victory was greater.

Imagine: if five hundred men were destroyed, that means in this city that at least this many people were against the Jews. Though the Jews had lived and worked quietly in Persia for many years, the atmosphere must have been some-what hostile. Though the city was described as "perplexed" (Esther 3:15) when Haman's decree was made known, there were many people in the city who were willing to carry out this order. Five hundred men in this one city alone, but Persia had 127 provinces other than Shushan as well. Think about this: five hundred men defeated in one city; and there are 127 other cities where this same battle is raging. We do not know the number of fatalities in the other cities.

Among the fatalities, the historian reveals specific identities.

> *Also Parshandatha, Dalphon, Aspatha, Poratha, Adalia, Aridatha, Parmashta, Arisai, Aridai, and Vajezatha — the ten sons of Haman the son of Hammedatha, the enemy of the Jews — they killed; but they did not lay a hand on the plunder.* Esther 9:7-10

The history list the ten names of Haman's sons. All ten of them were killed in addition to the 500 men killed in Shushan. The Jews did not touch the "plunder", even though the decree written by Mordecai had given them the right to take their possessions (Esther 8:11).

Just a little side note: in looking for definitions of the names of Haman's ten sons, two of the names reveal a little something. "Dalphon" (Strong's # OT:1811) means, "to... drop through, melt, pour out."[1] Also, Aridatha (Strong's # OT:717) literally translated means, "prolonged in the sense of violence".[2] Haman's atti-tudes and rebellion (his wife's as well) were most likely passed on to his sons, and so the evil and anger could have continued — *been prolonged and/or poured out* — had his sons been allowed to live.

The decree gave the Jews permission to keep any possessions of any people whom they defeated. The word plunder means "spoil" from a battle. Plunder can refer to properties stolen or seized by force during a war. However, the Jews did not keep any of these possessions for themselves. They were not fighting in order to gain wealth through this violence. For the Jews, the object of this battle was to *defend* themselves. This is another aspect of this situation that proves to us that the Jews were not out for revenge. They had permission from the king to take any pos-sessions of their defeated enemies. We might say they had a right to take whatever "plunder" was left, but they did not take anything. Their faith in God was strong, and they did not need to profit from the death of these men. God would provide their needs, just as He provided this victory.

Just a couple of things to think about....

Remember Abraham? In Genesis 14:21-22 (he was still Abram at this time), he refuses to take any possessions from Sodom, though the king offered. Perhaps the Jews are taking his example, and refusing to be made rich off the spoil of evil men.

In Persia, what about the women and children? What does the decree say about them in Esther 8:11? The Jews were given permission "to destroy, kill, and annihilate all the forces of any people or province that would assault them, *both little children and women*, and to plunder their possessions", but chapter 9 only tells us that five hundred men were killed. It is entirely possible that the deaths of the women and children were simply not recorded (that would not be at all unusual). However, try for a moment to consider the feelings and character of the Jews: they are not out for revenge, they are only trying to defend themselves. Is it possible that the Jews did NOT kill the women and children? Women and children did not participate in the battle. If the Jews are only defending themselves against people coming against them, perhaps there was no reason to seek out the women and children and kill them in this battle as well.

If the Jews did leave the women and children, is it possible that they left the "plunder" for them? Such an act of mercy may also be remembered by the women and children, and might prevent even further animosity between these two groups of people in Persia. (These are just my personal thoughts based on what we have read about the Jews and their character; not based in history or the Scriptures. It would not have been wrong for the Jews to follow Mordecai's decree to the letter and destroy the women and children and take the plunder).

> *On that day the number of those who were killed in Shushan the citadel was brought to the king.* Esther 9:11

King Ahasuerus is made aware of the Jews' victory in Shushan. We'll read his response to this news tomorrow!

Father, every good and perfect gift is from You. Without You on my side, there is no victory! Help me to trust You through the trials in my life, and help me to operate in wisdom through the victories that You bring to me. It is a gift to be Your child!

DAY FOUR: ESTHER 9:12-14

God is glorified as we are faithful — strive daily to reflect His character to the people around you! Allow the Lord to show Himself strong through YOU!

FRIEND TO FRIEND...

When we first planted the church, Michael was "bi-vocational". He held one job as the pastor of our new congregation, and the other was as a criminal investigator in the same county where he had once served as a deputy. I often wondered if the sharp contrasts between these two positions created any sort of confusion or difficulty for him. One day, I wondered aloud, and Michael had a powerful answer to my query.

Though holding two jobs was difficult, it was the contrast between the two that Michael loved. He told me, "Jennifer, I see people at their worst: selfish, degraded, driven to desperate situations and even criminal acts. I also see people at their best: giving, loving, making sacrifices for the benefit of others. I get to see all of this, often in the same day. Do you know what experiencing these vast differences in people teaches me?" I didn't, but after that beginning, I wanted to know. I shook my head, so Michael continued.

He told me: "The Holy Spirit uses these experiences to remind me every day that the possibility to be on either end of this continuum is in every single one of us. The difference between where any of us may land lies in our dedication to the Lord. Jesus makes the difference. Without Him, I could have one of those 'worst days'. Any good day is a result of His grace, and any bad day can be redeemed by His forgiveness."

Wow. I loved the mental picture Michael's explanation provided: a continuum, with our best possible on one end and our worst possible on the other. A continuum is defined this way: "a continuous sequence in which adjacent elements are not perceptibly different from each other, but the extremes are quite different." Think about it: "adjacent elements may not be perceptibly different". In a church, everyone may appear to be the same. In a jail, everyone may appear to be the same. Compare one to the other, and the differences between them may initially seem striking, but always bear in mind that we are all created by the same God, and that same God desires all people to live in a close relationship with Him (2 Peter 3:9). The possibility to succeed is in every one of us, just as is the possibility to fail. Praise God for the potential in you, and praise God for the days in which you reach that potential. Praise God when the people around you achieve their God-given purposes. Be gentle when they fail, as you would hope that they would be gentle when you fail. The potential for failure is there on your best day; the potential for greatness is there on your worst day. We are all on this "continuum" together.

I learned something else about my husband on this day. His answer explained more than just why he loved both of his jobs. His answer also explained to me the reason behind his openness in the pulpit. Michael has always shared openly from his pulpit. Triumphs and tragedies alike, they all make it into his sermons on a regular basis. Upon hearing some of his personal illustrations, I sometimes think to myself, "did he have to tell all that?". In the end, however, he is always right to share his heart. In sharing our good times, he gives his congregation an example of praising God and serving Him on the best days. In sharing our heartbreaks, he gives his congregation an example of praising God and serving Him on the worst days. As God is always the same, our response in either situation should be the same. Whatever the situation, it should always point us to Him.

Another valuable outcome of Michael's sharing his heart freely with his flock is that it makes him accessible. He demonstrates to the people who have been entrusted to him that he is Christian, like they are. Not "super Christian", not infallible, not above them or any better. He is simply giving them the opportunity to see his response to the best and the worst, and his example seems to inspire the congregation to put aside their own fears and be themselves: serving God and growing every day.

As members of his congregation follow Michael's example, hopefully they are able to share their best and worst with people among their own spheres of influence. This way, the cycle continues: in the good, God is praised; in the not-so-good, God is praised. People whom we may never speak to personally are touched and are pointed to Jesus because of Michael's showing the path to freedom: taking the words of Jesus to heart and truly living what He spoke to us: "Let your light so shine before men, that they may see your good works and glorify your Father in heaven" (Matthew 5:16). Jesus said "your good works" without qualifying when "your good works" should happen. Good works are not only expected in the triumphs; they are simply *expected*.

We need to back up and see this direction from Christ in its context. Matthew 5:13-16 reads:

> You are the salt of the earth; but if the salt loses its flavor, how shall it be seasoned? It is then good for nothing but to be thrown out and trampled underfoot by men. "You are the light of the world. A city that is set on a hill cannot be hidden. Nor do they light a lamp and put it under a basket, but on a lampstand, and it gives light to all who are in the house. Let your light so shine before men, that they may see your good works and glorify your Father in heaven.

"Let your light SO SHINE before men" (Matthew 5:16, emphasis mine). Do not allow the word of God and the action of God to become of no effect in you. Allow yourself to be open and transparent with the people around you, and share the difference Jesus Christ makes. Recognize your purpose, and who you are in Christ. You are salt: *to season, preserve, and protect.* Salt must touch food to be effective in preserving. You are light: *to reveal, illuminate, and show the way.* A lamp must be connected to a source of power in order to provide light. You are a city on a hill: *to offer a refuge, and provide a ground for unity.* A city must be *accessible* to provide refuge and protection. You must be genuine in order to be accessible. You must be accessible in order to be effective.

Esther has made herself accessible. Remember that without any guarantee of a favorable outcome, she exposed herself completely to Ahasuerus the first time she went into his chambers. Though Esther experienced favor with the king from their first meeting, imagine how much more he must admire her now that he has a truer understanding of her character. Now that the Jews have proven victorious over their enemies in a fantastic way, Ahasuerus desires to see Esther again. Let's join her in the throne room.

At the end of the day, the news of the battle in Shushan is brought to Ahasuerus. He must have called for Queen Esther, because she is there now speaking with about this turn of events. Though it may have been unusual for a king to consult with his queen concerning political policy and battles, Ahasuerus has a few questions of his own for Esther. Surely her wisdom, grace, and faithfulness (to God, to the Jews, AND to Ahasuerus) is opening this door for her with her husband, the king.

> And the king said to Queen Esther, "The Jews have killed and destroyed five hundred men in Shushan the citadel, and the ten sons of Haman. What have they done in the rest of the king's provinces? Now what is your petition? It shall be granted to you. Or what is your further request? It shall be done." Esther 9:12

The king tells Queen Esther of the victory for the Jews. He tells her that five hundred men in Shushan have been killed, as well as Haman's ten sons. Ahasuerus also wants to know if Esther has heard what has happened in the other provinces. In spite of the fact that these deaths represent his people in his own city of Shushan, and subjects all over *his* kingdom, he does not seem particularly upset by the news. Even though this tragic situation was created by Haman and then diffused by Mordecai, it can hardly be said that Ahasuerus played no part. It is amazing that Ahasuerus can stay this detached. It is also worth noting that the normally selfish Ahasuerus is not making any attempt to attribute this victory to himself. He has just learned of five hundred deaths in one city alone, and his response is to ask Esther if she has any other information. He then asks her if she has any further requests. A promise is made to Esther: any further request she may have will be granted to her.

Here is yet another example of God's providence. God is showing her favor once again and He is using the people around her to accomplish His divine purposes.

> *Then Esther said, "If it pleases the king, let it be granted to the Jews*
> *who are in Shushan to do again tomorrow according to today's decree,*
> *and let Haman's ten sons be hanged on the gallows."*

Esther 9:13

Because of Esther's faithfulness and perseverance, God has shown her favor yet again. She is invited into the king's chambers, and without prompting, Ahasuerus offers to grant another request. Esther asks that the king allow the Jews in Shushan to defend themselves against further attack again on the following day.

This seems an unusual request from Esther. We know she is not acting out of anger or some desire for more bloodshed; either would be out of character for her. Possibly she is wanting to reinforce to the people in the capital that the power of God is truly with the Jewish people. Perhaps she is desiring to show the people in the capital that Ahasuerus has given his support to the survival of the Jewish people. Esther knows that this show of power will surely be told in all of Persia. It is also possible that Esther senses that there are still people in this city who are against the Jews, and she wants to try to avoid problems before they have a chance to start.

Esther also asks that Haman's sons be hanged on "the gallows". We do not need to think hard to know to which gallows she is referring. Esther means the gallows that Haman built in his front yard for Mordecai. She means the gallows that Haman was hanged on himself. Even though she was given this property by Ahasuerus, she must have kept the gallows up as a remembrance to the inhabitants of Persia. To the Jew and to the non-Jew, the gallows must have made quite a statement. Seeing the bodies of Haman's dead sons on these gallows would make quite a statement as well.

> *So the king commanded this to be done; the decree was issued in*
> *Shushan, and they hanged Haman's ten sons.* Esther 9:14

Whatever Esther's reasons for these requests are, King Ahasuerus does what he promised he would do. He grants her request. Haman's sons are ordered to be hanged on the gallows prepared by their father, and another day of fighting is in store for the inhabitants of Shushan.

As Ahasuerus did for Esther, your King will do the same for you. You have a standing invitation to enter His throne room. You also have a promise that *as you are faithful*, He will grant whatever you request. As recorded in John 15: 7, Jesus says, "If you abide in Me, and My words abide in you, you will ask what you desire, and it shall be done for you."

"You will ask what you desire, and it shall be done for you." This is good news, but there is a condition. You must "abide" in Christ and let His words "abide" in you. When the word of God abides in your heart, you will make requests to your King in wisdom. Your prayers will have a purity that will be irresistible to your Heavenly Father. You will make *right* requests, and God will respond to you. Abide, as you may remember, means "to stay (in a given place, state, relation or expectancy)... abide, continue, dwell, endure, be present, remain, stand, tarry for"[3] — LIVE and CONTINUE in... you must plant the word of God in your heart. Once the word is planted, you must continue working to *keep* it there!

John 15:8 is a great verse for us to close with today:

> *"By this My Father is glorified,*
> *that you bear much fruit;*
> *so you will be My disciples."*

The Father is glorified as you continue to abide in Him: strive to glorify Your Father!

Bearing good fruit is a great outward sign that something is growing right on the inside... Well, depending on the fruit, it could also be a sign that (uh-oh!) something is growing wrong in the inside. Are you bearing fruit that is glorifying to Your Father? Pray for opportunities to please Him — and bear good fruit!

✿

DAY FIVE: ESTHER 9:15

As God is faithful, how will you respond? Continued trust in His goodness and power is the only right attitude, though Satan will try to tempt you into trusting in yourself. You are smarter than that, Woman of God! You are a daughter of the King — not a victim of a snake!

FRIEND TO FRIEND...

In thinking about Esther's initial response to the task set before her, I am again in awe of the change which the Lord has wrought in her. From the intimidated, alienated young queen in unfamiliar surroundings who told her cousin, "...any man or woman who goes into the inner court to the king, who has not been called, he has but one law: put all to death... I myself have not been called to go in to the king these thirty days" (Esther 4:11), an amazing transformation has taken place. Now, many months later, Esther stands before Ahasuerus, confident enough to request a second battle between the Jews and their enemies.

A few verses are brought to my mind as I consider Esther's commitment to the task set before her and the faithfulness she has demonstrated every step of the way. Jeremiah 42:6 says, "Whether it is pleasing or displeasing, we will obey the voice of the LORD our God to whom we send you, that it may be well with us when we obey the voice of the LORD our God." Initially when Esther learned what Mordecai expected her to do on behalf of the Jews, she was displeased with the task. After her fast, however, Esther obtained the same kind of resolve that this remnant had in speaking to Jeremiah: whether or not it seems to please us personally, we will obey the voice of the Lord. The only way to experience success and effect change is to obey God's voice. This was a principle that Esther understood and acted upon.

Proverbs 11:3-6 also seems to fit here:

The integrity of the upright will guide them,
But the perversity of the unfaithful will destroy them.
Riches do not profit in the day of wrath,
But righteousness delivers from death.
The righteousness of the blameless will direct his way aright,
But the wicked will fall by his own wickedness.
The righteousness of the upright will deliver them,
But the unfaithful will be caught by their lust.

Esther's integrity has guided her, while Haman's perverse and faithless spirit ended in his own destruction. While the Jews were delivered as a result of their righteousness before the Lord, Haman's riches could not save him. Esther, Mordecai and the Jews had their paths directed as a result of their blameless actions. Haman's wickedness caused him to reap wickedness and be caught in his own trap of lust for power, wealth, and recognition from men.

One more, and we will return to Persia to close out this week: "Hope deferred makes the heart sick, but when the desire comes, it is a tree of life" (Proverbs 13:12). Always bear in mind that the hope inside you was placed there by God. He knows your heart, and He knows that losing the thing for which you are hoping will make you sick inside. In His providence, He is continually working to create an atmosphere in which you can be successful. Trust His heart, and do not grow weary of waiting for your hope to come. God has given you a promise, and "though it tarries, wait for it; because it will surely come..." (Habukkuk 2:3).

Esther is seeing that the victory for which she carried so much hope has come. The promise made to her by God is being fulfilled before her very eyes. The battle that had at one time threatened her life has become a crown.

After the battle, Esther requests that the Jews in the city of Shushan be allowed to do the same "again tomorrow according to today's decree". King Ahasuerus grants her request.

> *And the Jews who were in Shushan gathered together again on the*
> *fourteenth day of the month of Adar and killed three hundred men*
> *at Shushan; but they did not lay a hand on the plunder.*
> Esther 9:15

Once again, the Jews "gathered together". Once again, UNITY helps them win the battle. As God provided the victory yesterday, He also provides the victory on this day. As the Jews were faithful to God through the first victory, they are faithful to God through the second victory. Another three hundred men are killed in Shushan, bringing the total in this city alone to eight hundred men.

Once again, the Jews leave the plunder. Even though they have experienced great victories twice in a row, they do not get "cocky". Their plan yesterday was to defend themselves and to trust their God. The plan did not change today. The plan was not altered at all by their victory. We see yet another example of what was discussed last week: if some situation has driven you *in* to the prayer closet, do not allow the relief of that same situation to drive you *out* of the prayer closet. The Jews did not falter in their faithfulness. They recognized that every victory came from the Lord. They recognized that without Him there would be no victory.

Sometimes people experience victories, and then begin to trust in themselves. The Jews did not fall into this trap. When they learned of their impending destruction, they prayed and trusted the Lord. When they learned of the opportunity to defend themselves, they prayed and trusted the Lord. By preparing and putting His principles to work, they were victorious. Their attitude did not change with the success God had given to them.

This kind of faithfulness is a trait we see in Mordecai as well. When he was an exiled Jew raising an orphaned cousin, he was faithful to God. When he was honored by the king, he was faithful to God. When he received the promotion to become "second-in-command" in Persia, he was faithful to God. Esther also has the same quality of steadfastness. As an orphan girl, she was faithful to God. As a "queen-in-training", she was faithful to God. When she became queen, she was faithful to God.

Take this lesson from Esther this week: wherever you are, let the Lord find you faithful. Whether His instruction is "pleasing or displeasing" to you, obey the voice of the Lord "that it may be well" with you!

Even in victories, do not fall into the trap of pride in SELF! In James 4:10 it is written, "Humble yourselves in the sight of the Lord, and He will lift you up." You are a gift and a treasure, woman of God! You have no need to trust in yourself — your God is in control!

❧

"The integrity of the upright will guide them, But the perversity of the unfaithful will destroy them. Riches do not profit in the day of wrath, but righteousness delivers from death." Proverbs 11:3-4

Father, Your love is without compromise. If I allow it to, Your love will free me.
Your love will free me from allowing circumstances or even the people around me
to sway me from my primary purpose: being faithful to You.
If I wrap myself in Your love, I will be released from the unreasonable fear that my witness or my integrity could be compromised
by the response of other people to You or Your word.
I recognize that my responsibility is to represent You well;
anyone else's reaction or response is Your responsibility.
This freedom will allow me to be patient with people, gentle with people, and unaffected in my own walk by the actions of other people.
This freedom will release me from judging people
(a selfish task — and one that does not belong to me).
To make it plain, Your love gives me the freedom to do my part faithfully, confident that You will "do Your part" in me and all the rest of Your children!

❧

1,2,3. (Biblesoft's New Exhaustive Strong's Numbers and Concordance with Expanded Greek-Hebrew Dictionary. Copyright (c) 1994, Biblesoft and International Bible Translators, Inc.)

ESTHER: CHAPTER 9-10
A Big Celebration

"Through many dangers, toils and snares..." Esther has traveled a long journey to come to today's celebration. She has trusted in the providence of God. She has allowed the love of God to push past her fear so that she could stand in the gap for her people. Though unexpected events came her way, she handled it all with grace and faithfulness. In doing so, she set a wonderful example for the people of Persia and for us. Considering a few events preceding Esther's ascension to the throne one more time will give us a broader picture of God's providence.

Around the year 606 B.C., the prophet Daniel came to Babylon (under Persia's control) with the Jews who were taken into captivity. About 20 years later, while the Jews are still in captivity, the prophet Jeremiah's ministry begins, and he encourages them that the Lord has good intentions toward them and will end the captivity at the right time (Jeremiah 29). Though Mordecai and Esther have remained in the city of their captivity, they have experienced firsthand His faithfulness. The Lord fulfilled His promise to His people.

Around 538 B.C., King Cyrus comes into power. King Cyrus is King Ahasuerus' (Xerxes) grandfather. As the prophet Isaiah had prophesied over him some 200 years before Cyrus ascended to the throne, he ends the Babylonian captivity (Isaiah 44:28-51). At the time of their release, Cyrus allows the Jews to return to Jerusalem, and also orders that work to rebuild the temple should begin (Ezra 1). Though his support to the Jews was initially strong, Cyrus loses interest at some point and work on the temple is stopped.

Some eight years after coming into power, King Cyrus dies. His son, Darius, ascends to the throne. King Darius is King Ahasuerus' father. During his reign, work to rebuild the temple begins. Beyond his order to begin work on the temple again, Darius finances the work (Ezra 6).

Around the year 486 B.C., King Darius dies. Now his son, Ahasuerus, comes into power. Three years into Ahasuerus' rather uneventful reign, Queen Vashti is dethroned. Four years after dethroning his queen, Ahasuerus' servants suggest a search for a new queen. Esther is brought to the palace, and after a year or so, is chosen to become queen of Persia. Though Ahasuerus' reign may have been somewhat disappointing, Esther's time on the throne is anything but that. She aids in averting an assassination attempt on Ahasuerus' life, exposes a terrible enemy, and comes to the rescue of the entire Jewish race.

The Jews' celebration was truly years in the making by our God of providence. Let's celebrate with them as we close out this last week!

DAY ONE: ESTHER 9:16-19

In Psalm 40:9, the psalmist writes, "I have proclaimed the good news of righteousness In the great assembly; Indeed, I do not restrain my lips"... As the Jews in Persia are celebrating, let us celebrate as well — do not restrain your lips from proclaiming His good news in your life!

FRIEND TO FRIEND...

Shortly after Michael and I moved to Miami, a woman came into the church offices. It seemed obvious to Michael that she was in desperate need of help. Sadly, he could not communicate with her: she spoke no English, and no one in the office was able to translate her Spanish. Michael phoned one of our youth leaders, fluent in both English and Spanish. Placing the call on the speaker phone, Michael asked our friend to translate the conversation. Speaking in her own language, this woman tearfully told her story. Once she was finished, still on the speaker phone, our friend communicated this poor woman's situation to Michael. She was in a new apartment, and her landlord required an immediate deposit or she would be evicted. The difficulty was that she would have no money for two weeks, when her Social Security check was expected. If Michael could loan her the money, she would pay him back as soon as her check arrived.

As I was working at the church myself, Michael called me to his office. Knowing she could not understand us, we spoke freely to each other in front of this woman. Michael had asked the pastor: the church had no benevolence for her. Heartbroken himself over her situation and full of compassion, Michael wanted us to help her personally. I asked him if he was certain; the amount for which she was asking us for was almost exactly the amount that we had in our small savings account. It was all we had. Considering the huge cut in pay that the move to Miami had represented for us, there was no guarantee that we would ever see this money again if she did not pay us back. It was a tremendous sacrifice on our part. I asked Michael if he was certain; with tears in his own eyes, he told me that he was sure. I looked at this woman and smiled at her. Normally I would not have continued such a private conversation with my husband in front of a stranger, but, after all, she could not understand us. I felt badly for her myself. If we *could* help her, maybe we should. I told Michael that he should act as he felt was right; I would be in agreement with him if he wanted to give this money to her.

Over the phone, our friend explained to her that we were going to help her. He also explained to her that this was our own personal money, rather than the church's money. I watched as Michael wrote out that check. I didn't feel as if he was wrong, but I still drew in a deep breath as I saw the number. It was all we had. He handed it to her, she spoke what seemed to be words of gratitude and left. We were quiet for a few minutes, but then Michael said, "Jennifer, if we ever make a mistake, let's err on the side of mercy." This time my smile was more genuine, and his sweet words brought tears to my eyes. Confident that we had been right, we went on about the day.

About three weeks later, Michael and I were out running a few errands. Walking toward the grocery store from our parked car, Michael began to run. I was confused by his sudden hurry and quickened my own pace. I stopped when I saw that Michael had run out in front of a car. A nice, new car. Green station wagon. The car stopped, and as Michael made his way to the driver's window, I knew why he had stopped this car: the driver was the same woman to whom we had given the money.

"Hello!" Michael greeted her. It didn't seem as if she recognized him, but she was very polite. "Hello! How are you?" she replied. "Hello" and "how are you", in perfect English, barely even an accent. As long as I live, I'll never forget it. While I thought my eyes might pop out of my head, Michael didn't flinch. He said to her, "I thought you didn't speak English, friend." Her eyes grew as big as platters as she began to recognize him . "Oh, well, I learned!" she offered to him, a little too eagerly. "Well, I'm proud for you. Have a good day. We'll see you soon.", Michael told her. "Oh you will, Pastor, you will! See you very soon!"

We never saw her again. Though she did not ever give that money back to us, the Lord has returned it to us a hundredfold over the years. We were young and easily taken in, our zeal for helping people and coming to the rescue of the weak in our new city overriding the wisdom that the Lord might have offered to us had we taken a few more minute to consider the sum. We have thought about that woman so many times over the years. Though now we are older and try to be more careful stewards, we will never forget our little commitment to each other and to the Lord on that day so many years ago: "if we make a mistake, let's make it on the side of mercy."

We have had many opportunities to help people over the years. Sometimes it was money they needed, sometimes it was time. Sometimes it was support, sometimes it was friendship. Every time, we gave. We gave as unto the Lord, and trusted Him for the return. Though sometimes it has come back to us through the same person to whom we gave, many times it was the Lord Who replenished our supply.

Every time Michael shares this story, people laugh when he recalls her saying, "Hello! How are you?" It does make for a comical story, but I cannot pretend that we have never been hurt. As pastors, we have seen people come and seen people go. At times, we have given all we had, only to watch people walk by us as if we were wallpaper on the background of their lives. At times, our hearts have been broken, and we feel as if we could hardly stand to make such an investment in someone else. Every time, we take our heartbreak to the Lord. Every time, the Lord asks us the same question, tailored to the situation. He will say, "Why did you give?" We answer as honestly as we can: "Because, Lord, we felt as if it was right. We felt as if it was what You would have us do. We gave because it was You Who sent them into our lives, even if only for a season. We gave because You provided the ability to give." Every time, the Lord offers the same soothing answer: "Then you were truly giving to Me. Satisfy yourselves in that, and let me heal you so you can give again." And again and again and again... Like Paul said, "I would gladly spend and be spent for the sake of your souls" (2 Corinthians 12:15). Our hearts are made whole again in the hands of the One Who created us; and we face the next need, whether it be our own or that of someone else, with no fear.

Jesus spoke of giving in Matthew 10:8. He said, "As you have freely received, freely give". Your life is a gift; do not hesitate to offer it back to the Lord. Sometimes that will require serving His people. In Luke 6:38, Jesus tells us to "Give, and it will be given to you: good measure, pressed down, shaken together, and running over will be put into your bosom. For with the same measure that you use, it will be measured back to you." You can be confident that what you give in the right spirit will be given back to you. However, there is no guarantee that it will come back to you from any specific source. Trust the Lord to provide for you, and give freely without expecting return from men.

In 1 Timothy 6:18-19, Paul writes about giving. He says, "Let them do good, that they be rich in good works, ready to give, willing to share, storing up for themselves a good foundation for the time to come, that they may lay hold on eternal life." You can expect a return, but you must understand that you are not only *giving*. You are *investing*. The Jews in Persia surely understand this principle of giving without fear of loss. We will see them demonstrate it beautifully today.

As Jews throughout all of Persia came together to defend themselves on the appointed day, they found their strength in the Lord and in their *unity*. Esther made another request of the king at the end of the day: that the Jews in Shushan be allowed to do the same the next day. She also requested that Haman's ten sons be hanged on the gallows. The king granted each of her requests. He commanded each of these things to be fulfilled. The day after the initial victory, the Jews in Shushan killed another 300 men (in addition to the 500 killed the day before). Haman's ten sons were hanged on the gallows. Again, they did not claim any of the plunder for themselves, though it was well within their "rights" according to the decree.

We have spent several verses talking about the Jews in Shushan. What about the Jews throughout the rest of the provinces of Persia?

> *The remainder of the Jews in the king's provinces gathered together and protected their lives, had rest from their enemies, and killed seventy-five thousand of their enemies; but they did not lay a hand on the plunder.* Esther 9:16

We have to appreciate the victory that the Jews experienced. Eight hundred enemies of the Jews were killed in Shushan. *Seventy five thousand* of the Jews' enemies were killed outside of Shushan on the appointed day. The Jews throughout all of Persia were not only unified in their defense, they were also unified in their *attitude*. No Jew throughout all of Persia laid a hand on the plunder. Maybe this was a message that the battle had not been about revenge for the Jews. Maybe it was a message to the unbeliever that they were completely dependent on the Lord. Their refusal to gain wealth as a result of another man's death must have been a very strong message, made all the stronger by their unity.

It is also interesting to notice that while the decree clearly gave all the Jews a right to take all of the plunder for themselves, *none* of them did. The Jews were so spread out over the provinces, it is nearly impossible to imagine that they were somehow able to communicate to every single Jews across Persia any intention to leave the plunder. As they were unified in their purpose, they were also unified in their devotion to the Lord. God can speak to His children, and His word never contradicts itself.

Psalm 25:14 tells us that "the secret of the LORD is with those who fear Him, and He will show them His covenant". The Jews in Persia have demonstrated quite emphatically by their actions over the past several months that they do fear the Lord. The word "secret" literally translated (Strong's # OT:5475) means, "a session, i.e. company of persons (in close deliberation)".[1] Possibly God spoke to everyone in this "company of persons", and placed in their hearts this gentle reminder: He alone had always been their source, and He alone would always be their source. The Jews had no reason to fear lack, therefore they felt no need to profit financially from these deaths.

God tells the Jews in Jeremiah 31:33 that He will form a new covenant with His people. He will put his "law in their minds, and write it on their hearts". His covenant is one of peace and provision, health and security, and much more; all our needs provided for in one perfect covenant between a loving God and His faithful people. Imagine if God had put this same thought in the minds and hearts of all the Jews in Persia: "Do not care for yourselves; I will care for you as I always have. No need for the plunder of evil men; I have riches beyond human comprehension for you!" At the moment that they needed direction, possibly reassurance, the Jews had it.

> *This was on the thirteenth day of the month of Adar. And on the fourteenth of the month they rested and made it a day of feasting and gladness.* Esther 9:17

The Jews outside of Shushan had rest from their enemies. They made this day a day of celebration. Feasting, light, and gladness made this a different kind of party than Ahasuerus was accustomed to throwing. This was not a party to celebrate a man: it was a time to celebrate what God had done for them. This was a celebration of praise to the Lord.

> *But the Jews who were at Shushan assembled together on the thirteenth day, as well as on the fourteenth; and on the fifteenth of the month they rested, and made it a day of feasting and gladness.* Esther 9:18

The Jews in Shushan celebrated on the fifteenth day. Remember, because of Esther's request, the Jews in Shushan had one more day of fighting than the rest of the provinces. They waited until their work was completely finished before celebrating. Even though there had been great victory for the Jews all over Persia, and even though others throughout Persia were celebrating already, the Jews in Shushan were not distracted from their purpose. As we read earlier, their determination and focus served them well, and they were successful a second time.

> *Therefore the Jews of the villages who dwelt in the unwalled towns celebrated the fourteenth day of the month of Adar with gladness and feasting, as a holiday, and for sending presents to one another.* Esther 9:19

For the Jews, this was a "good day", a day for feasting and gladness... Important to notice here is that it was also a day of "*sending presents to one another*". Did you notice that the Jews exchanged gifts? This is key: as they refused to profit from the battle (take the plunder) they demonstrated their faith in God to provide their needs. Beyond refusing to profit from the spoils of evil men, they even gave gifts to each other. On this day of unrestrained joy and praise, they gave freely of what God had *already* provided for them. What a fantastic way to express to the Lord gratitude over what He has done in your life: freely give. If we truly understood that God is ever our Source, as the Jews in Persia must have understood, then there would be no need to worry about giving.

Notice also that the Jews celebrated *immediately* the great victory the Lord had given to them. While the grace of God was fresh in the hearts, they turned their excitement over the victory into praise!

Before we close for today, take a moment to celebrate what God has done in you! Maybe you have experienced great victory in your life. Did you pray hard for the victory? Did you cry hard through the battle? Now that it is over and Christ has led you to triumph just as He promised, praise Him with the *same* determination and energy that drove you to pray during the battle!

This is a simple, but one of my favorites is Psalm 126:3 — "The Lord has done great things for us; and we are glad!" Isn't that true? Hasn't He done "great things" for you? Aren't you glad? Celebrate His goodness to you!

☙

DAY TWO: ESTHER 9:20-25

Father, Your mercy never fails — this must mean that there is never a moment when I do not have a reason to praise You! Let me take this opportunity right now: Thank You, Lord!

FRIEND TO FRIEND...

In 2 Corinthians 8:1-5, Paul writes about the churches of Macedonia. He writes,

> *Moreover, brethren, we make known to you the grace of God bestowed on the churches of Macedonia: that in a great trial of affliction the abundance of their joy and their deep poverty abounded in the riches of their liberality. For I bear witness that according to their ability, yes, and beyond their ability, they were freely willing, imploring us with much urgency that we would receive the gift and the fellowship of the ministering to the saints. And not only as we had hoped, but they first gave themselves to the Lord, and then to us by the will of God.*

Once these Christians in Macedonia were made aware of God's abundant grace, their response was to give *liberally*. Just as God's grace had been given freely to them, they gave freely to others. Liberality means *to remove or loosen restrictions.* They literally removed all restrictions on their giving. In the Strong's concordance, "liberality" is literally translated in this way: "sincerity (without dissimulation or self-seeking), or (objectively) generosity".[1]

The Macedonian Christians went far beyond generous giving. They gave with no concern for their own provision. Paul writes that these churches in Macedonia had extraordinary responses to extraordinary circumstances. First, they were in the midst of a great struggle. Their response to the great struggle was abundant joy. Paul writes that "in a great trial of affliction" they had an "abundance of their joy". Second, they were in the midst of great poverty. Their response to their lack? They *gave*. Paul testified to the Christians in Corinth that "their deep poverty abounded in the riches of their liberality".

As with so many areas of our Christian walk, the example offered by the Macedonian Christians seems to demonstrate a backward kind of logic. A financial advisor might tell you to take care of yourself before you begin to give. However, God tells us that He will take care of our needs. As you have received freely, give freely. The churches in Macedonia may not have been rich financially, but they were rich in other ways. They were rich in joy and rich in generosity. The love of God had made them so confident that they were able to give, even through their lack, without fear. Representing another contradiction is that the Macedonian churches give with no ulterior motive. They are not expecting a return from man. They are not giving to receive recognition or praise.

Paul wrote that the Macedonian churches gave "according to their ability" and also "beyond their ability" (2 Cor. 8:3). This type of giving certainly required an extraordinary faith in God's ability and desire to provide for them. They looked beyond their lack and were able to see what the Lord truly desired for them: joy, peace, love and provision. Once they felt confident in that knowledge, it became the very thing which they desired to see happen for other believers. Paul writes that they were "imploring... with much urgency that we would receive the gift and fellowship of the ministering to the saints" (2 Cor. 8:4).

What a beautiful picture! Once the grace of God has been revealed to us, our response should be the same: to share His grace with others. Remove the restrictions that you may have in your own mind about giving. Certainly giving can refer to financial gifts, but beyond that, you can give of your time, your knowledge, your talents or your resources. Having God's grace revealed to you fully should release you from fear. You no longer have to fear that your own needs may go unmet as a result of sacrificial giving. You can be confident that God is your provider at all times. You do not have to fear going unrecognized when you give of your time or talents, because you can be confident God will reward you. Imagine the unrestrained joy and confidence that comes along as a result of leaning fully on God's grace.

Once Esther and Mordecai realized that they were an integral part of God's plan to save the Jews from destruction, they were very deliberate and careful throughout the entire process. They depended on the Lord and sought His guidance at every turn. Esther and Mordecai also encouraged the Jews around them to do the same. Remember when Esther asked Mordecai to gather all the Jews present in Shushan to fast and pray for her before she went into the king for the first time?

Those prayers were certainly heard and answered, and probably in a much greater way than even the Jews had expected!

Just like Paul wrote to the Ephesians, "Now to Him who is able to do exceedingly abundantly above all that we ask or think, according to the power that works in us, to Him be glory in the church by Christ Jesus to all generations" (Ephesians 3:20-21). God surely exceeded Esther and Mordecai's expectations in Persia. Esther and Mordecai must be celebrating with great passion and joy like the rest of the Jews; maybe even more so because of all their hard work.

However, Esther and Mordecai still have work to do. As much as Esther desired to see her people rescued, she possessed a stronger desire to communicate to her people the faithfulness of God. Like the Macedonian Christians, this may have been Esther and Mordecai's way of imploring the Jews to recognize the hand of God in every step of the process, not only in the final battle. Perhaps this letter was meant to encourage fellowship among the believers in the full knowledge of what the Lord had done. Esther continually points her people to the Lord.

> *And Mordecai wrote these things and sent letters to all the Jews, near and far, who were in all the provinces of King Ahasuerus, to establish among them that they should celebrate yearly the fourteenth and fifteenth days of the month of Adar...* Esther 9:20-21

As the Jews are celebrating all over Persia, Mordecai writes the entire history in letters to the Jews. Of course, the Jews already know part of the story. They knew their lives were put in grave danger by the first decree written by the evil Haman. They knew they were saved by the second decree written by Mordecai. They knew it was God who gave them the victory. However, for the Jews, there must have been many "holes" in this story. When Esther asked Mordecai to have the Jews in Shushan pray, there were Jews all over Persia who were not made aware of the bravery of their queen.

Considering that even Ahasuerus was initially in ignorance of her heritage, it is possible there were people outside of the capital who were still unaware of the fact that Esther was Jewish. Mordecai wrote the entire history to "fill in the blanks" for the Jews all over Persia. Their celebrations were most likely made even more significant as they learned of everything that had transpired over these several months. For Esther and Mordecai, it was equally important, if not more important, for the Jews to celebrate the faithfulness of God as it was to celebrate the victory over their enemies. In order to truly appreciate how much they had to over come and how far the faithfulness of God had brought them, they needed to understand the whole story.

> *...as the days on which the Jews had rest from their enemies, as the month which was turned from sorrow to joy for them, and from*

> *mourning to a holiday; that they should make them days of feasting*
> *and joy, of sending presents to one another and gifts to the poor.*
> Esther 9:22

Mordecai is not only telling the Jews their story, but he is also instructing them to celebrate every year on these days! "*Make this a tradition! God has turned your sorrow into joy!*" Mordecai tells them to make feasts on this day each year. He also tells them to send presents to each other and to give gifts to the poor. In the King James version, the word "presents" is translated as "portions", which suggests a measured amount of food. The word "gifts" suggests a sacrificial gift. Certainly this was meant as a way of remembering that God is their Source. The Jews were sharing amongst themselves out of the abundance that God had provided, and giving sacrificially with the knowledge that God would return their "gifts" to them. "Freely you have received, freely give"! According to Mordecai's instructions, the Jews were to put this principle into action every year.

Let's adopt this same tradition of giving in our own lives — God loves a cheerful giver!

> *So the Jews accepted the custom which they had begun, as Mordecai*
> *had written to them...* Esther 9:23

"So the Jews accepted the custom which they had begun". They were united in their obedience to the Lord throughout the conflict, and now they are united in their attitude of praise to God! Their celebration is made all the more special because of their new knowledge from Mordecai: their *entire* story!

> *...because Haman, the son of Hammedatha the Agagite, the enemy*
> *of all the Jews, had plotted against the Jews to annihilate them, and*
> *had cast Pur (that is, the lot), to consume them and destroy them;*
> *but when Esther came before the king, he commanded by letter that*
> *this wicked plot which Haman had devised against the Jews should*
> *return on his own head, and that he and his sons should be hanged*
> *on the gallows.* Esther 9:24-25

Many of the Jews probably did not know Haman had cast lots against them to determine the day of the intended destruction. Many probably did not know that Esther had gone before the king to stand in the gap for them. Many probably did not know that the destruction which Haman had meant for Mordecai had fallen on his own head. Many probably did not know that Haman's sons were hanged on the gallows in the capital. Now that they have received Mordecai's letter informing them of the *entire* history, they are able to celebrate the entire history!

What has God done in your life? How has Christ led you to triumph? Consider your entire history as we close out today, and thank Him for all the events in your life (even the times that you would have skipped over had you been given a choice) that brought you to *today*. This is the day that the Lord has made, and you should rejoice and be glad in it!

God is good! Whether or not we are aware of everything He has done for us, we have so many reasons to praise Him. The Jews began praising God before they had the whole story, imagine how much more reason they had to celebrate once they received Mordecai's letter!

Father, You are so good to me! Let me join the psalmist today and say to You: "You have turned for me my mourning into dancing; You have put off my sackcloth and clothed me with gladness, To the end that my glory may sing praise to You and not be silent. O LORD my God, I will give thanks to You forever!" Psalm 30:11

DAY THREE: ESTHER 9:26-28

Recognize that what God is doing IN you, He is also doing THROUGH you! Do not allow His faithfulness to stop with you — pass it on!

Friend to friend...

At specific times each year, I go on a twenty-one day fast. A couple of years ago, I felt as if my children were ready to share this time of sacrifice with me. Knowing that it would be unsafe to ask my three little ones to go without food, I determined another type of sacrifice that we could make together: we would go twenty one days without "eating out". It may not seem like much of a sacrifice, but we enjoy going out to eat. With our busy schedule, it has even become part of our routine. Lindsay and I always eat at our favorite "fast food" restaurant on Tuesdays in between violin lessons and cheer practice; Tyler and I like to go to breakfast together before his karate class on Saturday mornings. Once a month, Michael and the children get up early and go out for chocolate chip pancakes before school.

For a few weeks, we forego these little parts of our routine. They become built-in teachable moments between us and our children. While Lindsay and I have a sandwich in the car on the way to cheer practice, we can talk about how Jesus fasted. We pray together. Over breakfast on Saturday morning with my son, I can explain to him how the fast works. While we are making this sacrifice, we take these opportunities to make a "trade" of sorts with the Lord: every time we think of going into a restaurant, we are reminded of our fast and we take an opportunity to pray instead. We try to have a specific area of concentration of our prayer together during our fasts. While my children and I agree on something specific, I also pray that their faith will be strengthened by the opportunity to see the Lord move.

In Psalm 78, the psalmist writes about the importance of passing on the faithful works of the Lord from generation to generation. He writes in verse 4, "we will not hide them from their children, telling to the generation to come the praises of the LORD, and His strength and His wonderful works that He has done." The faithfulness of the Lord is not to be hidden; from our children or from any person that the Lord has put in your path.

Psalm 102:18 states, "This will be written for the generation to come, that a people yet to be created may praise the LORD". We have discussed this principal in depth, but let's say it again: whatever God is doing *in* you, He is really doing *through* you. This is not about you: the Lord is blessing you so that you can be a blessing to others... so a "people yet to be created may praise the Lord!" It represents such an awesome responsibility should you choose to accept it: the Lord, capable of using any thing to achieve His purposes is choosing you to further His Name. Rise to the challenge, and recognize the honor it is to serve Him.

The Word of God tells us that we overcome "by the blood of the Lamb, and by the word of their testimony" (Revelation 12:11). Just as sharing your testimony will offer strength and build the faith of the hearers, you will be strengthened by sharing what the Lord has done and is doing in you. People will be encouraged by what God is doing through you. He is no respecter of persons. What He does for you, He can do for anyone! If you are willing to be genuine and open, you can *give freely* to others the encouragement that you have received.

Just a few weeks ago, I was fasting again. I had decided not to share my fast with my children. This is not at all unusual, and had always gone unnoticed by my sweet little ones. On Tuesday afternoon, Lindsay and I drove through our regular fast food place. I ordered her usual, and ordered a bottle of water for myself. After she prayed over her meal, Lindsay asked, "Mommy, are you fasting?" I explained to her that I was, but that this fast was between me and the Lord. She seemed to understand as much as her young mind could understand. It brought tears to my eyes when she asked what I was fasting about, and if she could pray with me sometime. She understood more than I had given her credit for; she knew I was "making a trade", as I had explained to her many times before. She recognized that I was giving up something that I wanted for something that I wanted even more: a closer relationship with the Lord.

Maybe one day she'll explain it to her daughter, and the cycle will continue. Perhaps one day my sons will come to a crossroads, and remember the value of sacrifice. One day they will be able to teach someone else how to depend on the Lord, and they will testify to His faithfulness. "Great is the LORD, and greatly to be praised; And His greatness is unsearchable. One generation shall praise Your works to another, And shall declare Your mighty acts" (Psalm 145:3-4).

As we discussed before, what God is doing in you is not only for you. God may be working things out for you that will also benefit the people coming after you. God worked through the Jews in Persia, but this tremendous success was far reaching. The affects of Esther's faithfulness, Mordecai's faithfulness, and the faithfulness of the Jews in Persia would impact generations and generations.

Mordecai and Esther saw the importance of preserving this day. They took measures to ensure that the truth they experienced first hand would not wane with time or be forgotten altogether. As Jews all over Persia "have rest from their enemies" and celebrate the victory that God has provided, Mordecai writes a full history to send out to all the provinces. Esther and Mordecai knew that it was extremely important for the Jews to know the complete truth of their deliverance. However, Mordecai had more than one reason to write these letters.

So they called these days Purim, after the name Pur. Esther 9:26a

These days were aptly named "Purim". "Pur" means to cast lots. If you remember, casting lots was the way in which Haman determined the day on which to eradicate the Jews (Esther 3:7). The name "Purim" was meant to remind the Jews of the power of God over the power of evil, and Jewish people celebrate the "Feast of Purim" even today!

> *Therefore, because of all the words of this letter, what they had seen concerning this matter, and what had happened to them, the Jews established and imposed it upon themselves and their descendants and all who would join them, that without fail they should celebrate these two days every year, according to the written instructions and according to the prescribed time...* Esther 9:26b-27

Mordecai and Esther had a second reason for writing this history to the Jews. The first reason, of course, was to let the Jews know the whole story so they could praise God for all that HE had done for them. The second reason was to preserve this history for all generations. Esther and Mordecai wanted to ensure that God's work on behalf of the Jews was never forgotten. God had not only preserved the Jews who lived in Persia on the "thirteenth day of Adar"; He had preserved all the generations of Jews who would follow them. This great victory was for all of the Jews, their children, and their children's children and so forth...

> *...that these days should be remembered and kept throughout every generation, every family, every province, and every city, that these days of Purim should not fail to be observed among the Jews, and that the memory of them should not perish among their descendants.* Esther 9:28

Mordecai was giving encouragement to the Jews, but he was also admonishing them: "these days *should* be remembered". The memory of this victory should not perish among the descendants of these Jews who were saved on this day. Without a tradition of celebrating this victory — without a conscious effort on the part of the Jews to remember the great things that God had done for them — this great victory would be reduced to a forgotten memory. After a generation of Jews, this victory might never have been remembered again had it not been for Mordecai and Esther recognizing that it was important to preserve it in this letter.

Mordecai and Esther understood that theirs was a small part of a BIG plan. However, I don't know if even they understood how big this plan was! When the Jews were saved from total annihilation, Mordecai and Esther probably had no idea that generations and generations later, two *Jewish* people in a small city called Nazareth would be among their descendants. You know to whom I am referring: a young, devout girl named Mary and a poor carpenter named Joseph. Esther and Mordecai had no way of knowing that through these people would come the true Savior, and that He would come not only to save the Jews, but all people everywhere. What a tremendous responsibility and beautiful heritage!

Just as Esther and Mordecai felt a responsibility to preserve this history for the generations to come, we should feel a responsibility to preserve it as well. "Purim" is a day of remembrance of what God did for us through Esther and Mordecai's obedience, but let me encourage you to remember God's faithfulness to you EVERY DAY! Just as the psalmist wrote "one generation shall praise Your works to another", purpose in your heart that you will be part of the generation that praises the works of God to the people who will come after you. Look for new ways to preserve the memory of God's goodness in your life. Look for new ways to encourage the people around you. Let everyone know that what God is doing for you, He can do for them as well!

Encourage the people around you: "If He did it for me, He'll do it for you!" God is no respecter of persons, and that little knowledge might mean the world to someone in your life who feels defeated. Pray that God would place you on the right path to touch the right person at the right time!

❧

DAY FOUR: ESTHER 9:29-32

Having the tenacity to follow through is such a great quality! If you have it, praise God for that characteristic! If you do not have it, pray that God would help you to develop this important trait! It's important to start strong AND to finish strong!

FRIEND TO FRIEND...

Sitting at the kitchen table, staring at his math workbook and those unsolved problems, Jacob was absolutely miserable. As I began to prepare dinner, I wondered how long I should let him sit there and sulk before I intervened. The struggle can be good at times, but it seemed to me that Jacob was struggling unnecessarily.

As I considered going to the rescue, I remembered. We were all good until the long division. Until then, three times three equaled nine or two plus two equaled four, and we were done. Memorized. Short and sweet. What could be simpler? Now that there was long division, there was a process involved: to reach the quotient, we have to divide into a digit or two. Then we must multiply, then subtract. Subtraction might involve the dreaded borrowing, and once we are done with subtracting, we must bring another number down and begin again (and possibly again) until the problem is solved. To find the answer, we had to commit to the process.

For Jacob, committing to the process isn't always easy. One reason Jacob has a hard time with the process is that he cannot see the end from the beginning. For him, the end is the unknown quantity that is lurking out there, threatening and making him nervous. He looks at that math page, and is already worried about the end result: "What if I don't finish? Mom won't let me play video games. I won't be allowed to have friends over. I might have to go to bed early. What if my brother gets done and I am left to work all by myself? Tyler might get to play outside and I won't be able to go with him..." By this time, Jacob has already worked himself into a panic because of his lost play-over, and he hasn't even taken the first step!

When Tyler finished and went outside, I thought that Jacob might just start crying. Now one of his fears about homework this afternoon had been realized: he was alone. I decided he had been sitting there long enough.

Knowing what his struggle was, I sat down at the table with him and started to speak gently. It was the *process*. I tried to help him understand how doing each step well would produce a positive outcome. I told him again that the Bible teaches us that the "end of a thing is better than its beginning" (Ecclesiastes 7:8); this was not the first time that he had heard that from me. After my little "let's get this done" speech, I looked at his workbook, ready to help him figure out what to do. The bad news: it was long division. The good news: there were only six problems.

Six problems? Now I was a little frustrated, realizing Jacob had spent the last thirty minutes staring at his workbook, and had worked himself into this state over six problems. The fact was that he would have been done ten minutes ago had he just started working when he started *worrying*. I took a deep breath. "Son, do you understand what you are supposed to do?" "Yes, ma'am." Deep breath, long pause, gritted teeth. "If you understand, son, why are we sitting here and not working?" Now came the tears. "Mom, I have to multiply and divide and subtract and borrow and bring down and do it all again. This takes a really long time, and I'm already sitting here by myself because you let Tyler go outside."

Because *I let* Tyler go outside? I let that one go, and took another deep breath. I explained to Jacob again that performing each step well would end in a positive result. I knew that Jacob was worried about the length of time between now and the end. I explained to him that the most important thing to concern himself with at the moment was finishing *step by step*. As I sat beside him for the next few minutes, offering the needed encouragement at each step rather than help, Jacob completed his six problems and was outside riding bikes with his brother in no time.

I hoped that Jacob would remember more than just the long division. I hoped that he would recognize that in tackling his problems step by step, little by little, he had been able to complete the task. Later in life, long division would be solved by a calculator; more significant problems would be solved by the ability to commit to the process. As important as it is to *begin* strong, it is infinitely more important to *finish* strong.

The Bible has wisdom to offer on finishing strong. In the book of Ruth, Boaz praised Ruth for her attitude at the *end* of her struggle. He said to her,"Blessed are you of the LORD, my daughter! For you have shown more kindness at the end than at the beginning" (Ruth 3:10). Proverbs 20:21 tells us that "an inheritance gained hastily at the beginning will not be blessed at the end". From the very beginning, we must understand that God's timetable is not the same as ours. This knowledge should encourage rather than cause undue worry, creating in us an inward resolve to remain faithful as God is faithful. Rushing through and skipping necessary steps in the process will result in a decreased blessing at the end.

One more verse about an end, and this one contains a precious promise: "Though your beginning was small, yet your latter end would increase abundantly" (Job 8:7). As a result of faithfully committing day by day, step by step to the process that the Lord has placed before you is an abundant increase at the end.

Today it's long division, Jake. Learn the value of committing to the process, and tomorrow you'll conquer the world.

Esther is experiencing today the rewards of remaining faithful. Her beginning was small, but as she remained faithful every day, God has continued to increase her. Esther made a commitment to the process, and she kept that commitment until the end. Her struggle was hard, but it was purposeful. Esther did not struggle unnecessarily.

Now that the Jews are rescued and are enjoying their day of rest from their enemies, it might seem that Esther and Mordecai's work is finished. Things are not always what they seem: their work is not yet done! Mordecai and Esther intend to see this work all the way to completion.

Esther and Mordecai, once again, present a sharp contrast to King Ahasuerus. Unlike Ahasuerus, they do not grow complacent. Unlike Ahasuerus, they do not tire easily of the situation at hand. Unlike Ahasuerus, Esther and Mordecai do not look back and "re-play" all the things that they have done already and decide for themselves whether it is enough. Esther and Mordecai know their work is not done, and their intention is to follow God's direction as long as He has work for them to do.

> *Then Queen Esther, the daughter of Abihail, with Mordecai the Jew,*
> *wrote with full authority to confirm this second letter about Purim.*
> Esther 9:29

After Mordecai sends out letters to all the Jews to establish Purim as a holiday, Queen Esther also sends out a letter to confirm what Mordecai has written. With Mordecai's help, she wrote her own letter to her people. "With her full authority" probably means the holiday of Purim was established permanently.

This certainly is a stark contrast to Ahasuerus' style of leadership. Esther sends out a letter to her people, and shows a great interest in their knowing what happened. Ahasuerus hardly knows what is going on outside the palace gates, and doesn't show much interest in his people at all. We see his lack of interest demonstrated several times throughout the book. Remember when he was easily swayed by Memucan to de-throne Vashti? He made a quick decision without considering the feelings of his wife. What about when he allowed Haman to publish the decree against the Jews? Ahasuerus made a decision based only on what one man said to him without researching the situation for himself. The destruction of an entire race of people in his kingdom might have warranted a little consideration on his part, don't you think? Instead, he sits down to a drink with Haman. Ahasuerus would not even write the decree himself to destroy the Jews or the decree to allow them to defend themselves. He had Haman write the first, and Mordecai write the second. This is not someone who would have written a letter to his people for any reason. Esther's letter may have seemed unnecessary to Ahasuerus; Mordecai had already written a letter, right? He may be wondering why Esther feels it important to go to the trouble of writing her own letter to the Jews.

It is important to notice that since she became queen (ever since God gave her this measure of authority), Esther never detached herself from the people as Ahasuerus did. Over and over again, she went "the extra mile" to ensure the safety of the Jews. When Ahasuerus was looking out only for himself, Esther was looking out for the needs of her people. When Ahasuerus was too lazy or too complacent to "inconvenience" himself with the troubles in his kingdom, Esther had a passion for people. She let that passion be the determining factor in her decision making — not personal loss or gain. Esther knew the people in Persia would be blessed once the grace of God was made known to them, and she had confidence that they would be trustworthy with this information.

You have been given a measure of authority in your life as well. What are you doing with the authority that God has given to you? Let Esther be your example of responsible authority!

> *And Mordecai sent letters to all the Jews, to the one hundred and twenty-seven provinces of the kingdom of Ahasuerus, with words of peace and truth.* Esther 9:30

Mordecai sent letters to all 127 provinces with words of "peace and truth". Some Bible scholars suggest that Mordecai wrote the book of Esther. Some of them suggest that the book of Esther is the letter that Mordecai sent to all the Jews explaining to them the entire history (9:20). I can't argue with them — I'm not a bible scholar! But considering the time line of Esther — the events in this book (as we have discussed before) happen in between those of Ezra and Nehemiah. God's name is mentioned *everywhere* in those books and present a striking contrast to the book of Esther, where His name is never mentioned. We have gotten to know Mordecai a little over the past ten weeks.... it seems "out of character" for him to write a history to the Jews and leave God out of it. Other bible scholars think this was copied from Persian records. To me, that seems to fit better with what we have learned about Mordecai.

> *And Mordecai sent letters to all the Jews, to the one hundred and twenty-seven provinces of the kingdom of Ahasuerus, with words of peace and truth, to confirm these days of Purim at their appointed time, as Mordecai the Jew and Queen Esther had prescribed for them, and as they had decreed for themselves and their descendants concerning matters of their fasting and lamenting. So the decree of Esther confirmed these matters of Purim, and it was written in the book.* Esther 9:30-32

The letters that Mordecai and Esther sent out after the victory were to inform the Jews of the entire history, to confirm with words of peace and truth what the Lord had done, and to decree these two days as holidays to all generations. The words "it was written in the book" suggests that this was a decree, written into history. Once again, Esther and Mordecai are showing that they are trustworthy in a position of authority.

This verse says that Mordecai used words of "peace and truth". How can you use words of peace and leave out the Prince of Peace? How do you write the truth and leave out the Way, the Truth, and the Life? It seems his faith was so deep that it might have even been impossible for him to write a history in its entirety and not mention God. Possibly more likely is the idea that Mordecai wrote his letter, filled with the "peace and truth" of the Almighty God, and left the historical writings to someone else. Would it be impossible to write your history and not mention God? Does your life reflect His power and purity so much that it would be impossible to leave Him out?

In these letters, there is something else that is addressed: "matters of fasting and lamenting". It may seems out of place in the midst of all of this celebrating, but Esther and Mordecai did not want the Jews to forget: their faithfulness did not depend on their circumstances. There are appointed times for celebration and sadness alike, and we serve the same God through them both.

Lord, thank You for the measure of authority that You have given to me... Help me to follow-through even when it may seem that my task is over! Help me to remember that You always have a purpose for my life. Though my purpose may change from time to time, though I may complete one task and move on to another... You have made a commitment to completing Your work in my life. You are never finished with me!

※

DAY FIVE: ESTHER 10:1-3

Father, thank You for imparting wisdom and knowledge! I desire with my whole heart to live a life full of Your favor and full of Your grace... use me, Lord. I give myself completely to You!

FRIEND TO FRIEND...

Thinking back on the extraordinary circumstances of Esther's life, it becomes clear that Esther's life was, in every possible way, unexpected. Unexpected by the people around her, unexpected by the king who chose her, unexpected by the Jews whom she rescued, even unexpected by Esther herself.

Surprises and changes can be difficult to handle, but this simple truth can make it easier: there are no surprises to the Lord. In His providence, "that continuous agency of God by which He makes all the events of the physical and moral universe fulfill the original design with which they were created"[2], every detail is covered. Throughout the Bible, we see demonstrated over and over again that God must delight in seemingly impossible people and situations. How about a young man slaying thousands with only a donkey's jawbone as a weapon (Judges 15:16)? How about that same man years later: blind, weak and frail bringing down an entire temple (Judges 16:28-30)? Samson lived it. How about an adulterer becoming a man after God's own heart (Acts 13:22)? Though David may have seemed an unlikely role model to some, God knew best. What about an enemy to Christians becoming one of our greatest missionaries and writing more than half of the New Testament (Acts 9)? All Christians are strengthened today by the inspired writing of Paul. What about a young virgin finding herself carrying the Messiah (Matthew 1:18)? Sounds unbelievable, but Mary would testify to the truth. "With men it is impossible, but not with God; for with God all things are possible" (Mark 10:27). How about an entire race of people rescued by the bravery of a young, inexperienced queen? An orphaned Jewess and her displaced uncle are probably not the instruments that you would have expected such wonderful things to happen through. To God be the glory!

Paul wrote in 1 Corinthians 1:26-30. "For you see your calling, brethren, that not many wise according to the flesh, not many mighty, not many noble, are called. But God has chosen the foolish things of the world to put to shame the wise, and God has chosen the weak things of the world to put to shame the things which are mighty; and the base things of the world and the things which are despised God has chosen, and the things which are not, to bring to nothing the things that are, that no flesh should glory in His presence. But of Him you are in Christ Jesus, who became for us wisdom from God — and righteousness and sanctification and redemption — that, as it is written, 'He who glories, let him glory in the LORD.' "

Why does the Lord choose these things which we would not expect to achieve His purposes?

"That no flesh should glory in His presence." It is a powerful statement, and one certainly personified in Esther and Mordecai. Their letters could have been about all the things that *they* had accomplished. They could have taken credit for the Jews' deliverance, but they gave all the glory to God. They recognized that apart from the Lord there would have been no victory at all.

Let's return to Persia for the last time.

And King Ahasuerus imposed tribute on the land and on the islands of the sea. Esther 10:1

Ahasuerus imposed a heavy tax on all the inhabitants of Persia. History tells us that once again Ahasuerus led Persia in a war with Greece around this time period. Once again, trying to succeed where his father could not. Once again, experiencing a miserable failure. It was also a costly failure, so that may explain the tax. In the missing years in between chapters one and two, he may have been coming off another failed attempt to take over Greece, explaining his depression at that time. His father, Darius, had led a couple of attacks against Greece, and had not been successful either time. Except for these attacks against Greece, Darius' reign had been very successful. Maybe Ahasuerus was making one more attempt at something that his father had been unable to do because he wanted some sort of legacy of his own. His reign wasn't really noteworthy — without Esther, he hardly would be remembered at all.

> *Now all the acts of his power and his might, and the account of the greatness of Mordecai, to which the king advanced him, are they not written in the book of the chronicles of the kings of Media and Persia?* Esther 10:2

Our Persian chronicler tells us the other acts of Ahasuerus are recorded in another book of chronicles of the kings of Media and Persia. It is possible he was gently letting the reader know: "We're not going to spend time on this here." Whoever it was that wrote this book, we have seen that he "cuts right to the chase". Leaving out years here and months there, he only records what he considers necessary. Apparently Ahasuerus did not do much that "made the cut" in the eyes of our chronicler; maybe because there was nothing truly noteworthy. While it is true that the entire first chapter of Esther is devoted to Ahasuerus, do not overlook the content of that chapter: Ahasuerus' party. The historian might have known his audience was being given a fairly revealing picture of Ahasuerus' character from the very beginning.

Interesting also is the fact that the chronicler mentions the "greatness of Mordecai" in the same verse with Ahasuerus. A displaced Jew mentioned as being great next to a king? That is an awesome example of how the Lord uses *people* whom the world would not expect in *ways* which the world would not expect.

> *For Mordecai the Jew was second to King Ahasuerus, and was great among the Jews and well received by the multitude of his brethren, seeking the good of his people and speaking peace to all his countrymen.* Esther 10:3

What a beautiful benediction for Mordecai: he was "seeking the good of his people and speaking peace to all of his countrymen." How could someone like that not be well received by Jews and non-Jews alike? That is the favor of God! Wouldn't it be nice for words like these to be included in your benediction as well?

Is anyone else bothered by the fact that we finished the book of Esther with a chapter that does not even mention her? I have to admit that I was bothered by this omission. She was not mentioned in the first chapter either. As I puzzled about it, a little thought popped into my head (or maybe into my spirit?): *the first and the last*. Esther's name is left out of the *first* chapter and the *last* chapter possibly because she is *not* the First and the Last! She served Him, though, and she served Him well. Esther put God *first*, and as her final act recorded in the book of Esther (9:29-32), she made sure that the memory of what God had done for the Jews in Persia would *last*....

What about Esther's legacy? In the beginning of our study, we read through Ezra 6:1-14. When the temple was finally completed, Ezra recorded the work was completed at the command of "the God of Israel, and according to the command of *Cyrus, Darius, and Artaxerxes*" (Ezra 6:14, emphasis mine). Seemingly, that verse seemed made a big statement about Ahasuerus (or Xerxes). His grandfather, father, and son are mentioned, but Ahasuerus himself is left out entirely. Consider this: Artaxerxes (the son of Ahasuerus, mentioned in the) is the step-son of Queen Esther. He was raised in the palace with Esther for the better part of his life. Ahasuerus certainly was not a role model of great authority — but Artaxerxes was blessed to have had a great role model nearby in Esther! It is feasible that Ahasuerus' son may not have helped the Jews complete the temple without Esther's influence. Artaxerxes was blessed to be a first hand witness to Esther's extraordinary life. We are blessed as well to have her example recorded for our benefit today.

Years after Esther's triumph, King Ahasuerus dies. Sometime around 465 B.C., his son Artaxerxes ascends to the throne. You may remember that the events recorded in Esther happened in between the events recorded in the books of Ezra and Nehemiah. Ezra records events around 536 — 450 B.C. Nehemiah picks up the story, and comes to Jerusalem with the purpose of rebuilding Jerusalem. He completes the task; not only with Artaxerxes' permission, but with Artaxerxes' funding. Perhaps his favor toward the Jews was as a result of Esther's influence.

Though she is not mentioned anywhere else in the Bible, this is one woman who made a tremendous impact for the kingdom of God. Let me challenge you to sit down sometime and read the book of Esther in its entirety. Even though we took several weeks to get through it, Esther is a relatively short book. With the knowledge that you have gotten from the Lord over the last several weeks, re-reading the book as a whole would be a great way to end the study.

I believe your impact for the kingdom of God can be just as great. Be encouraged that the Word of God is true. Rejoice in the fact that you will ultimately experience success as you follow the Lord "because He who is in you is greater than he who is in the world" (1 John 4:4). God is no respecter of persons (Acts

10:34); what He did through Esther, He can do through you.

Take an example from Esther, and take your world by storm!

Father, speak to me daily and challenge me to think outside of myself... Never allow me to become complacent or satisfied... I submit my life to You — Lord, have Your way in me!

❧

being confident of this very thing, that He who has begun
a good work in you will complete it until the day of Jesus Christ
Philippians 1:6

Father, Your love is constant and faithful.
If I allow it to, Your love will free me.
Your love will free me from
frustration or impatience while I am on my journey with You.
As I wrap myself in Your love, I am released from frustration with myself,
because I recognize that I am a "work in progress"
that You are committed to completing!
I am released from impatience with the people around me as well -
I can choose to recognize them as Your work also!
Confident that my faithfulness will help me achieve Your goals for my life,
I can work toward becoming the woman that
You intend me to be —
without compromise, without apology,
and without fear that I will be left unfinished!
I am Your child, and Your love is all I need!

❧

---

1.   (Biblesoft's New Exhaustive Strong's Numbers and Concordance with Expanded Greek-Hebrew Dictionary. Copyright (c) 1994, Biblesoft and International Bible Translators, Inc.)

2.   Dr. Augustus Hopkins Strong, Systematic Theology, p. 420.

AFTERWORD

Dear Friend,

These weeks have gone by quickly for me... It is my sincere prayer that the Lord has been able to speak to you through the life of Esther. As soon as I completed the study myself, "I am going to miss Esther!" Almost immediately, however, I felt a little check in my spirit. The truths that I have learned during the past several weeks and the virtues that I have seen demonstrated though the life of this queen will stay with me. When we started this bible study, I asked you to find a quiet corner and get ready to meet a new friend. I suggested that you might find that you have a lot in common with this orphaned Jewess . I hope that you have found common ground with her; that something in this study sparked you to say, "I can relate to that!"

Esther, generations before the birth of Christ, mirrored so many of His qualities. Remember when Esther said, "I will go to the king...and if I perish, I perish!" (4:16). She went to the king and stood in the gap for all the Jews who could not approach Ahasuersus on their own. What did Jesus do? He said, "Father, if it is Your will, take this cup away from Me; nevertheless not My will, but Yours, be done" (Luke 22:42). Jesus knew that His mission required His death. Still, He went to the King and stood in the gap for all of us who, before His sacrifice, could not approach Him on our own. Esther rescued the Jews in Persia. Jesus Christ rescued all mankind. Are you mirroring these qualities as well?

The possibility for greatness is already inside you; tap into your potential in God. Just as the acorn has everything it needs inside it to become a mighty oak, God has placed in you all the qualities that you need to grow. All you have to do is believe, confess, receive, obey... Commit to the process. Allow the roots of your life to grow deep and spread wide. Allow your branches to yield fruit and provide protection. Be encouraged that all you need, every single thing, is already inside you. Before you were born, there was a plan. At the moment you came into existence, the God Who sees the beginning from the end placed inside you the very specific items that you would need in order to experience success and serve your purpose. Find confidence and peace in that knowledge, and grow strong.

To be honest, God is not through with me yet. As we began the book, I'm not sure that I had anything in common with Esther, but I did observe many qualities in Esther that I desire to see duplicated in my life. I pray that I will be a "living sacrifice": someone willing to make the sacrifices needed to find God's will and walk it out. I pray that I will not crawl off the altar as God daily re-creates me into the woman that He would have me be. I hope that the next time I read the book of Esther that I will be able to say, "That's just the attitude that I would have had!" or "I would have made that decision the same way Esther did!" I am praying that these lessons will stay with me... submission to authority, respect, faith, character, operating in wisdom, operating on God's "timetable", patience, trusting the Lord with the consequences of obedience, depending on the Lord whole-heartedly, serving the Lord without fear, refusing to compromise, refusing to give up or give out....

What did you learn from Esther? Days or weeks ago, you opened this book as a student. I hope that you are leaving as a friend. "He who is in you is greater than he who is in the world" (1 John 4:4-5), my friend. He who is in *you is greater...*

Blessings,
Jennifer